THE EDIBLE GARDEN

THE EDIBLE GARDEN

ROB HERWIG & HANNELIE BOKS

HAMLYN

Edited by Alan Toogood
Translated from the Dutch by AGET
Language Services
Photography by Rob Herwig

First published by Zomer & Keuning-Ede
under the title
Handboek voor de moestuin
© Copyright 1985 Zomer & Keuning
Boeken B.V., Ede
This edition published in 1986 by Hamlyn
Publishing,
Bridge House, London Road,
Twickenham, Middlesex, England

© Copyright 1986 English language edition
Hamlyn Publishing, a division
of The Hamlyn Publishing Group Limited

ISBN 0 600 30682 8

Phototypeset in England by
Wyvern Typesetting Limited, Bristol
on Linotron 202 in 9 on 10 pt Times New
Roman

Printed and bound by
Graficromo s.a., Cordoba, Spain

Contents

Before we start

We've all heard the story of the modern market gardener: every day he strides up and down the green rows, busily spraying and scattering artificial fertilizer, so that his wares glisten in their crates and the supermarket is delighted with the deliveries he sends them. But just next to his house he has a little plot of vegetables fed only on farmyard manure. That's where he grows the food for his own family!

Of course, the reality isn't always like that: there are plenty of environment-conscious growers, who try not to grow just for outward appearances. But they are very much in the minority – growing with 'chemicals' is always cheaper, and if shoppers continue to buy just on appearances these conscientious gardeners will not be around much longer.

There is a trend these days for our food to become more and more manipulated. Not just by spraying and over-fertilizing: we are also seeing more and more 'prepared' foods in the shops. Kale is sold cut into small pieces, carrots are scraped, quite a few vegetables come from the deep freeze at a time of year when there are plenty to be had fresh from the fields. To our way of thinking, this is a disturbing development, and to a degree it is due to laziness on the customer's part.

Obviously, you are not as lazy as that, or you would not have bought this book. You can count yourself among the growing number of people who are sick of growers' tricks, people who want to give their families food they know is good for them because they grew it themselves. 'Growing it yourself' has become the 'in' thing.

One thing particularly strikes us about this self-sufficiency movement: these days, people can hardly be doing it to save money, as they generally were 50 years ago, because in comparison with other types of food, shop vegetables are not expensive to buy. No, they are doing it because vegetables from your own garden are healthier and, above all, tastier, and because gardening is a great hobby, and one that gives you quick results.

For us, growing our own vegetables, combined with writing this book and taking the photographs for it, has been a delightful task.

Hannelie Boks
Rob Herwig

How plants work for us

Every plant is a highly efficient factory in miniature, which takes all manner of substances from its surroundings and converts them into products that we find useful or decorative.

One of the most important features of plants is their ability to produce oxygen from carbon dioxide. As you no doubt know, human beings and animals do the opposite: they use up oxygen and breathe out carbon dioxide. Plants and people are actually helping each other to stay alive by working in opposite ways like this: a world with too much carbon dioxide or too much oxygen would be deadly to both.

Plants we can eat, which is what this book is about, help us in another way: they produce cells which serve us as food. With some plants it is the leaves that we eat, sometimes we take the roots, and in a good many cases we pick the fruit. This book is mainly organized according to what part of the plant we eat.

How does it work?
A plant consists of roots, stems and leaves.

Roots are designed to take in water from the soil, along with the food dissolved in the water. They also act as an anchor for the plant to stop it falling over.

The intake of food is through extremely fine hair roots. The minerals dissolved in the soil moisture then find their way into the vascular system of the plant, a network of tubes which distributes them to the leaves.

It is in the leaves that assimilation takes place. 'Assimilation' means 'making similar' or 'making the same'; and all the plant is doing is turning the food it has absorbed into the material it already consists of, so that it becomes part of the plant itself. The real miracle at the heart of all this is photosynthesis.

The plant absorbs carbon dioxide from the air through tiny pores; then, with the help of sunlight and chlorophyll (the green pigment in the plant) the water taken in through the roots is split up in the leaf cells to form hydrogen and oxygen. The carbon dioxide from the air, together with the freshly-formed hydrogen, is then reduced to a carbohydrate, and the oxygen is given off into the air.

If this is not getting too complicated, I'll go a bit further into it. During the day carbohydrates are produced, but overnight photosynthesis comes to a halt and carbohydrates are delivered to every part of the plant, where they are used as fuel. Any surplus is stored as a reserve, for example in the tubers of potatoes.

Another activity going on in plants is nitrogen absorption, a very complex process whereby nitrates from the soil (and therefore nitrogen) are converted into amino acids. These in turn are converted to proteins. This is another of the unique abilities of plants: they are the only form of life that can produce proteins directly from the minerals found in the soil. Animals (which includes human beings) cannot do this, so they can only stay alive by eating each other – or, of course, by eating plants.

Which brings us back to our main subject: we eat plants – the plants we call vegetables – to stay alive. That goes for the vegetarians among us, at least. Most other people get the bulk of their protein from animal foods, and vegetables come second as far as protein is concerned. It's a matter of choice – animal proteins are not indispensable.

Plants usually produce flowers as well; and although we may well eat some of them (artichokes, for example) they are more important in the vegetable garden for the part they play in reproduction. That is, assuming we let things go that far; more often we either pick the plant before it flowers or we eat its seeds.

Sex comes first for vegetables
Whatever kind of sex education you had you will certainly have heard of 'the birds and the bees'. Inside each flower there are stalks called stamens which produce male pollen; this is carried – either by the wind or, yes, by insects and birds – to pistils, stalk-like female organs inside the flower, where the pollen is absorbed into the female cells. The direct outcome is not a new plant, but a seed that will eventually grow into a new plant.

This, of course, is a process we have to deal with in our vegetable garden practically every day: nearly all vegetables are grown from seed, and quite a few of the vegetables we eat are actually seeds themselves – think of peas and beans, for instance.

Some flowers pollinate themselves – the pollen is passed to their own pistils, and often this happens before the flower even opens. Peas and beans are examples.

Cross-pollinating plants, on the other hand, make more of a meal of it: their pollen has to travel some distance until it lands on a different flower – but still a flower of the same species. Brassicas (cabbages, cauliflowers, etc.) and onions are examples of cross-pollinators.

This cosy, olde-worlde beehive stands right next to our vegetable plot. There is constant 'traffic'.

If you look at freshly germinated beans you can see the two seed-lobes quite clearly.

Collecting your own seed

It doesn't take much thought to realize that you'll have more success collecting your own seed from self-pollinators (peas, beans, lettuce) than from cross-pollinators. With cross-pollinators there is always a good chance that a speck of pollen may be blown or carried across from a plant with poor characteristics. The result is a degeneration in the stock, and 'mongrels' of this sort are nearly always less productive or less tasty than their parents. So if you're working with cross-pollinators (endive, beet, brassicas, leeks, radishes, spinach, onions, chicory, carrots) you're far better off buying seed.

Seed selection

Great Britain is famous for seed selection. Long ago growers started crossing vegetables with each other to produce better varieties. What is a 'variety'? It is a named hybrid created by man, which will give reliable, unchanging results

when grown. Often some variation can, in fact, arise: in that case we are not looking at a 'clone' (100 per cent matching inherited characteristics) but at a group of hybrids (inherited characteristics not 100 per cent identical). For instance, carrots of the 'Nantes' variety belong to a group which can still give rise to new and different varieties.

F_1 hybrids need to be created afresh every time by the seed producers from two established parent strains. This can only be done by removing the stamens from one strain so that these flowers may then be pollinated with pollen from another strain. This is all done by hand, and that is why F_1 seed is more expensive. However, the following generations stay identical to the parents, and very often they are stronger, bigger and tastier – in short, better than ordinary varieties. And for this reason F_1 varieties are becoming more and more popular. Taking your own seeds from F_1 hybrids is not advisable because you will nearly

always end up with inferior plants.

When seed growers carry out their selection and cross-breeding they have quite a number of things to pay attention to. These include: early or late ripening, resistance to disease, large plants or large fruits, colouring, climate, soil type, liability to premature seeding, etc.

Organic seed

This is the name given to seed grown without artificial fertilizer and without the use of pesticides. Organic growers believe that these seeds produce stronger plants. It is very difficult to prove this one way or the other.

Premature seeding

Premature seeding (or 'bolting') means that a plant flowers before we want it to. When we grow lettuce, for example, we want to harvest an edible crop, not flowers.

Early seeding can be caused by one of two things. First, the length of the day. Plants come in two types: the long-day plants and the short-day plants. The long-day plants flower when there are more than 12 hours of daylight each day, and the others when there are less than 12 hours. Most vegetables are long-day plants, so early spinach, for instance, will flower if you sow it in the summer.

Secondly, plants may bolt as a result of cold. The cause is usually sowing too early, when the ground has not warmed up enough. Chinese cabbage grown below 16°c (60°F) will surprise you with a fine flower instead of a crop.

Fortunately, the seed growers have done something about this – if they had let things stay as they were, you wouldn't be able to harvest a crop of lettuce in the summer, and spinach would certainly be out of the question. They have turned many long-day vegetables into plants that are fairly indifferent to the amount of daylight, or at least are slow to seed. Also, in many cases, they have reduced the sensitivity of vegetables to low temperatures.

There are not many short-day vegetables. Butter beans certainly started off that way, but now – happily for us – they flower with long days too.

It all depends on the soil

Is the soil in your garden suited to growing vegetables, or isn't it? That is what it all depends on. Not all vegetables have the same needs, so it's a matter of adapting the soil to suit the vegetables you want to grow. Potatoes require a fairly acid soil, so don't add lime to it; on the other hand, a dose of lime will do brassicas the world of good. This gives us a few more things we need to look at.

What is the soil made of?

All types of soil owe their origins to weathering of the earth's crust. This wearing down by the elements causes the mineral-bearing soil particles to disintegrate; the more they have been worn down, the finer the particles are.

If you take a handful of fairly moist soil from your garden you have enough of a sample to find out roughly what type of soil you are working with. Work it into a ball. If it falls apart again as soon as you open your hand, and if you can distinctly feel the soil particles as tiny grains, you are dealing with a sandy soil. If small particles stick to your fingers, there is some loam or clay mixed in.

If you can easily make a ball out of the soil and even roll it out fairly thin, after which the whole thing crumbles again, there is rather more loam or clay mixed in, and you have a medium loam soil – a sand and clay mix.

If you can knead it between your fingers so well that you could, if you wished, model it into a small figure or the like, you are dealing with either heavy clay or pure loam.

Besides the mineral content the soil can (and must) contain decayed plant and animal matter, known as humus. Peaty soil consists of humus and nothing else; heathland soil is sand mixed with peat.

The mineral particles making up a soil type can be classified according to their grain size. Next to stones and sand grains, which cannot provide any nutrients to the plant roots, we can also identify particles smaller than 0.016 mm, which constitute silt. These are particles we come across especially in clayey and loamy soils; near the roots, it does not

take very long for them to get worn down further, until they are small enough to be absorbed by the plant. A high percentage of silt particles makes the soil fertile.

You can see the organic matter we call humus: it looks like tiny sponges. Humus can take in a lot of moisture, along with the nutrients dissolved in it, and hold them for a long time. Pure peat contains very little food, but we can easily add some with the aid of artificial fertilizer or organic manure, and this will instantly make the same soil ideal for plants. Potting compost is often made up in this way.

Besides minerals and humus, the soil also contains thousands of millions of tiny creatures such as worms, bacteria, insects and moulds. In every 100 m² (120 sq yd) of soil there are some 25 kg (½ cwt) of these assorted creepy-crawlies and their friends. And they keep themselves busy all day (and all night) with all manner of useful activities, such as eating each other and converting materials into other materials, with, it seems, just one driving aim: to produce food for the plants. Their role in life is to bring up the rear of the unfathomable underground war machine and eat up the scraps.

Now add air and water

Minerals, humus, bugs – all of this would be useless but for another two very important ingredients: air and water. There must be a good proportion of these in the soil, otherwise there would not be many vegetables we could grow. Where the air is, there can't be water, and vice-versa. The most important

A well-known source of green-manure, and a very attactive plant to bees, too: *Phacelia tanacetifolia*, a hardy annual.

ingredient of air is the oxygen that the insects, but also the roots, need to live. And water is important to make up losses caused by the evaporation the plants suffer above ground.

Well, now you know – more or less – what it's all about: minerals, humus, creepy-crawlies, oxygen and water. Together, these all decide the quality of the soil. Let us have a look at a few gardening terms used in this connection:

Available silt. These are the very fine mineral particles. Clay may contain more than 60 per cent of this; in loamy soil the figure is between 10 and 30 per cent. In sandy soil it is below 10 per cent.

Humus content. The percentage of organic matter in the soil. The ideal is 4–10 per cent, in clay and sandy soils. Peaty soil contains more than 30 per cent humus.

Structure. The degree to which soil particles are bound together. The coarser the particles, the better is the structure. The structure is also improved by humus. If the soil has a good crumbly structure air can readily penetrate and excess water can easily drain away.

Porosity (or permeability). The extent to which water and air are allowed into the soil – very closely connected with the structure. The opposite of a permeable soil is a water-retaining soil.

In a long spell of dry weather, clay soil produces typical patterns of cracks. Working the ground after this often presents problems.

Moisture raising ability. The strength with which a soil type can transport water upwards from deeper levels. This phenomenon is based on the capillary effect: the fact that very narrow channels transport liquids. The narrower the channels, the better the moisture-raising ability. You can see from this that soils with plenty of small particles (clay soils) have an advantage here over coarser soils (sandy). Soils with a good measure of humus will also raise moisture.

The ground water level

The ideal state of affairs for vegetables is a ground water level which is reasonably constant at a depth of about 1 m (3–3½ ft). Given this, it then depends on the moisture-raising ability of the soil whether the water is raised sufficiently.

If the ground water is too high, many roots (black radish, for instance) cannot penetrate deep enough; if it is too low, we have to do a lot of watering.

Now for the acidity

Finally, we turn to the last of the many factors deciding the quality of the soil: its acidity or alkalinity. Technically, the acidity – or pH – is a measure of the concentration of hydrogen ions in the soil. The more of these ions there are, the more acid the soil is. Hydrogen ions are found in acid rain and in some artificial fertilizers, among other places. The pH figure tells you how acid your soil is:

pH 7 is neutral, 4 is very acid, 10 is extremely alkaline.

Peaty soil is by nature acid; dune soil (not often found in Britain) is alkaline. Clay soils are generally alkaline, but can also be acid. Sandy soils are usually on the acid side, especially when nothing has been grown in them for a long time.

The ideal pH for sandy soil lies between 5.3 and 5.7 and for clay between 6.3 and 6.8. But you will need to pay careful attention to the needs of particular plants, which can be very different. We prefer to grow brassicas, for instance, in an alkaline soil, to reduce the risk of clubroot (a fungus disease). But potatoes are unhappy in soil with a high percentage of lime, and fairly acid soil is more what they need. When we come to describe the individual vegetables, we will include the pH value whenever possible.

Improving the soil

If your soil contains enough available minerals, if there is a proper quantity of humus, if the life under the soil is proceeding happily, if ground water and drainage are in the best possible condition, and, finally, the pH value is just what you need, then is it unnecessary to improve your soil.

You will have realized that this ideal situation is not met with very often! So improving the soil is practically always a first requirement.

Digging (see page 18) improves the structure, and allows more air to get into the soil. At the same time, fertilizer or compost can be turned in. Well-rotted farmyard manure (preferably cow dung, but pig manure or chicken manure will do) gets the life in the soil started, and the manure also contains available minerals. Working in rough manure also adds humus.

The best source of minerals is artificial fertilizer. As for which artificial fertilizer you use, it all depends on the kind of gardening you are going in for (see page 12). For organic gardeners, chemical compounds of nitrogen are nearly always taboo, but basic slag (with a lot of phosphate in it) is often allowed. The table on pages 180–182 lists the main substances used as fertilizers.

A thoroughly natural way of getting more nitrogen into the soil is the use of green-manure crops. These are specially chosen plants which are sown in the new garden to be dug in after the summer: vetch, clover, rye grass, turnip, etc. This also improves the structure and stimulates the soil life. The disadvantage of this is that you lose a whole year; and that sort of patience isn't too thick on the ground when a new garden is being set up!

Humus, as we said, can be obtained from rough manure; we can also get it from garden compost, peat, leafmould, etc. These organic materials can be worked under during digging.

If the pH needs raising or lowering this can be done at the same time as the soil is being improved. Often it is a matter of adding lime – for instance to sandy and loamy soils. Be careful not to add lime at the same time as farmyard manure, as the manure will break down too fast under the effects of the lime. The lime needs to be dug in at a good depth, so

that it dissolves slowly.

The best procedure is to dig in the lime two spits deep (i.e. to twice the depth of the spade) in the autumn; then add the well-rotted manure one spit deep in the spring.

If the soil has too much lime already, working in acid materials to improve the soil, such as peat, can help. Sulphate of ammonia, a strong acid artificial fertilizer, also lowers the pH level.

Vetch (*Vicia sativa*), a green-manure plant related to the broad bean. It is not suited to acid soils.

Not by air and water alone

Most vegetables are pretty demanding. They need quite a variety of foods on their menu; and if we don't keep things well topped up it can soon put an end to our crops. On this page you will find a short summary of the most important nutrients (plant foods).

Plants take their hydrogen, oxygen and carbon from air and water; their other nutrients usually come from the soil. We divide these mineral nutrients into major elements and trace elements. Trace elements are required in such small quantities that a mere 'trace' of them is all that is needed in the soil, hence the name. First the major elements.

Nitrogen is needed for plant growth. On page 7 we mentioned that nitrogen plays an important part in the production of protein – and without protein plants cannot make any new cells, so they cannot grow. A shortage of nitrogen also leads to poor development generally, especially in leaf crops (brassicas, lettuce, etc.). Too much nitrogen is also a bad thing: this results in over-luxuriant, limp growth, which reduces the sturdiness of the plant. It also makes plants easier for biting and sucking insects (greenfly, caterpillars, etc.) to eat.

Phosphorus helps the development of roots, tubers and seeds. A shortage of phosphorus leads to retarded growth – the leaves turn pale green, the plants mature too late and produce less protein. An excess of phosphorus in the soil is rare.

Potassium (or potash) regulates the intake of water by plants as well as the transport of carbohydrates. Potash deficiency can be recognized by a yellow or reddish-brown discoloration of the leaf, beginning at the edges. Once this appears, the leaves will soon wither. Too much potassium can cause burning, as well as hampering the intake of magnesium.

Lime (calcium) is mainly useful for regulating the acidity of the soil (see page 10). Besides this, small amounts of calcium are absorbed by the plant, and help to keep the cell walls strong. A shortage of calcium produces limp plants with weak roots.

An overdose of calcium can bring about too high a pH figure, which is not good for plants preferring more acid soil, such as potatoes.

Magnesium is found in chlorophyll (the green pigment in plants). A shortage results in chlorosis: pale green or pale yellow blotches appear between the veins of the leaf. When this happens less carbohydrates are being created in the plant. An excess of magnesium rarely occurs.

Sulphur helps, among other things, in the formation of proteins. Shortages are not common.

Trace elements include: boron, cobalt, copper, iron, manganese and zinc. Most organic manures contain trace elements, as do many fertilizers. There are proprietary compounds available, too, which supply trace elements.

Too much nitrogen in the soil has made this dill plant too limp. The plant collapses after a shower.

The best way of getting a new garden going is to give it a good covering of farmyard manure.

It's a matter of balance

All the nutrients, trace elements included, must be present in the soil in the proper proportions. Too much of one element can lead to a shortage of another. Thus, too much iron in the soil can result in phosphates not being absorbed; and then again, too much phosphate can bring about a lack of copper. Excess nitrogen threatens the intake of potassium; and so on.

You can see, then, that it's well worth knowing just how much of any given fertilizer you need to add to the soil. And you can only find this out by means of a soil test.

Soil testing

It is possible to have the soil in your garden examined by a laboratory. They will not only tell you precisely how much of each of the major elements and trace elements you have in your soil, but also give you advice on improving it (that is, if it needs it – but there is usually some deficiency or other).

You can also buy yourself a soil-testing kit, which will enable you to find out the most important things for yourself – as far, that is, as the pH and the content of the major elements; but the result will not be as exact as a laboratory can give you.

Healthy soil – healthy plants

It will be common knowledge by now that not only in farming, but in market gardening as well, the growers work with an eye to efficiency and labour-saving, and with profits coming first. We can't blame them for that; but one of the inevitable results is that they have to resort to artificial fertilizers and pesticides. In a small garden, which is what we are dealing with in this book, efficiency can take a back seat: we can get along with a little less output, slightly smaller

You can do your own soil test with a simple kit; but the results are not 100 per cent reliable.

crops or the odd one or two pests, if the reward is a better taste and a smaller risk of finding undesirable chemicals in our food. As long ago as the turn of the century, as it became more and more apparent that the use of artificial fertilizers – especially nitrogenous fertilizers – led to a reduced resistance to attack, growers started looking for alternative growing methods. Some returned to the old ways, the methods used before the invention of artificial fertilizer. Others looked for outside factors that might influence plant development and growth. Nowadays, there are dozens of alternative ways of growing vegetables: we will describe the most important ones below.

The biodynamic method

Invented by Rudolf Steiner (1861–1925) as a component of his anthroposophical doctrine. It is essential in this method of gardening that proper account is taken of ethereal forces (as manifested in the elements earth, water, fire and air) and astral forces (deriving from the planets). Indispensable manures include: cow-dung mixture (a cowhorn is filled with cow manure, buried for a few weeks, then the contents mixed with plenty of water, given a good, long stir and sprayed over the plants). Silica mixture (a cowhorn again, but filled this time with finely ground rhinestone, buried and mixed as before and likewise sprayed on the plants). Equisetum mixture (meadow-horsetail made into a 'tea', boiled for a very long time, and again sprayed). Various composts, made from camellia, stinging nettles, dandelion, oak bark and valerian juice. Com-

post preparation plays a very important part in the biodynamic method of gardening. When sowing and harvesting, special attention is paid to the position of the moon and the other planets. Digging is perfectly permissible. Chile saltpetre can be used for short periods, and basic slag, magnesium, lime and patent potassium also have a place in the biodynamic recipe book. Green-manure plants are used a good deal. Pesticides are not totally forbidden, but they must be biological in origin, like herbal teas, preparations containing pyrethrum and derris, etc.

Organic–biological gardening

Also known as the Mueller–Rusch system. Here, everything revolves around the 'living substance', a kind of macromolecule that can occur in both a superior and an inferior form. Logically enough, the idea is to encourage the superior form, since this is the one responsible for keeping plants and people healthy. As the only thing that can keep the living substance in its superior form is a good team of soil organisms (see page 9), it is a matter of respecting and helping these soil organisms. This is done by administering bacterial preparations. Besides this, digging is forbidden, because it mixes up different levels of soil and causes a partial dying off of the soil organisms. The ground is not allowed to lie fallow: there must always be something growing in it or lying on it (such as manure). The pH of the soil has to be kept on the high side, generally between 6.7 and 7.0. This encourages the bacterial life. Manuring: good, old, well-rotted farmyard manure, bonemeal and fine grit containing plenty of silica and magnesium. Green manuring: mixtures of oats and particular clovers: this gives the soil plenty of nitrogen. Green manuring with spinach is also used a good deal. Pesticides are used with great circumspection – only one organic preparation is used.

Macrobiotic gardening

The emphasis in the macrobiotic garden is on the trace elements (see page 11). These can be added to the soil with a special concentrate. Compost is important – well-rotted manure is worked into the soil. The ground is covered with a mulch in the autumn. Earthworms are

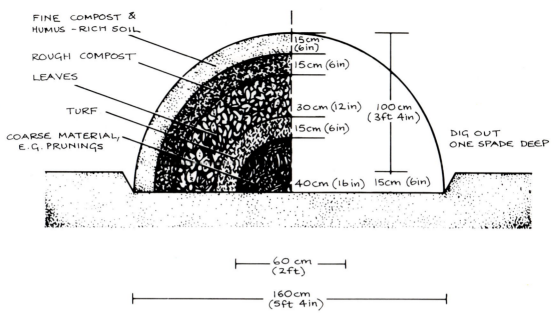

Raised mound beds are built up in layers. In dry weather they need frequent watering. Some gardeners swear by them, but making a bed like this means a lot of work.

FINE COMPOST & HUMUS-RICH SOIL

ROUGH COMPOST

LEAVES

TURF

COARSE MATERIAL, E.G. PRUNINGS

15cm (6in)

15cm (6in)

30cm (12in)

15cm (6in)

100cm (3ft 4in)

40cm (16in)   15cm (6in)

DIG OUT ONE SPADE DEEP

60 cm (2ft)

160cm (5ft 4in)

bred separately, to improve the structure of the soil.

The teachings of Zen Buddhism are applied in the macrobiotic method of growing. The male force, yang, and its female counterpart, yin, at work in both the microcosm and the macrocosm, are part and parcel of the method. Some plants are typically yin, and must be sown on yin days, while some are yang and are sown on yang days.

The Lemaire–Boucher method
Using this system, the soil must not be worked deeper than 15 cm (6 in). Much use is made of compost, which must not be more than four weeks old. Lavish use of calcified seaweed is central to this method. The material is worked into the soil.

The Ruth Stout method
Mrs Stout makes much use of mulching – covering the ground with a thick layer of organic waste material. Hay, especially, is her favourite. The layer of mulch keeps down weeds and encourages soil organisms. The method can be labour saving, but tends to look rather untidy. Complementary planting also plays its part in this system of gardening, which is rather out of fashion at present.

Raised mound bed
A rather specialized method of gardening makes use of the raised mound bed,

built up from different layers of organic waste. Its width is 1.8 m (6 ft), and the bed is some 80 cm (2 ft 8 in) high. First, the soil is dug out to a depth of 20 cm (8 in). Then a 40 cm (16 in) thick layer of twigs is placed in the middle of the bed. Over this is laid a 15 cm (6 in) layer of turf. After this, a 30 cm (12 in) thick layer of leaves. Coarse, half-rotted compost comes next. The bed is getting wider and wider as this goes on. Finally, the bed is covered with the soil that was dug out to start with: it should now be semi-circular in section. This shape increases the surface area of the bed, so that in theory more crops can be grown per square foot. The rotting of the waste material built into the mound also produces a very rich soil. The drawback is that when the weather is dry the mound needs a lot of watering.

The mound is planted with all kinds of vegetables, preferably complementary crops. It all amounts to a lot of work, and the question is whether it's really worth all the effort to grow vegetables this way. But if you are the kind of gardener who likes to experiment, raised mounds could be just up your street.

Our system
There are still other ways of growing vegetables, but it may be interesting to say something about our way of growing at this point. It's something of a hybrid of the systems we have just mentioned.

We only use deep digging when laying out a new garden or when, for one reason or another, it looks as if the soil is not at its best any more. The way we go about this is shown on pages 18–19. Apart from this, we only do shallow digging, in autumn or spring, and when the weather is fairly dry we use a rotary cultivator. Our favourite fertilizer is old farmyard manure, along with calcified seaweed, basic slag, ash from the fireplace (for the lime), concentrated trace elements, and blood, horn and bonemeal. After the first harvest some dried blood is added, to be sure of sufficient nitrogen for later growing. We never allow chemically prepared nitrogen into the garden. Compost is only worked in under the soil when deep digging, to prevent weeds from germinating. We have tried mulching, but the beds got untidier than we liked, and in wet weather weeds even managed to grow on top of the mulch layer. Insects are attacked only with pesticides that do no harm to the environment.

We don't think this system of gardening needs a name of its own – as we see it, it's simply a 'commonsense method' which aims to achieve the healthiest possible product with the least possible effort. We reject all the extreme methods, which sometimes seem to be more like cults – not because we think they are no good, but simply because we haven't the time.

13

Compost

As we have seen on the last few pages, composting is essential to most alternative vegetable-growing methods. Every alternative persuasion has its own way of preparing compost, but it would be too much of a digression to describe them all. If you are interested in one particular way of doing things, you would be far better off buying a book about that method, where the finer points of composting will be dealt with along with everything else.

Compost means 'put together'. A good compost, then, is put together out of as many different, easily rotting materials as possible, which will make for a good fertilizer once they have rotted. In itself, compost is not too rich in plant food, so very often bonemeal or some other substance is added. The main advantage of compost, in fact, does not lie in the nutrients it provides for the plants so much as in its enriching the ground with humus and the different kinds of organisms which help to keep the soil healthy.

You can make compost from both garden waste and kitchen waste. You can throw a lot more things on the compost heap than you think: all your vegetable waste, including potato peelings, ash from the fireplace, unprinted cardboard, throw-away paper bags from the vacuum cleaner, in fact anything you think will rot. All you have to watch out for are things that have been treated with preparations to slow down the rotting process. Oranges, for instance, have nearly always been treated with a fungicide, and potatoes from the shop will have been sprayed with a product to stop

them sprouting. If you think your peelings may have gone through a process like this, don't use them in your compost. If a piece of plastic gets into the compost by accident, by way of the vacuum-cleaner bag for example, that's no problem: when the compost is ready, you can simply sift out whatever has not rotted. We've recovered a good few knives and forks this way! Not that it does the silver any good – in an efficient compost heap, even glass is attacked. From the garden, you can use remnants of plants, grass cuttings (in moderation), fallen leaves, dead twigs, weeds, etc. But you have to be a bit more careful than in the kitchen. In some cases, plant diseases can survive in the compost. You don't have to keep every sick or attacked plant away from the compost, however; but cabbages with clubroot, for example (an ugly and very persistent fungus disease), are best put out for the dustman. Remember, too, that seeds often come through the composting process unscathed. So if you throw weeds on to the compost heap just as they are coming into seed, you could find, later, when you put the compost to use, that these seeds will start germinating and make you a lot of extra work. It is possible to make compost that is practically free of weeds, but you will need to select your garden waste very carefully.

Now to describe how we prepare compost. It's the most common system, and produces a very serviceable compost.

To start with you will need two compost bins. For a small garden these should have a floor area of about one 1 m² (10 sq ft) each. The best thing is to

build them yourself – plastic always breaks down in the long run, and metal containers rust. You can see in the photographs how the compost bins are made. The front is open and has been closed off with planks. This makes it easier to empty the compost bin. Gaps have been left in the walls so that air can get in. Too much air is not a good thing, as the outside of the compost heap will dry out – for this reason, wire-netting containers are useless.

In the kitchen we have two good-sized rubbish bins, of the sort that a standard plastic bin-liner will fit into. One bin gets all the waste for the compost, the other takes the rubbish that goes out for the dustman (and you could, if you like, have a third bin, for glass). Dividing things up from the start can save you a lot of unpleasant work later. When the compost bag is full it is emptied on to the compost heap, where, as far as possible, the waste from the kitchen is mixed with the waste from the garden. Inside the bin a layer of waste is built up to a thickness of about 15 cm (6 in). Mix this up well with a fork; then scatter a thin covering of lime over it, and possibly some blood, horn or bonemeal as well. Give the pile a few good whacks with the fork so that the lime and the bonemeal sink into the waste a little. Find a lid for the compost bin (plywood is ideal), as otherwise the rain might make the compost too wet, or the sun could dry it out too much. You should aim to keep it 'fairly damp' all the time, neither wet nor dry, in which case the system will stop functioning. Continue building layer by layer until the bin is full. As there is no floor, worms can crawl up from the ground and go to work, along with their soil-eating friends – centipedes, moulds and micro-organisms – to rot the waste.

Some composting systems advertise that their process takes only a few weeks, but we don't really see what the hurry is. We have left some compost heaps for as long as four years, and they have been no worse for it. Under normal conditions you can count on the first half of the rotting process taking about six months, or a little less if you fill your first

FAR LEFT: The solid, practical compost bin we made ourselves.

LEFT: A bin made from a kit.

bin quickly. Now you have to turn the compost heap over – that is, transfer it from the first bin to the second. When you do this you will very probably disturb a pack of busy worms: this is a sign that everything is working well. Lift the contents of bin one out into bin two, and again scatter a layer of lime over every 15 cm (6 in) layer.

The first bin is now free for use again, so you can continue dumping rubbish in it. Once it is full you can empty the second bin and pass the contents through a sieve. The best for the purpose is a very coarse sieve with about a 1 cm ($\frac{1}{2}$ in) mesh, which you can fasten to a wooden frame measuring 80 × 150 cm (about $2\frac{1}{2}$ × 5 ft). Set this up at an angle of 45° and throw the compost over it with a fork. Everything that falls through can be used immediately and whatever stays on top will have to be sifted through. First of all, put any pieces of plastic or metal and knives and forks on one side, then throw the large pieces of waste which have not yet rotted properly on to the new compost heap.

That's how easy composting can be. There's certainly not much work in it, and you always come out of it with the satisfying feeling that you are not throwing away anything that can still be used for the garden – and not just for the vegetable garden, of course! If you suspect that there are unwanted seeds in your compost, which you can easily check on by taking a sample indoors to see if anything grows, it makes sense to work in the compost about a spade deep. In that case the seeds should have little chance of germinating. If you are working according to a no-digging system, the best thing to do is to spread the compost over the garden very early in the autumn, around the end of September. Most seeds should then germinate before the winter starts, and given that young plants are generally not hardy, they will be killed off by the first frost.

It is also possible to sterilize the compost by heating, but that is a big job, and very costly in energy.

If your garden is short of worms, these can be bought and added to the compost. It is also possible to breed your own worms, and breeding kits are available.

Vegetables and their food values

In this age of informed eating and attention to the figure, it is always useful to know what your food consists of. If you grow organically it is comforting to know that, at any rate, no harmful substances have found their way into your vegetables.

At the same time you should bear in mind that vegetables only make up a very small proportion of our total diet. An average portion of vegetables provides us with at best some 70 kilojoules (17 kcal) out of the roughly 10,000 (2 400 kcal) we need per day. The amounts of minerals and vitamins are mostly small, too, with the exception of vitamin C.

Let's start with the total energy, nowadays given in joules, or to be precise, kilojoules. Since 'kilo' means one thousand, this means we are counting in units of one thousand joules. Previously, we used kilo-calories, but this is now being slowly given up. One old kilo-calorie (kcal) equals 4.184 kilojoules (kj).

We divide the energy we get from a given product – that is, our kilojoules – into protein, fat and carbohydrates.

The best sources of protein are broccoli, Brussels sprouts and broad beans.

No vegetables are rich in fat, but those with the most are borecole or kale and sweet corn.

The most carbohydrates are found in potatoes, sweet corn and scorzonera.

Next come the minerals, which are present in considerably smaller amounts.

The largest amount of calcium is found in cress and borecole. There is a relatively large amount of phosphorus in broccoli, savoy cabbage and Brussels sprouts.

Parsley has by far the most iron, which is also abundant in beetroot, broad beans and corn salad.

We get most sodium from self-blanching celery and above all beetroot.

Potassium mainly comes from celery, parsely, purslane, spinach and potatoes.

Even smaller amounts are involved when we turn to vitamins. There is no vitamin A in plants, but there is β-carotene, also known as provitamin A. Root vegetables have most provitamin A, but borecole and spinach also contain relatively large amounts.

Vitamin B_1, also called thiamine, is mainly found in green peas.

Vitamin B_2 (riboflavine) comes mostly from parsley.

Vitamin B_6 content is limited even in raw vegetables, and after cooking it is even less. There is most in potatoes and Brussels sprouts.

Lastly, vitamin C, also limited in uncooked vegetables. Brussels sprouts and red peppers come top, followed by parsley and borecole. It's worth pointing out that the energy, mineral and vitamin content does not seem to be the same throughout Europe. These differences are partly due to the way the figures are arrived at. But when the variations are often as high as 100 per cent you had best take the reported figures with a pinch of salt!

Finally, as to what all the minerals and vitamins are good for, that is something you can find out more fully from a book on food and diet, as it is outside the scope of this work.

Scorzonera is rich in carbohydrates.

How gardening keeps you fit

Hannelie on healthy exercise

I think that keeping active and busy is the basis of human well-being. In our welfare society we can see a lot of problems that derive from bad habits: poor posture and poor carriage. Back complaints, flat feet, flabby stomach mucles, breathing difficulties – I see them all daily in my practice as a physiotherapist.

It's by no means a bad thing that many people have realized that they don't get enough exercise and are taking up sport, aerobic dancing or fitness training.

But it seems to me that you can also try to get some exercise out of your every-day activities, and that is much more efficient.

I'm going to talk specifically about the kitchen garden, which is what this book is about, after all. To start with, let's take 'normal' posture – or, to put it better, 'correct' posture. What does this boil down to?

You could say that it falls somewhere between the 'military' bearing, stiff and taut, as we see on army parades, and a relaxed posture, which gives the straining back and leg muscles some rest.

With a bed 1.2 m (4 ft) wide, many people can still manage this spread-legged position. It's good exercise for the legs.

BELOW LEFT: If you often bend like this you would see a lot of your physiotherapist.

BELOW RIGHT: Always try to squat by bending your knees: this spares your back.

The most important jobs in the vegetable garden

Digging is without any doubt the worst job. But any healthy person can dig without difficulty if he or she uses the right spade and puts the right load on the back. The shaft of the spade must come up to the bottom rib, and the blade must not be too big (small for clay, larger for sandy soil). Hoeing is much lighter work, but it often produces tired backs because a lot of gardeners bend over to hoe. That is the wrong way to do it. If the hoe is at the proper angle to the shaft and the shaft is long enough, you can stand up straight to hoe. It's good exercise for the oblique stomach muscles (to keep a slim waist!) and first-class exercise for

the arms, especially for the muscles at the back of the upper arm and the shoulder, which don't often get much of a look-in in normal life.

Pushing a wheelbarrow is easier if the wheel is in the right place (not too far to the front) and if you walk upright, with your stomach muscles tight.

Now for bending, which you will do a lot of when you're sowing or weeding. I recommend that you bend at the knees, if this is not too difficult for you. Not everybody is comfortable working in a squatting position, but it is far better for your back. Often all you will need to do to keep your balance is to support yourself with a couple of fingers.

Finally, a few tips on exercises you can do in between jobs. When you first go out into the garden, start with a few breathing exercises. Breathe in through the nose: first fill your stomach, then press your ribs out – and make sure you keep your shoulders low.

Breathe out through the mouth: first relax your stomach, then let your ribs fall.

After this, do a few deep knee-bends – you can pick out a few weeds while you're doing these. Then hoe between the rows for a while: this will not only give you a chance to get your breath back, but it will also keep your stomach muscles busy.

Now some stretching exercises: point your arms skywards and make yourself as tall as you can. Spread your legs and – without bending your knees – stretch your fingertips to your left and right foot alternately.

If the seed bed is 1.2 m (4 ft) wide, most people will be able to stand spread-legged across it. This keeps the thigh muscles in trim, and you can reach the middle of the bed very easily, too.

I am sure that if you pay a little extra attention to proper posture you will find much more pleasure in growing your own vegetables; and I wish you every success.

LEFT: If you dig like this, back pain will often be the result.
RIGHT: Digging with a straight back causes far fewer problems.

LEFT: Wrong hoeing position.
RIGHT: A long-handled hoe allows you to stand upright while you work.

Working the soil

Working the soil has always played an important part in vegetable growing – we can see that this was true even back in prehistoric times. The last hundred years have seen a good deal of argument about working the soil: is it necessary or not, should it be shallow or deep, what with, etc. On pages 12–13 you can read more about the most important alternative ideas on how the soil should be worked.

In this book we shall not only be looking at the alternative ways of working the soil, but at orthodox ones, too.

Digging

The most common way of working the ground in small gardens is digging by hand. It is especially important when a new garden is being started, as you can then be certain of what lies underneath the surface layer, which often looks perfect in itself. For instance, it's the usual practice on building sites to bury rubble. If you buy a new house and try to grow on that patch, your kitchen gardening will certainly be a flop. There's nothing for it but to get rid of it all.

Another result of building work is that the soil will more often than not have been consolidated under the weight of the builders' machinery. This means there will be less air in it: the structure is 'spoiled', as we say.

It's not unusual for the garden of a new house to have been raised, most probably by a hidden filling of sand.

How is this raising done, and what kind of sand is used? You can safely work on the assumption that the cheapest available solution was chosen, and that the idea that you might want to get healthy vegetables out of your garden was not uppermost in the builder's mind.

All in all, digging is nearly always the best option when you have to work fresh ground. Larger areas can be attacked with a mechanical digger, but enclosed gardens have to be dug by hand. You can farm out the work to someone who does it on the side, or to a gardener, but it makes sense in that case to pay by the hour rather than a flat fee for the job, otherwise it's likely to be botched.

Even if you are not planning, or not able, to do the work yourself, it is still a good idea to read the following paragraphs, as then you'll know what to look for, at any rate, while someone else is doing it.

Sandy soil is the easiest to dig and for this reason professional gardeners of earlier days always used enormous spades, so that the work was done faster. For clay, on the other hand, a special, extremely small clay spade was used, and sometimes, as well, a fork with four flat prongs. Besides this, they waited until the clay had just the right amount of moisture, as clay can't be dug well when it is too wet or too dry.

Since a hard frost can do a lot to improve the structure of a clay soil it's best to dig this type of soil just before the winter. Sandy soil can be dug just as well in the spring.

There are different ways of digging, which are indicated by the depth the soil is worked to. Thus, we talk of single digging, double digging and treble digging. The reference is to how many 'spits' deep you dig, a spit being the depth of the spade's blade, usually 25–30 cm (10–12 in). Treble digging, then, will loosen the soil to a depth of 90 cm (3 ft). Generally, we do not dig deeper than two spits (double digging), which is where, if there was a fair growth of weeds, we lay the weed layer that we skimmed off the top of the soil (roots and all).

When you are double or treble digging you can switch round the top and bottom layers. But you should only do this if the ground has recently been disturbed, for instance, during building activity. Otherwise, keep the top layer on top and the underneath layer underneath – mainly because the upper layer has most wildlife in it. The soil organisms could have the stuffing knocked out of them if they were buried that deep. And this is precisely why the no-digging lobby object so strongly to digging in the first place: they reckon that any disturbance of the layers of the soil kills off soil organisms.

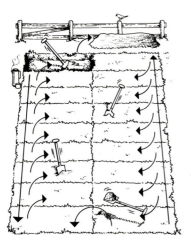

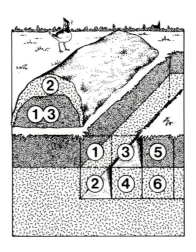

FAR LEFT: Soil dug out of the first trench has to be carried over to the spot where the digging finishes. You'll have least transport to worry about if you work up and down in narrow strips, as the drawing shows. This way, the wheelbarrow can stay in the garden shed.

LEFT: In the double-digging method, spits 1 and 3 (upper layer of soil) are dug out and set on one side. Spit 2 also comes out and is likewise kept aside. Then 4 takes the place of 2, 5 takes the place of 1, 6 takes the place of 4, and so on. For adding manure in between, see the photographs opposite.

When you are double-digging, first dig a trench. You can see from the picture that the first trench is dug two spits deep. The earth that has been dug out is piled up in the foreground – this is where we shall work our way back to after digging two parallel beds. Digging narrow beds up and down across the plot is easier than trundling soil from one end to the other.

Only the first spit is dug out of the second trench. This is the spit numbered 3 in the drawing. The digger is standing inside the first trench and does not have to bend down so far. This soil joins the rest on the pile of dug-out soil. Hannelie is using a stainless-steel spade, an expensive piece of equipment, but very good to work with.

A shovel is used to give a neat finish to the section that has been dug out. This gives you the 'steps' effect in the drawing. This finishing is not absolutely necessary, but very useful if you are digging for the first time, as it helps you to get a clear view of the stages of the work. The process of digging soil out is now finished: the rest will be turned over where it is.

The lower spit of trench 2 (spit 4 in the drawing) is now turned over and takes the place of spit 2 in the drawing, below where spit 1 originally was. The spade is pushed into the soil with the foot. If it is good and sharp at the digging end, it will cut like a knife through butter – in sandy soil, at least.

Farmyard manure which is standing by in the wheelbarrow is laid on top of the new lower spit of trench 1, using a dung fork. In this way the manure will be about 25 cm (10 in) below the surface, which is the most important rooting level for vegetables. This method is only recommended for mature farmyard manure: fresh manure is better mixed into the soil.

The upper spit of the third trench (spit 5 in the drawing) is laid on top of the manure. At first, the soil will lie much higher than it was, but it will settle. The first leg of your spit digging is now completed; now go back to the third photograph and repeat until the garden has been dug or until you're ready to call it a day.

A small garden cultivator will work the soil to a shallow depth. It is ideal for working manure into the top layer.

Single digging is the easiest kind of digging: the soil is simply turned over and put back where it came from. You don't really need to dig up the soil, lift it out of the trench and throw it back in. If you are wearing stout gardening shoes or boots you can lean the shaft of the spade against your foot and simply twist the blade over. The soil will then fall into the gap, upside down, without your having to take the weight. There's also a very clever mechanical spade which does the same thing.

For double or treble digging, you first have to dig out one or more trenches completely before you can start. The drawings and photographs on pages 18 and 19 explain how to do it.

If you have never done any digging before, do only a very small patch on the first day, to get your body used to what is really pretty hard work. Once you've got the hang of it you will probably find it very good exercise. You'll be working off about 900 to 1200 joules (200 to 300 calories) of fat per hour – useful for people who are carrying a little too much weight.

It's true that a lot of older gardeners have ended up with a round back from digging, but this is because they have never had a chance to read Hannelie's tips on proper posture (pages 16–17). It need never happen to you!

Levelling

It is possible to level out uneven ground during digging. This is done by adding extra soil to the lower spit, or taking some away. A practised digger will often do this while working, without realizing it, but it's a bit more difficult for the beginner. The main thing is never to even out the soil by adjusting the topsoil, as this will make the cultivation layer thicker in one place than in another.

Improving the soil

If the soil isn't 100 per cent fertile (which is nearly always the case), digging gives you the ideal opportunity to improve its condition. You can add all sorts of things to it to increase the humus content, for example, or to raise the fertility, change the acidity level, and so on. These substances are never put in deeper than the roots will grow, and for vegetables this is seldom more than 60 cm (2 ft), which is the same as our two spits. We call this depth the cultivation layer.

Nearly all soils will benefit from humus, which can, for example, take the form of peat, leafmould, farmyard manure, mushroom compost or garden compost. About 5–10 m³ of one or more of the soil improvers mentioned can be added to each 100 m² of surface (177–350 lb per 120 sq yd). This would produce a layer anything up to 10 cm (4 in) thick, which is a fair amount. Only a true peat soil has absolutely no need of additional humus.

Soil with a poor structure, such as clay, can be perked up marvellously by adding humus, especially peat or compost. Lime can also improve the structure of a clay soil.

Lime, which usually comes as hydrated lime, is principally used to raise the acidity (pH) of the soil. Acid soils, particularly sandy types, but also clays, need some lime, especially if plants are to be grown in them which can't stand a low pH, which includes many vegetables. Follow the advice you are given after the soil test. As lime is poor at spreading through the soil it is very important to add it during double digging. But there is a snake in the grass: it is not advisable to add manure and lime at the same time, as this will bring about a chemical reaction, and as a result the manure will decompose too quickly. So if lime is needed work it in while you are digging, wait up to six months, and then work the manure into the surface layer only.

You can see from the photographs what is involved in working manure (or other improvers) into the soil. If you want the stuff right at the very bottom of the trench, spread it on the second or third spit (a dung fork is as good as anything) before you turn it over; then it will be up-ended along with the soil. If organic material (farmyard manure, for example) needs working only into the top spit, the entire surface can be covered before digging.

Loosening

If you don't want to do any digging it's advisable at least to loosen the soil in the spring so that air can penetrate. The tool generally used for this is a digging fork. It is stuck in the ground and pulled backwards and forwards. Then rake the soil surface level to obtain a fine tilth and it's ready for sowing.

Cultivators

More and more amateur gardeners are buying small rotary cultivators. These machines have advantages and disadvantages.

The possible advantages are that working the soil takes less effort and, above all, fertilizers and other materials for improving the ground can be mixed very intensively into the soil. However, the machine does not cultivate very deeply – 15 cm (6 in) would be about the best – so that the deep digging called for when starting a new garden could not be done with a cultivator. But it is fine for the regular annual working-over. Even some no-digging fanatics approve of cultivators, because very shallow work – 5–10 cm (2–4 in) can be done with them, which they don't consider disturbs the soil organisms.

The disadvantage is that machine cultivating on wet soil can result in a packed, hard surface layer, through which moisture cannot penetrate. For this reason cultivators should only be used on soil which is dry or only slightly moist.

Space for your vegetables

Vegetable growing needs space: that goes without saying. This book is designed both for someone who wants to grow a few heads of lettuce on a balcony and for the enthusiast with several acres of land.

Keep them separate

It is usual to grow vegetables in a separate part of the garden. Under the fruit trees, for instance, there would be too much competition for rooting space, and if planted in the border our vegetables would quickly be overgrown by their decorative neighbours, resulting in poor performance. This, however, does not change the fact that it can be very refreshing to grow a few artichokes or even a few heads of red cabbage among the border plants. Odd corners of the garden can easily be used to grow relatively undemanding plants, including many herbs.

But on the whole, preference should be given to growing vegetables in beds, more or less in rows, which, needless to say, makes the task of looking after them much easier.

Vegetables can quite successfully be accommodated in the flower garden; the concrete ring provides an interesting texture and the red flowers of the runner beans are very decorative.

BELOW: As far as possible, the kitchen garden must be protected from the wind and receive plenty of sun: this produces a favourable micro-climate.

Position

Vegetables are very demanding, not only as regards the soil, as you can read on page 25, but also with respect to the micro-climate. Protection from the wind is appreciated by most plants, and a sunny position is advisable for nearly all vegetables. You will have to bear in mind these needs when you plan your garden, or you could run into problems. When setting up a new garden, whether it belongs to a new house or you're adapting an existing garden, it's always as well to plan things out beforehand. Graph paper makes this easier. Try to include an indication of which parts of the garden are in shadow and which receive plenty of sun. You can do this by marking in where shadows fall at three different times of the day. The best places to grow vegetables are those where no shadow falls between 9.00 in the morning and 5.00 in the evening. Very often we discover this area occupied in existing gardens by the lawn.

Think hard about whether that lawn is really giving you all that much enjoyment. It needs a fair bit of work to keep it in trim, it takes up quite a portion of your land, and despite this it is often too small to play games on. Many people who have thought it over have decided to dig up their lawn (or part of it) to grow vegetables. Now, for a good part of the year and for practically the same amount of work, they can enjoy beautiful vegetables from their own gardens.

It may be that you have the use of a plot of land away from your house, possibly on an allotment. The same tips apply: check out the position and the sun and shade – these factors are just as

ABOVE: Growing vegetables on the compost heap: ideal for lazy gardeners, but the plants are liable to attack by diseases.

LEFT: You can grow a good supply of vegetables on a small balcony.

BELOW: Why not dig up part of your lawn? Growing vegetables is more fun than mowing.

important as soil type and manuring.

Always lay out the kitchen garden so that you can get at it easily; herbs are best planted near the kitchen door, so that even in the winter you can nip out for a sprig of parsley.

Size of the garden

If you are short of land you can grow vegetables in tubs. These can stand on the balcony, for example, or on a flat roof. Vegetables which do not grow very tall can be grown quite successfully in plastic flower pots. A depth of only 20 cm (8 in) is often sufficient. Larger concrete containers or wooden tubs are also very suitable. A position against a wall will allow you to grow berry or stone fruits; you need no more space than the roots take up.

But you must understand that growing vegetables and herbs that way is not a serious way of doing it. You should never expect a few square metres (yards) of garden to provide any significant

proportion of your food needs. If it's more or less a question of feeding your family from your kitchen garden then you should be thinking in terms of around 50 m² (60 sq yd) per person, for the vegetables alone. If you are also aiming to grow berry fruits you have to add 30 m² (36 sq yd) to that. For top fruits (apples and pears) you'll need another 50 m² (60 sq yd). Add on another 1 m² (10 sq ft) for herbs, and you end up with a total of 130 m² (156 sq yd) per person, or some 500 m² (600 sq yd) for a family of four. And then, of course, you have to add space for paths, a compost heap, a shed, and maybe a greenhouse or a growing frame, and it's already adding up to 600 or 700 m² (700 or 850 sq yd). If you're limiting yourself to vegetables, herbs and berry fruits, some 400–500 m² (500–600 sq yd) would be enough to make you completely self-sufficient.

In practice, you will find that you will grow some of your vegetables yourself, and buy the rest. It is very difficult, especially in winter and spring, to supply your table with the vegetables it needs from your own garden. Your money will go to the greengrocer until the first fresh spinach arrives at your table from the garden, which is usually sometime in May. So we will work on the basis that you have a kitchen garden with an area somewhere between 25 and 400 m² (30 and 500 sq yd).

Our vegetable garden has an area of 500 m² (600 sq yd), including the paths and the greenhouses. We also have about a thousand square yards available for potatoes and other plants that need a lot of room.

The famous vegetable garden in Wisley, with its eight-sided greenhouse and glass cloches.

BELOW LEFT: Vegetables in separate wooden troughs.

BELOW: Tomatoes in growing-bags.

Laying out your garden

Once you have decided to lay out part of your garden as a kitchen garden, try to form a picture in your mind of what you want. Think of the old-fashioned country gardens, where vegetables used to be grown in a really pleasant style. In fact, you still come across them. A simple division by means of low hedges, a well in the middle, a few benches to rest on – it's all so much nicer than a rectangular plot of land and nothing more. A vegetable garden will fit just as well into a stylish modern garden: with the help of a low hedge (to cast less shadow) it can be divided from the ornamental part of the garden, and then a neat path of attractive flags or other stones can be added to link the two.

Vegetable gardens are usually laid out in rectangular beds with a width of 1.2 m (4 ft). The average person standing at the edge of a bed of this size can just reach the middle with his or her hands

The toolshed can be a very attractive element in a small garden.

flagstones, for example. This is what we did – in fact, the paths are 50 cm (1 ft 8 in) wide, because we didn't have to worry about the odd few inches. The advantage of this is that you can always keep your feet dry, which is not to be sneezed at in the winter. One disadvantage, however, turned out to be that adding compost and manure gradually caused the surface of the beds to rise, so that the soil ended up a little above the level of the paths. This means that we have already had to raise the paths of couple of times, which is quite hard work. A second disadvantage, which particularly applies if you're working the ground by machine (with a cultivator), is that hard paths can get in the way. So think twice before you spend good money on flagstones.

Not just beds

The beds of vegetables and the paths between will take up most of the space in your kitchen garden, but not all. You will have to keep your tools somewhere, for a start. A special shed is very handy for this, if your garden has the space. Another useful addition is a greenhouse or a frame, for raising seeds in the spring. If you are taking an organic approach to your gardening, you won't be able to do without a compost heap. And think about the supply of water and electricity. A tap and hose are particularly important, because plenty of watering will be needed in dry weather.

When the work's done you'll want

These raised beds can be reached with ease from a wheelchair.

somewhere to rest: you'll get a lot of enjoyment from a small bench or some other kind of seat, from which you can survey the garden. It could be partly in the shade.

If you have children, bear in mind how useful it can be to introduce them to the wonders of nature at a very early age. Even children of one or two years of age can keep themselves quite busy in the garden, in their own way, and a few years later they will have no problems growing simple vegetables like cress, radishes or lettuce. They enjoy seeing the quick results: that is one of the nice things about vegetables, and it is a great stimulus.

without stepping on it. Try it out for yourself: 1.2 m (4 ft) doesn't sound much, but it is quite wide enough. Gardeners who are not so tall might prefer a bed width of 1 m (3 ft 4 in). A reasonably fit person can also stand astride the bed to work, as shown on page 16.

If possible, the beds should run north–south. There is practically no limit to the length, but it is best to have them no longer than 10 metres (30 feet), otherwise you'll be forever walking round them. Ideally, too, the tallest plants should be on the north side and the lower ones towards the south so that they will all get the full benefit of the sun. Between the beds are the paths: 30 cm (1 ft), the width of a small flagstone, is wide enough for these. At right-angles to these paths you can lay a main path, which would thus run east–west in the ideal layout.

It goes without saying that this is just one of countless possible solutions: what you choose will be decided by the lie of the land and your personal taste. In our garden, for example, we chose slightly curved beds forming part of a very large circle. You can see what this looks like from the photographs. Other people prefer to have an old-fashioned country-style garden.

You can consider whether or not to give your path a hard topping, with

You can catch children's enthusiasm at an early age by letting them sow their own names. This one is in mustard seed.

Plan your gardening

When you have prepared your garden and laid it out, and have made sure the soil is in good fettle, you haven't finished. We have now come to one of the most complicated parts of the whole business of vegetable growing. You don't have to master this section all at once, at least not in your first year in your new garden; but in later years you will be glad to have read about it so that you can prevent your crops becoming smaller year by year. The subjects of this section are successional sowing and planting, complementary crops and crop rotation. Three very important rules for the grower, which prevent soil from becoming exhausted and plants from falling victim to all kinds of diseases.

Successional sowing and planting

In one year you can grow several different vegetables one after the other on the same piece of ground. We call these the early crop, the main crop and the late crop. We also have 'catch crops': different plants grown on the same piece of ground at the same time (also called 'double cropping' or 'intercropping'). These should not be confused with complementary crops, which we will come to later. Before you become dizzy with all these new terms, here are a few examples. If you sow kohl-rabi in March, you can harvest the vegetables at the beginning of June. Then you still have time to sow dwarf French beans. You pick these when they are still very young, at the end of August or early September, and after that you can still sow corn salad, which can be picked well into the winter, especially if you grow under a cloche. An example of inter-cropping is the planting of pre-sown lettuce under the runner bean supports. The lettuces grow faster than the beans, and by the time the beans begin to deprive the lettuces of light they will have been harvested.

So far it all looks pretty simple. But now comes the problem that you can't grow any vegetables in any order you like. Some, such as leaf vegetables and brassicas, take a vast amount of nitrogen from the soil. If you now try to grow

Cabbages planted among the lettuce – an example of intercropping that requires some extra nitrogen.

Beans between rows of green vegetables: a good intercropping combination requiring no extra fertilizer. The green vegetables are harvested before the beans become fully grown.

plants which need a lot of nitrogen, you will not have much success. So after early cabbage you must not grow summer spinach, or sow lettuce after spinach. And you must also make sure that the sowing and harvesting times match up well. Celeriac (turnip-rooted celery), a vegetable with a long growing period, doesn't really leave room for any other crops in the same year.

Some vegetables are only suitable for growing as the main crop, while others can be either early or late crop, for example spinach, radishes and corn salad. Generally speaking, it is unusual to be able to grow three crops one after the other; more often we are limited to two, and then in only 40 per cent of cases, so that we can use the garden as a whole to 140 per cent. In this book we have included against every vegetable the crops you can grow before or after it. This will help you to draw up a growing plan.

Complementary crops

Growing different vegetables together in one bed may be intercropping, as we mentioned above, but it may also amount to 'complementary' planting. This looks much the same, but with complementary crops we make use of the fact that certain vegetables have a positive effect on each other, or fight each other's pests and diseases. For example, the smell of onions or garlic acts as a repellent to the root fly, which likes to lay its eggs in young carrots; and for this reason onions and carrots are often grown together. Another example is lettuce grown on the lee side of a row of peas. The pea twigs will keep off the wind, which helps the lettuce to grow.

Complementary planting can also affect the taste of vegetables. Chervil, for instance, makes radishes taste sharper, and garden cress improves the taste of radishes, too. The roots of one vegetable can release substances into the soil that can be put to use by another plant. Bacteria on the roots of peas produce nitrogen which is very welcome to leaf greens.

A lot has been written about complementary cropping and the mutual effects of plants on each other, but little real research has been done. Most of what we are told goes back to stories passed down by older gardeners to their children and grandchildren. Sometimes they work; sometimes they're simply old wives' tales. We have given favourable and unfavourable complementary combinations for every vegetable in this book, which we have collected from a large number of books. When different authors contradict each other we have recorded the combination as 'disputed'. Try out some complementary crops for yourself and form your own judgment. The soil type needs taking into account as well: what's good for one garden may be wrong for another.

Crop rotation
Certain vegetables take the same nutrients from the soil all the time. If this is carried on for a number of years serious shortages can occur.

Other plants are sensitive to diseases that may persist in the soil. If you grow the same vegetable in the same spot the next year the attack becomes worse.

If we grow brassicas in the same place for several years we end up with incurable clubroot, a fungus disease which, on sandy soil in particular, can lead to a complete loss of the crop.

To avoid all this misery various schemes of crop rotation have been worked out. These make sure that you

only come back to the same place with any plant after a number of years. The longer you can leave it, the better – some crop-rotation plans run to eight years! In a private garden, however, three years is generally as far as it goes; and that is often enough of a problem, because you have to keep very precisely to the plan.

The easiest way of going about it is to divide the garden into three sections of equal size, called 1, 2 and 3. The vegetables are divided into three groups, and we shall call them A, B and C.

A is the group of plants that use a lot of nitrogen, which we can only grow, therefore, after a good application of nitrogen fertilizer. These are potatoes, leaf vegetables, brassicas, gherkins, courgettes, cucumbers, melons, celeriac, leeks and tomatoes.

B are root crops such as beets, fennel, carrots and onions.

C are the leguminous plants (peas, beans) which constantly produce nitrogen via their root nodules.

The plan now looks like this:

In the fourth year you start at the beginning again. Apart from that, it's simply a matter of remembering where everything was last year.

Crop rotation in action: first row leaf vegetables (lettuce), second row root crops (onions), and finally peas.

Don't be discouraged
Just to recapitulate: in planning your kitchen garden you will have to take account of:

1. Successional planting.
2. Complementary crops
3. Crop rotation.

Nearly all the plants should receive plenty of sun and – something we think is important – the overall effect must look good. This is a practically impossible task and you must not let yourself be discouraged by the flood of demands. We grew vegetables for years without paying too much attention to all these rules and the result was indeed that some crops fell off and some diseases hit harder than we expected. But 80 per cent of the crops came up marvellously, and 10 years on the trot, to boot. When you consider that the best professionals rarely achieve better than 90 per cent we'd gladly put up with 10 per cent less in output and a lot less work!

But this doesn't mean we think you should pay no attention to planting combinations and crop rotation, which are very good things in themselves. We just don't want to discourage the beginner by laying too much stress on it.

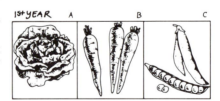

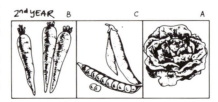

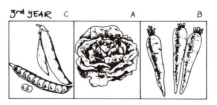

Making it easy

When we are growing vegetables we can make use of a number of growing aids which will give us earlier crops or protect the plants. Mostly this is a matter of improving the micro-climate by keeping the wind off and letting the sun through.

Plastic sheeting

Surprising results can be achieved with plastic sheeting. Usually this means simple horticultural polythene sheeting. It is available in widths up to 8 m (26 ft). Polythene is not perfectly clear, which is just what we need, since this shields the plants from the fiercest of the sun's rays. Strong polythene can be used several times. It can be laid directly on the ground, or you can make tunnel cloches from it (see below). The most common use of transparent sheeting is as a covering for newly sown beds, to accelerate the germination process. Under the polythene the temperature rises while the humidity level is preserved, and this helps the seeds to germinate quickly – especially in spring, when the weather is still cold. It is important, however, to keep a close eye on what's going on under the plastic, because as soon as the plants start growing they touch the sheeting, and if the humidity is too high this can lead to fungus diseases: the seedlings damp off, as gardeners say. If you want to, you can string the sheeting above the ground, but then you have effectively produced a tunnel cloche, of which more below.

You can also obtain perforated plastic sheeting specially made for vegetables.

Expanding plastic sheeting has thousands of small slits, which open as the plants grow.

The holes ensure airy conditions underneath and so the sheeting can be left over the plants for a longer period. An even better idea is slitted plastic, which starts off closed but opens as the plants grow. This not only gives more ventilation but also stretches with the plants. Not readily available everywhere, but very useful if you can find it.

An extra advantage of plastic sheeting is that it protects the seeds and young plants from birds, which are always glad to find seeds to eat early in the year.

A different application for plastic sheets is offered by black mulching polythene, which is used to suppress weeds. This is handy, among other things, for growing strawberry plants, which are planted through small holes cut in the plastic.

Netting

Netting has partly the same effect as plastic sheeting, but it lets more air through, as well as rainwater. The main use of netting is to keep pests away. There are various sorts, but very fine mesh is needed to keep out insects.

A different sort of netting is bird netting, designed to keep birds off fruit bushes, strawberries and brassicas, for example. It's a good idea to fix this netting tightly across a framework of laths or pipes, because if you throw it loosely over the plants birds will become caught up in it.

Cloches and tunnels

We now come to a growing aid for the kitchen garden which is probably the most important of all. Unfortunately, too many people still do not realize how much one can advance crops by using cloches or tunnels. And speeding up the crops is one of the best ways of avoiding a huge number of pests, because very often everything has been picked before they wake from their winter hibernation.

Ingenious inventors have come up with many ways of producing tunnels. Glass cloches are very popular in Britain, often made of plain window glass. The sheets of glass are held together with special clips, so that long tunnels can be built. We are not very enthusiastic about this system, because if just one pane breaks you're back to square one: so every piece has to be carefully removed from the garden and stored somewhere safe from accident. Besides this, clear glass does not give full protection, so the sun can burn the plants.

FAR LEFT: Strawberry netting as protection against birds.
LEFT: Insect netting on a frame of plastic electric conduit.

Then there are sturdy tunnels made from polyester and other kinds of rigid plastic. If your seed beds happen to be just the right width these are very handy to use, since you can lift up one section to hoe or harvest underneath. Unfortunately, this kind of tunnel is very expensive.

Then we come to the most popular cloches: those made from plastic sheeting. They can be bought in the shops. A version which sells very well consists of flexible wire hoops which are placed across the bed. The plastic rests on these hoops and thinner ones are bent over the top to hold the plastic tight. Drawbacks: the hoops go rusty very quickly, and the sheeting is usually too narrow, at 1.2 m (4 ft), which is not enough for a bed of the same width. Also, a ready-made tunnel is not cheap.

We have developed a better system,

A frame with soil and space heating provided by electric cables.

which you can see in the photographs. Instead of wire hoops we use plastic electric conduit, which will last several years. This tubing, with a diameter of 15 mm ($\frac{5}{8}$ in) or possibly a touch thicker, say 19 mm ($\frac{3}{4}$ in) is supplied in lengths of 4 m (13 ft). Saw them in two, so that you have pieces 2 m (6$\frac{1}{2}$ ft) long; then, 25 cm (10 in) from each end, drill a hole, and insert a brass bolt as shown in the picture.

To build a tunnel, the ends of the conduit are pushed into the ground exactly as far as the bolt, that is, 25 cm (10 in) deep. The length of the tube spanning the bed is then 1.5 m (5 ft). Buy horticultural plastic in a 3 or 6 m (10 or 20 ft) width, and cut strips 1.5 m (5 ft) wide. These are now laid over the plastic supports, which you have positioned along the beds 50–75 cm (20–30 in) apart.

To hold the plastic down we use nylon cord, which is fixed crosswise over the tunnel between the brass bolts. At each end of the tunnel a stake is set in the ground, and the sheeting is fixed to it.

By pushing the plastic up between the tubing and the tightly stretched cord you can hoe underneath with ease, or ventilate the bed in warm weather.

A general disadvantage of bow-shaped tunnels is that the plants at the edges do not get a lot of room to grow. No problem: you can also make rectangular tunnels from electric conduit. You can buy corner pieces which the tubing exactly fits into. But you will now have to work out exactly what width your plastic sheet will need to be, which will depend on the height of your tunnel. This kind of rectangular tunnel is very

good for growing cabbages, not just under plastic, but under insect netting as well.

In autumn, winter and early spring you can cover the tunnels with bubble plastic (the type used for greenhouse insulation) instead of ordinary plastic: it provides better insulation and is heavier and stronger.

Cold and heated frames
Until recently a frame was always a construction of wood topped with a standard pane of glass in a frame measuring 1.5 m × 80 cm (5 ft × 2 ft 8 in). This is still an excellent design, though we would now suggest they should be built from concrete sections (available ready-made) and the glass frame from hardwood (often to be found second-hand). Not many professional

A small cold frame made from aluminium and glass, available as a kit.

Reliable greenhouse heating with a thermostatically-controlled fan heater.

An electrically heated propagator.

Aluminium greenhouse built from a kit and sprayed with a liquid shading material to protect plants from the sun.

gardeners use frames these days, because the bending needed to work with them is not very efficient in business. For an amateur gardener this doesn't matter so much.

Alongside these standard-sized frames we are now seeing a good many aluminium frames in kits, in all shapes and sizes. Usually the walls as well as the top are glass. These are well suited to balconies and other small spaces, but if you have a vegetable garden we would still recommend a good old-fashioned frame, because they are cheaper, more durable and easier to look after.

If you simply set up the frame in the garden as it is, you have what is called a cold frame (that is, an unheated one). The warmth then has to come from the sun, which usually means waiting until March. The plants can be protected from too much sun with shading netting or proprietary liquid shading material.

On warm days the frame is opened to the air, and when there is danger of overnight frost a piece of old carpet or newspapers are laid over it.

If you want to start using the frame earlier in the year it makes sense to heat it. Formerly this used to be accomplished by putting down a layer of fresh horse manure, which would heat up – the original "hot-bed", also known as a manure bed, early frame or forcing frame.

Nowadays we can provide heat much more easily by using electric heating cable laid zig-zag fashion on a sheet of polystyrene foam. The cable is covered with a 5 cm (2 in) layer of sharp sand and on top of this are placed plastic trays of seeds, young plants, etc. There is no need for a thermostat (which is expensive) to achieve excellent results. If the loops of cable are spaced about 10 cm (4 in) apart, the average rise in soil temperature will be about 10°C (50°F).

The ideal: a greenhouse

Nearly everyone who grows vegetables for a hobby dreams of owning a greenhouse to get seedlings off to an early start and to grow tender plants later in the season.

We could write a huge amount about greenhouses – in fact, one could fill a book. That's not what we aim to do, so we will limit ourselves to the most important facts.

A greenhouse does not have to be in full sun: a touch of shade when the day is at its hottest is no bad thing. The door will usually be on the south side. If the garden is next to the house, try not to set up the greenhouse too far away. Think of the gas, electricity and water supply and protection from icy east winds.

The type of greenhouse is usually aluminium these days, which is cheaper than wood and lasts longer. Anodized aluminium can be very attractive. Aluminium greenhouses are delivered in kit form, and the assembly is an easy matter for a DIY enthusiast. There are freestanding and lean-to versions.

The equipment you need in a greenhouse mainly consists of staging so that you don't have to bend down all the time you are busy. In a typical vegetable greenhouse you will probably set up staging on one side for plant raising and grow at ground level in the normal way on the other side. This is fine for taller plants, such as tomatoes. An electrically heated propagator is also useful for early sowings. Again, think of the electricity and water supply.

Heating is not absolutely necessary in a vegetable greenhouse but without it you won't be able to leave anything in it over the winter, because it will get just as cold inside on a frosty night as it does outside. If you want to start sowing very early you have to be sure of a temperature at least 5°C above zero (41°F). This is most easily assured with an electric fan heater, but it runs up a big electricity bill. Gas is a cheaper means of providing heat. Paraffin heaters are far less useful for greenhouse heating – the fuel is forever running out just when you need it.

As soon as the sun begins to shine a greenhouse will rapidly warm up: this warmth is free and is a big help in the spring.

Insulation is a major preoccupation at the moment, and rightly so with high fuel prices. One shouldn't really be building greenhouses with single glazing any more, but use double glazing. If you have a greenhouse with single glazing it is a great help during the winter to line it internally with bubble plastic.

Lean-to greenhouse from a kit, in brown-enamelled aluminium.

Propagation

By the propagation of vegetable plants we mean here not only growing from seed, which is by far the most common method, but also other ways of multiplying, such as dividing and taking cuttings.

Growing from seed

Nearly all vegetables are grown from seed. On pages 7–8 you can read how a plant develops from its seed. You will also find there special information on growing from your own seeds, on F_1 hybrids, on bolting, etc. Here we will be dealing specifically with the techniques of seed-raising.

Most seeds prefer to germinate in a moist, fairly warm environment. But there are exceptions. Lettuce seed, for example, requires a temperature below 20°C (68°F) to germinate. This is why many lettuce sowings turn out poorly in warm, sunny weather. There are also seeds that need to go through a cold period first before they can germinate. Primulas are a good example of this. In the vegetable garden we don't have a lot to do with cold-germinators of this sort. Seeds that germinate at low temperatures (sometimes only one or two degrees above zero) are usually sown early, and seeds that only germinate when there is plenty of warmth are sown late. By providing extra heat (e.g. in frames or the greenhouse) we can get warm-germinators going much earlier.

Because ordinary, sandy garden soil dries out very quickly in warm weather, at least in the upper levels where we have sown the seed, we can expect summer sowings to give poorer results than seeds sown in spring, when the soil is steadily moist. Fortunately something can be done about this – read on.

Sowing out of doors

If we sow our seeds directly in the garden we call this sowing in the open. Usually this is done at the spot where the plants are to be left to grow until they are harvested. Alternatively, we may sow in a separate outdoor seed bed, from which the plants will later be moved to their final position. If the soil is dry and sandy we can mix in some humus-rich material such as peat, potting compost or garden

A small propagator, ideal for raising early vegetables.

compost with the top layer. The moisture will then be retained for longer.

If there has been no rain you must give the ground a thorough watering before sowing. Watering after sowing is not advisable, since the seeds might be washed away, and the soil might become compacted at the surface.

There are three methods of sowing: in rows, broadcast and in groups. Each method has advantages and disadvantages.

Rows make gardening easy: the rows are spaced a hoe's width apart. And you can see which are the plants you have sown as soon as they show their shoots, because weeds never arrange themselves in rows.

Broadcast sowing is only used for plants that do not grow very tall, such as spinach and purslane. This will give you a greater yield per square foot than sowing in rows. But if many weeds come up at the same time you can spend a lot of time sorting out one from the other.

When sowing in groups, one or more (often 5) very large seeds are sown very close to each other. The next batch is then sown a fair distance away.

In this book we tell you the distance to leave between rows or groups of seeds. If broadcasting is better, we will say so.

Don't sow too densely. Beginners nearly always sow too many seeds. This does not matter too much with broad beans, because they are so big you can make practically any mistake you like with them; but the finer seeds – like

Ventilation is necessary when the sun becomes too strong. This can be achieved by panes you can open (ventilators) or by using an electric fan. There are ventilators which open automatically according to temperature, and the fan can be controlled by a thermostat. Very useful, this, because you only need to let ventilation slip your mind for a minute and the temperature can very quickly jump to over 50°C (120°F), causing considerable harm to the plants.

Shading also helps to keep the temperature down and it prevents the plants from becoming scorched. We are not keen on roller blinds because you spend half your time rolling them up and letting them down. A much easier method is spraying the greenhouse with a proprietary liquid shading material which becomes clearer when it rains, but is not washed away.

Other points. Buying a greenhouse kit is not all there is to it. Whatever kind it is, solid foundations are needed, either of brick or made from wooden sleepers, otherwise the building may blow over in the first strong wind, or subside. Staging is never included in the price, nor is heating, automatic ventilation nor connections for electricity and water.

Growing in the greenhouse. Details of this on pages 44–45.

carrots and lettuce – are often sown too close together. This makes for extra work when they germinate, as the seedlings have to be thinned out. If the thinning out is not done early, the growth of the young plants will be held back. So try sowing fine seeds so sparsely that they seem to you to far too thin on the ground. You will probably still have quite a bit of thinning out to do!

A method often used to ensure fine seeds are well spread out is to mix them with silver sand. A packet of seeds is mixed into a few kilos (lbs) of sand, then the resulting mixture is sown. One advantage of this is that it helps you to see more easily where you have already sown seeds.

Instead of sowing directly from the packet you can also use a seed sower, a simple piece of equipment that gives you a bit more control over your work.

For larger seeds you can use a seed drill, which guarantees you a regular spread. This is especially useful if you are sowing large areas, such as $100 \, m^2$ (120 sq yd) for the freezer. You can also use it without bending down, which is another nice thing about it.

Fluid sowing. A method which is becoming better known in Britain. The seed is mixed into a harmless jelly, such as wallpaper paste (free from fungicides!). The mixture is poured into a plastic bag and a small corner is snipped off. Then the mixture is squeezed from the bag at the spot where it is wanted.

Tape and pellets. Many amateur gardeners are still wrestling with the problem of sowing too densely, and the seed companies are always coming up with new ideas. Very fine seeds are put

through a machine which covers each with a layer of material to produce small pellets, which are much easier to sow. A good idea, but a bit more expensive. The same goes for seed tape, containing seeds spaced out the right distance apart.

Sowing depth. Large seeds must be sown deeper than fine ones. A good average is 1 to 2 cm ($\frac{1}{2}$ to $\frac{3}{4}$ in); very fine seed should lie 0.5 cm ($\frac{1}{4}$ in) below the surface, while larger seeds, such as peas and beans, can be pushed in to about 5 cm (2 in). Early in the year, when the soil usually has plenty of moisture, you don't need to sow as deep as in the summer, when the ground is often very dry as a result of the warm, sunny weather. By sowing a little deeper during the summer you will give the seeds a better chance of germinating, because the deeper you go the moister the soil.

Better germination out of doors. There are a few ways of helping your seeds germinate better out of doors. We have already mentioned the trick of

Sowing in the open, left to right: first make a good straight drill (furrow) with a board or the back of a rake. The depth of the drill depends on the size of the seeds. Then sow, here with a special tool. Broadcast sowing, straight from the packet.

mixing some moisture-retaining material with the topsoil. To make a seed bed we often tip out a bag of potting compost over the ground and sow in that. There are two advantages: better germination and absolutely no weeds!

Another way of preventing the ground from drying out is to cover the seed bed with a wet sack. This works well provided you check every day to see when the seeds have germinated. When that happens the sack must be removed because the plants must have light to grow properly. You can make things a

LEFT: Cover the seed bed with a sack to prevent drying out.
RIGHT: Fluid sowing with wallpaper paste.

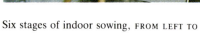

Six stages of indoor sowing, FROM LEFT TO RIGHT.

THIS PAGE: Seed trays are filled with seed compost. Press down well. Then scatter the seed evenly over the compost. Shake silver sand over the surface until the seed is covered.

bit easier by covering the seeds with a clear plastic sheet. This also has to be taken off once the seeds have sprouted, but it's less critical. If you want to keep in an extra bit of warmth and moisture after germination, use a tunnel cloche, as described on pages 27–28.

To prevent the seed bed becoming too warm (useful for all kinds of lettuce), you can cover it with a piece of polystyrene foam or use the wet sack as before.

Protecting your seeds. Most seeds are a great delicacy for birds: they sit and wait until you've sown those lovely peas, and then pick them out again the next morning. To stop this happening you must protect the seed bed with a length of wire netting until the shoots have appeared (if it's not already covered with a plastic sheet).

Thinning out. However thinly you may have sown, the plants are sure to be too close together. This cannot always be prevented because there is always a proportion of seeds which will fail to germinate, and you have to allow for this when sowing.

Thinning out should always be done in stages – you never know whether something might go wrong later, and there's always time to remove a few more.

Thinning is not desirable for carrots. Harmful insects can latch on to the smell of the plants which is spread by loosening the soil when the seedlings are pulled out. With carrots, at least, you will have to try to sow so that no thinning out needs to be done.

Sowing indoors

As we said, nearly all seeds germinate quicker and better if they are given more warmth. The best temperature varies from plant to plant and is given in the individual descriptions, but in general it is between 10 and 25°c (50–77°F) for vegetables. Besides warmth, successful germination also requires moisture and air, so we set the seeds in a mixture which provides for these needs: that is, an airy, moisture-retaining mixture. A proprietary seed compost is suitable.

Light. Light is not needed for seeds to germinate, but once the shoots show it is of vital importance. Not fierce sunlight, but filtered light. Too much sun will scorch the delicate seedlings, while too little light will cause them to grow tall and spindly. This also happens when the days are still short: plants sown too early have no strength and will collapse. Artificial lighting can help to prevent this trouble, but it is most unusual in vegetable growing. Your best bet is to keep to the sowing times given.

Warmth. There are several ways you can provide extra warmth for the soil you have sown your seeds in. The simplest method is simply to put the pots or trays somewhere with heating. Cover the containers with plastic, as otherwise the compost will dry out far too quickly, with the inevitable result: poor germination. Using this system, you also have to ensure the heating is not too strong,

because the compost must not be warmer than 25°c (77°F). Above 30°c (85°F) germination will take place too quickly, and above 45°c (113°F) everything will die. A small thermometer is not a luxury when you are starting out. In a frame or greenhouse the environment will be warmer, but in the early spring the soil will not easily rise above 10°c (50°F). Soil heating is the answer here. The best way to provide this is with a heating plate or heating cable, sold specially for this purpose in garden centres.

You can install heating cable on part of your staging, so as to make a sort of 'propagator' which is always ready to get seeds sprouting quickly.

Hardening off. This is the process of getting young plants used to lower air humidity and lower temperatures. It is the lower humidity, especially, that they have trouble with. Take the plastic cover off a tray of seedlings, set them in the sun (in dry air), and after a few hours they will be punch drunk. This is not the way to go about it. Slow but sure is the motto here, and keep a careful eye on progress. You wouldn't take a baby straight outdoors from a bath, either, without drying it off and putting its clothes on first.

Pricking out. Plants start by producing two seed leaves if they are dicotyledons (cotyledon = seed leaf) and just one if they are monocotyledons (e.g. leeks). After their two seed leaves, the dicotyledons produce two true leaves, which look completely different. Now they can be pricked out. Pricking out means transplanting seedlings separately or further apart. Monocotyledons can be pricked out as soon as they are big

enough to look after themselves.

We do our pricking out in inexpensive, square plastic pots, measuring 9 × 9 cm (3½ × 3½ in). Ready-grown plants are nearly always supplied in these, so most people will have plenty of them lying about; and if not, they can be bought very cheaply. The pots are filled with potting compost and the seedlings are then pricked out in them. These pots will fit into seed trays.

After pricking out, the seedlings are kept in warm humid conditions for a while (i.e. under glass or a plastic sheet) to help them through the shock of transplanting. As soon as you can see them growing again you can start hardening off.

Other methods of propagation

There are other ways of propagating plants besides starting from seed. Methods we can use in the kitchen garden are: planting, dividing, taking cuttings, layering and grafting.

Planting is as simple as it sounds: planting out vegetables or herbs that you have bought. Strawberries, for example. Onions and shallots are often planted, too. These are small bulbs that the grower sows for us the year before, to make it a little easier for us. It takes less time to grow onions from a bulb than from seed, and is especially recommended for poor soil.

Dividing is used for perennials, such as rhubarb, artichokes and various herbs. In October, or in March and April, the plants are dug up and divided into a number of pieces. This is done in such a way that each piece has at least one shoot and a few roots.

Now re-plant, and the pieces should each grow into a new plant. Nothing could be simpler.

Taking cuttings is a bit more complicated. We can use this method for perennial herbs, such as tarragon, marjoram and sage. Young shoots which have not yet become woody are snipped off below a bud and set in a mixture of potting compost and sharp sand. Soil temperature should be around 21°C (70°F). Cover with glass or plastic film. After a while roots will develop. Harden off and plant in the garden. Root cuttings can be taken from horse-radish, among other plants. Fair-sized pieces of root are put into the ground, and new plants should grow from them. Best done in spring. Sea kale can also be grown from root cuttings, see page 34.

Layering is something strawberries do for themselves. The long shoots root at a bud where they touch the ground. Later, cut the shoots and plant the young,

Sowing seeds indoors, continued: Let the tray soak in water. Label it and wrap it in plastic to prevent drying out. Finally, cover with a newspaper to stop algae forming. Remove this as soon as shoots appear.

rooted plants separately.

Other perennials will have to be helped to layer themselves. With sage you can bend a shoot and bury part of it in the soil, where it can be secured with a wire peg. After some time roots will form.

Grafting is particularly applied to gherkins, cucumbers, melons and tomatoes. Grafted plants grow better and are often less susceptible to disease. Grafting is

LEFT: Once the seedlings have two true leaves they can be pricked out. Lift from the tray carefully, so that the roots are not damaged.

RIGHT: Each seedling is set in its own 9 cm (3½ in) pot.

Root cuttings of sea kale can be made by cutting the roots into pieces.

the combining of two different but related plants. The strong grower is used for the root system; for cucumbers it is *Cucurbita ficifolia*, a variety which is sown normally. The scion (which forms the top growth) is also first sown. The stem of the root stock is cut through diagonally, level with a node. The lowest leaves are usually left on for a while. The scion loses its roots and only the upper part is kept. Again, it should be cut through diagonally at a node. The two parts are then pressed together with the cut faces meeting and held with a strip of plastic tape. Given high temperatures and humidity, the two plants will fuse together. After hardening off they are transferred to the garden.

Grafted cucumbers can very often be bought at garden centres.

Looking after your garden

Research has been carried out in a number of countries on the size of gardens and the time needed to keep them in order. If we make as much use as we can of double or treble cropping and complementary plants (see page 25) an area of $40\,m^2$ (48 sq yd) per person is enough for annual vegetable plants. The yield will then be around $100\,kg$ (220 lb) of vegetables (excluding potatoes), which should to be enough for a full year. We have not checked these calculations. If you only want to take part of your supply from the garden, $30\,kg$ (65 lb) of vegetables should be sufficient, and this amount can be supplied by intensive cultivation of $20\,m^2$ (24 sq yd). This assumes that the kitchen garden is fertile, lies in the sun, sheltered from the wind and that nothing goes wrong.

Further arithmetic of the same sort brings us to a garden of $160\,m^2$ (192 sq yd) for a family of four. This will feed them the year round. For potatoes we need to add another $200\,m^2$ (240 sq yd), and if you also want to grow some strawberries, rhubarb and asparagus we find ourselves with a total of $400–500\,m^2$ (500–600 sq yd). If you only want to grow part of your food in the garden, $80\,m^2$ (96 sq yd) will be enough, but this is without counting potatoes and perennials. All these figures are arrived at without allowing for paths!

So how much work is all this? We reckon on 35 to 40 minutes per square metre (a little over 1 sq yd) per year. For a garden of $160\,m^2$ (192 sq yd) this would add up to all of 100 hours per year. Taken over the period from March to October, this averages out at half an hour a day. The potatoes (working without taking double cropping into account!) need much less work, which means that you can get by on something like five hours per week with a garden of $400\,m^2$ (500 sq yd).

It's worth mentioning that comfortable sums like these take no account of holidays, stopping for a cigarette, chatting with the neighbour, etc., because you would no doubt do all of these whether you had a garden or not.

If you want to fit in a holiday it is a good idea to sort out your crops so that there is no sizeable harvesting to be done while you are away. In fact, long holidays are not all that good for the kitchen garden, or for your flower borders.

What tools?

To start off and keep up a kitchen garden you will need tools, and there are all sorts for you to choose from in the garden centres and hardware shops. We list below the most important ones, those that we have had good experiences with. This may not mean a lot in itself: every gardener has a favourite type of spade, hoe, rake or cultivator, which he or she wouldn't be parted from for love or money. However, we have tried out any number of different tools, and these are the ones we held on to.

Spade. For digging you will need a spade, which should have a straight blade, and not too hollow in shape. For heavy soils (clay) the blade should be comparatively small, while for light soil (sandy ground) it can be very large, and triangular in shape. We are mad about our expensive spade, with its stainless-steel blade and plastic handle. This sort of spade never rusts, so it slides easily through the soil. With careful use it should last a lifetime. Sadly, the handle is not always designed for tall people. If you stand upright, the handle of the spade should come exactly up to your bottom rib. If it does, it is the right length and will put the least amount of strain on your back.

Garden shovel. This comes in different shapes, more like a spade or more for shovelling (rounder in shape). On light soil you can just as easily dig with a spade-type shovel. Apart from this, shovels are mainly used for moving soil about. The hollow shape means that soil does not easily fall off. You would use a shovel rather than a spade to fill a wheelbarrow, for example.

Digging fork. Used for digging heavy soil, but also for loosening the ground (instead of digging over) as is common in alternative gardening. There are digging forks with round and with flat prongs.

Manure fork. Usually with four or five round-ended prongs, and used to lift manure, compost, hay, etc. Forks with more prongs and with blunt prongs are used, among other things, to lift potatoes.

Spade (stainless steel).

Garden shovel.

Digging fork, for clay and heavy soils.

Manure fork with six prongs.

Rake with interchangeable handle.

Wooden rake for making beds even.

Ordinary push hoe with long handle.

Wave-cut weeding hoe.

Stainless steel draw hoe.

Rake. Needed in the kitchen garden to keep the seed bed even. There are various types, with curved or straight, long or short prongs, and all of them come in a number of widths. We prefer to use one that is not too wide, and galvanized or (for a better appearance) made of stainless steel. Also a good old, wide, wooden rake with iron prongs. This two-sided rake is fastened to the handle by means of a hook. You can make the beds lovely and flat with it, but it's a hefty thing to use.

Hoe (push hoe, weeding hoe, Dutch hoe). You must be able to move your hoe backwards and forwards just under the surface of the soil to remove the weeds. A very important point is the angle at which the blade is fixed to the handle. If you stand upright and hold the hoe, the blade should be perfectly horizontal as it moves through the soil. Very often the angle is wrong: the blade points slightly upwards or slightly downwards, in which case you will find it difficult to work with.

The old-fashioned hoe has a straight or slightly curved blade and a wooden handle, which is fixed to the middle of the blade. Modern hoes have wave-cut, serrated blades with the handle attached at each end. The handle is made of aluminium. We prefer the latter type, because the upright sides mean you can see exactly where you are going under the soil. This means you can work much closer to the plants without risk of cutting them.

The blade of the hoe must be sharpened to a good edge both back and front. Stainless-steel hoes have their advantages: they can't rust and so they glide through the soil more easily. Hoeing is done walking backwards.

Draw hoe. Designed for the same purpose as the push hoe: fighting weeds and keeping the topsoil loose. Mostly used on clay, and used while walking forwards. Various types are available, some with stainless-steel blades.

Cultivator. Also well suited to fighting weeds, but designed in the first place for keeping the top layer loose. There are cultivators with one, three and five prongs, and on some the spacing is adjustable so that you can easily work between the rows.

Handles. A word about the handles attached to hoes, rakes and cultivators.

Formerly these were always made of wood, mostly ash. In recent years, however, more and more are being made with aluminium handles, sometimes interchangeable. This interchangeability often falls short of expectations: after a year or so the handle is usually inseparably stuck. However, aluminium is an excellent material for handles. Because it is light in weight, much less energy is needed for hoeing, and that's a great comfort if you're faced with a fair-sized area of potatoes.

All the tools we have mentioned – hoes, rakes and cultivators – are also available with a very short blade for use in a squatting or kneeling position.

Ridger. We use this to heap extra soil round the plants. Mainly with potatoes, but also with other plants, such as peas, root fennel and brassicas. You can also make furrows with a ridger, where, for example, you can plant leeks or self-blanching celery.

Wheelbarrow. The bigger the better. You don't have to fill it if you're carrying heavy materials, but if you're dealing with weeds or twigs a larger volume is a definite advantage. Whether a wheelbarrow is easy to wheel depends on where the wheel is. It is often too far forward. If you lift a loaded wheelbarrow and stand with your back straight, it should balance precisely over the axle, so that you hardly need take any weight. Try it out. A wheelbarrow with a polyester body will last longest.

Garden line and dibber. A simple garden line is useful to help you keep your plants or seeds in a neat row. A dibber is handy for planting onions, leeks and the like. There are hollow dibbers and pointed ones. The hollow ones are better for a beginner, because the hole is less pointed and the soil is less compressed.

Trowel. A cheap but indispensable piece of equipment. Be sure to get one made from stainless steel: it will be much more enjoyable to use.

Furrow opener. Not indispensable, but a useful tool. Adjustable, to draw four or more furrows at a time. You can sow directly into them.

Row dibber. A home-made piece of equipment consisting of a piece of wood 1.2 m (4 ft) long, with dowel rods hammered in. With the back you can form a sowing drill across the bed, and with the

dowel side you can make small holes for pricking out or planting onions.

Mechanical help. In the vegetable garden we do not have a lot of use for motor-driven machines. There is one exception, however: the rotary cultivator. This is a machine with curved blades which till the soil, sometimes to a depth of only 5 cm (2 in), but they can go as deep as 30 cm (1 ft). If organic matter, such as manure, has been spread on the ground beforehand, the cultivator will mix it in with the soil very well indeed.

There are very small electric cultivators which you can also use to fight weeds between the rows, but also larger, petrol-driven models, working to a width of as much as 40–60 cm (16–24 in). In general, they work between 5 and 30 cm (2 to 12 in) deep.

We get a lot of pleasure out of our rotary cultivator in the autumn, when a new lot of manure needs to be worked in. Also in spring, when we want to loosen up a neglected bed. One thing we have found out, though, is that the machine should not be used on wet soil: the result is a hard, compacted layer which water cannot penetrate.

Single-share cultivator (aerator).

Three-prong cultivator, non-adjustable.

One handle serving several tools.

Ridger being used between potatoes.

Wheelbarrow with plastic body.

Garden line to ensure straight rows.

Hollow dibber, to make planting holes.

Various stainless-steel trowels.

A row dibber of our own design.

Keeping down weeds

In this book a weed means any plant that grows where you don't want it. Mostly these are wild plants, such as couch grass, dandelions or stinging nettles, but a plant you have put into the flower border can also become a weed if it turns up in the kitchen garden.

Any soil is full of seeds and pieces of root left by weeds. And if there should be no seeds, they will soon be blown over or brought in by birds. When starting a new garden, on old pastureland, for example, you can be driven to desperation for the first few years by the weeds that are forever appearing. And because the seeds can crop up at surprising depths and survive for years on end, every time you dig the ground a little deeper a new batch of seed will come to the surface.

If you don't keep the weeds at bay they will starve out the vegetables; and this is why fighting the weeds is an absolute necessity in a kitchen garden.
Hand weeding. There are different ways of going about this. Simply pulling out the weeds is fine, but very time consuming if the weeds are small and numerous. Hoeing, combined with pulling out by hand (where the hoe can't reach), is more usual. After hoeing you can rake off the weeds if there are a lot of them, but we usually let them lie. If it rains a few of them start growing again,

Tree-bark is a perfect material for mulching.

Onions 'Sturon' planted through holes in black plastic.

which is regrettable, but we can put a stop to that as soon as we hoe the soil again. In rainy weather the whole garden is hoed over at least twice a week.

Now, wise old gardeners will tell you: never hoe in rainy weather – but we'd like to see their gardens after it has rained for four weeks with hardly a break, which is not unusual. Of course, hoeing is much more effective in dry, sunny weather, and we don't deny it; but it helps in wet weather as well.

It is often claimed that growing potatoes on a fresh piece of ground will keep down the weeds. Rubbish. It's not the potatoes that get *rid* of the weeds, but *you*, because you have no choice – if you didn't nothing would come of your potatoes.

So that we can act against the weeds at an early stage we very often sow in straight rows and mark each end with a small stick. This way, we can get right down to hoeing even before there's anything to be seen. Sometimes we add fast germinators (such as garden cress) to slow-shooting plants (such as celery) to act as markers.
Mulching. You can also fight weeds by smothering them. We call this mulching. It can be done with black plastic sheeting (see the section on strawberries, page 157), but also with organic material such as shredded bark, hay, grass cuttings,

straw or sawdust. The soil will not get clogged, and hoeing becomes unnecessary. The mulch can be applied as soon as the young vegetables have grown reasonably tall. Don't do it too early, when the ground is still cold, as the soil will then stay cold all the longer as a result of the insulating effect of the mulch. The organic material will rot and supply more food for the vegetables in the process. All in all, it often results in a yield increased by some 20 to 50 per cent.

So why is so little mulching done by the amateur? Many gardeners find a mulch unpleasant to look at. It strikes them as a lot of work getting hold of material for the mulch and then applying it. They have noticed that a lot of snails and even mice find shelter in the mulch and use it as a base from which to attack the vegetables. They also observe that after a time the weeds start to grow on top of the mulch, so that a new layer has to be added.

A thick layer of straw can also keep weeds down very well.

Other routine tasks

Watering

It will be necessary to water plants from time to time, certainly while raising young plants, but also while they are in full growth. For this reason no kitchen garden can do without a water supply.

There must always be a balance in the plant between the amount of water taken in by the roots and that evaporated by the leaves. Just after transplanting or pricking out this balance is usually upset: we have destroyed (not deliberately) a number of root hairs, which has limited the plant's ability to take in water. We can now water the ground for all we're worth, but if there are not enough roots all our watering is wasted effort. It is much better in such cases to limit the evaporation through the leaves, which is the other way of restoring the balance. You can do this by providing shade, by building a tunnel cloche from plastic sheeting over the plants, or by spraying the leaves with a fine mist.

You can also reduce the evaporation from the soil by mulching. Covering the ground with black plastic, hay or grass cuttings can help quite a bit.

It can make quite a difference what sort of soil the kitchen garden is on. Clay retains moisture so it is not necessary to water as often as on sandy soil, with its coarse structure.

When it rains, or when you water the ground, the soil clogs up: the grains on the surface lie closer together, and this can produce a sort of crust which can make it difficult for air to get into the soil. That's why you need to hoe the soil after every shower and every time you water, except when a mulch has been applied. Hoeing also helps moisture to rise from lower levels.

Most plants will let you know when they are thirsty. The leaves and shoots will hang limply and look sorry for themselves. Give them water or shade at once. You can water with a clear conscience when the sun is shining; it is an old wives' tale that this causes scorching. It is when the sun is shining that the evaporation is at its greatest, and that is when watering is most needed.

What do you water with? If you have no water supply for your garden a watering can is the obvious choice. Usually made from plastic and holding 10 l (2.2 gal). There are also some very attractive watering cans made from galvanized steel with brass roses. They will last for decades. Always point the rose upwards, so that the water falls on the ground with less force. Direct the water on to the soil around the plants, less on the leaves. Thoroughly soak the soil and afterwards dig a small hole to check penetration. Very often gardeners stop watering too soon: then only the surface is moistened and the water does not get down to the roots.

If you have access to a tap use a garden hose with a fine rose, or cover the whole garden with a sprinkler. We are very happy with pulsating sprinklers. The spread of the water is better than with any other kind. We also have a weakness for sprinklers which rotate very quickly and spray just a little water. You can happily leave them working all night.

Regular manuring

We make a distinction between manuring when setting up a new garden (which you can read about on pages 19 and 20) and regular manuring. And the latter can be further divided into the major annual manuring exercise (including digging over and working in compost) and minor manuring work.

Extra manuring is called for when you are following an early crop with another crop. This extra manuring is certainly necessary if the second crop consists of leaf vegetables. If enough potash, phos-

In dry weather the garden must be watered at frequent intervals.

The water gun is a useful aid to watering by hand. By squeezing the trigger harder you can change the jet from wide to narrow.

phate and lime has been added during the big annual round of manuring, a little extra nitrogen will suffice during the growing season. We prefer to add this in the form of dried blood which contains 12 per cent nitrogen. It is a joy to see how well spinach sown in August grows after such a dose. We also provide extra nutrients for plants which consume a lot of food, such as brassicas, courgettes, melons, celeriac, etc. In the middle of the growing season they get a scoop of dried blood which is watered in well. To prevent leaf vegetables in particular from containing too much nitrate when they are picked, you should not be too generous with the nitrogen, and certainly not put on any more manure within three weeks of harvesting.

Needless to say, you can add the extra nutrients in the form of artificial fertilizer, if that appeals to you more. Use sulphate of ammonia if you are only concerned with nitrogen, Growmore if you think some potash and phosphate would be useful as well. A general-purpose liquid manure is useful to liven up seedlings which are a little slow to grow.

You will need to add extra fertilizer more frequently on coarse soils poor in humus than on fine (clay) soils, which already contain a good amount of humus. These soils always hold the nutrients for a longer period.

Tying and supporting

There are quite a few vegetables that will not stand up by themselves. For these we have to provide support, otherwise they will lie flat on the ground, which usually does the harvest no good. Peas and beans are the best known of the vegetables that need support. Even if the packet claims to give you 'bush' beans or peas, it is still best to give the plants some support, especially if by mischance the soil contains too much nitrogen. You will find more about support given under

Rotary sprinklers spray a small amount of water, but distribute it very finely.

ABOVE: Liquid manure can be distributed by means of a measuring jar on the garden hose.
ABOVE RIGHT: Spread dried blood to provide extra nitrogen.

each plant. Tomatoes, peppers and aubergines also need to be supported with a cane. In the greenhouse, melons and gherkins are often supported on wires (see pages 146 and 147).

However you choose to support or tie your vegetables, make a secure job of it, because – especially after rain – they are heavier than you think.

Ridging
With ridging soil is pulled around the stems of plants. This is done for a number of reasons. With brassicas and bush beans it is mainly to give them more stability. With potatoes and carrots we do it to prevent parts of the tubers or roots showing above the soil (which results in a loss in quality). With beetroot we do it to prevent them being pecked by birds. With blanched vegetables, such as asparagus, blanching celery and root fennel, the purpose is to keep more of the plant growing in the

Tying a courgette plant to a stick with twine.

Ridging young sweet corn plants to encourage growth.

Unwanted side shoots on a tomato plant

This is one way to protect young bean plants from night frost.

dark, so that it stays nice and white and, as a result, is tastier.

Ridging can be done with a shovel or with a hoe, but there is also a special tool for the job – the ridger, a kind of small hand-held plough with which you draw a furrow. The soil becomes piled up against the plants on either side.

Ridging also takes care of weeds for a time, while the plants quickly make extra roots in the piled-up soil, and this helps them to grow better.

Stopping, side shooting and pruning

Stopping a plant means pinching out its top shoot. Young plants are stopped to encourage them to grow side shoots. For example, if we want to grow three shoots on an aubergine and it only produces one stem, stopping will make it throw out more shoots. Stopping is also useful with melons.

Older plants are sometimes stopped to fight disease. Broad beans, for instance, often have their tops removed to fight off blackfly. This is not terribly clever, because the yield per plant will fall off. Blackfly on broad beans are actually better dealt with by using an insecticide. Even soapsuds and methylated spirits can help a lot.

Stopping Brussels sprouts makes the top sprouts larger, so that the whole stalk can be picked at the same time. But stopping too early is a bad thing. The right moment is when the sprouts at the bottom are just 1 cm (a little under $\frac{1}{2}$ in) in diameter. However, topped sprouts

are less resistant to frost.

Stopping gherkins grown in the open results in a big reduction in the yield. The less leaves, the less fruit. Leeks often have their leaves and roots cut back before being planted out. Cutting back the leaves reduces evaporation, so it can be useful. But there is no sense in cutting back roots. In fact, cutting at either end will reduce the yield.

As tomato plants grow the side shoots must be removed from the leaf-axils (the axil is the angle of the leaf-stalk). This activity is called 'side shooting'. If it is not done, the tomato plant will get too bushy, and the quality of the fruit will leave much to be desired.

The pruning of berry fruits has two aims: (a) achieving or maintaining a good shape to the bush, so that the light can get in, the plant can easily be tied and the fruit can be picked without trouble, and (b) producing as many flower buds as possible. The way of going about it is different for each plant, so you will find more details about pruning under the individual fruit.

Protection from frost

There are very few vegetables that survive the winter or which we grow through the winter months. For those we do, protection against sharp frosts may be necessary—for example, for chicory, if we want to force it in a shallow hole. When there is a frost the hole is covered with insulating material such as straw, leaves or peat.

Night frost can be more of a problem,

and can cause a lot of damage as late as the middle of May in this country, especially away from the coast. Some vegetables are very resistant to night frost – there are peas, for example, that can withstand temperatures as low as $-12°c$ (10°F, or 22 degrees of frost). Plants like these can be sown as early as February without problem. Other vegetables are very sensitive, and for these a late date for sowing is indicated, as with beans, for example.

If you have been tempted to start growing your crop too early, you could be faced with a nasty surprise around the beginning of May.

If you have heard that there is frost in the offing (you will be warned of it in radio and TV forecasts, and you can also expect it on clear, still nights), there are some precautions you can take. The easiest is to set up a few sprinklers in the kitchen garden and let them run all night. They will spray at the most 100 litres of water (20 gal or so) per hour, so that there is no danger of puddles forming. The plants and flowers will be warmed up a little by the water and will not freeze. A more usual method is covering the plants with plastic sheets or flowerpots turned upside down.

Harvesting and preserving

Vegetables from your own garden have the one great advantage that you can eat them immediately after picking. In fact, the best time to pick them is first thing in the morning, when they are still fresh from the dew, but if you're not going to eat them until evening it's not such a good idea.

We usually decide which vegetables to eat during the afternoon, and they are then picked and prepared for the table. That way, they don't lose many of their vital ingredients.

There is a definite science to picking vegetables when they are just at their best. In general, they are at their most tasty when they are in a young, half-ripened state. This certainly applies to peas, beans, courgettes, radishes, carrots, etc.

For typical storing or preserving vegetables like potatoes, celeriac, brassicas, onions and winter carrots, we start from a fully ripened product.

By sowing quick-growing vegetables in small portions we can spread the harvest over a long period. It makes quite a lot of sense to sow a few rows of radishes and a few rows of lettuce every week.

When picking your crop, of course, you should always take the most fully grown plants first; the others will then have a little more space to grow.

Another way of picking vegetables in small portions can be used with spinach: only pick the outer leaves. The plant will keep on developing as before, and fresh, new leaves will take the place of the missing ones. You can just pick leaves from lettuce, too. There is even a special 'non-hearting' or 'Salad Bowl' type for the purpose.

Be very careful how you pick peas and beans. Often they are torn from the plant too roughly, leaving wounds. This makes it easier for fungus diseases to get into the plants, especially in wet weather.

Many kitchen gardeners who are new to the business are so busy growing that they forget to pick the crop in good time! Spend a little time every day checking on this, especially with vegetables like broc-coli, which are liable to turn over-ripe from one day to the next.

In warm weather far more vegetables will ripen than you can possibly eat. The temptation when that happens is simply to leave them on the plant, with the result that the taste is no longer at its best.

It is better to pick the vegetables when they are just right and either give them away or put them in the fridge. We keep asparagus in water in the icebox, where it will stay fresh for up to five days. Courgettes are best picked when small and kept refrigerated. Tomatoes, on the other hand, are tastier if they are left to ripen on the plant (commercial growers can't allow them to do this, as they would not be able to transport them) and this is why tomatoes you have grown yourself always taste better.

Picking late is also good for vegetables such as kale and sprouts: they become more tasty after a frost, because this causes more sugars to be formed in the plants. Some root crops also taste better for being picked late: parsnips are a good example.

Herbs that you want to preserve must be picked just as they are starting to flower. They can then be dried.

When we talk about preserving vegetables, many people immediately think of freezing or bottling. But there are other methods. Potatoes are usually stored in a cool, dry room, as are storing brassicas. Other vegetables, such as beets, celeriac, turnips and winter carrots, are better kept in sand. They can also be stored in pits in the garden.

Easier still is simply leaving storing vegetables in the soil. Scorzonera, for example, will never freeze. Similarly, winter carrots, celeriac and parsnips can be left in the garden provided they are covered with a mat during sharp frosts. A vegetable like winter leek, which only begins to grow in the spring, can be left unprotected in the garden over a normal winter. Winter cauliflower is far less able to stand frost. In fact, it can only be grown near the coast.

Conserving methods, including freezing, are not dealt with in this book.

After the first harvest a cabbage stem often throws out fresh shoots and produces a number of miniature cabbages.

This broccoli is too 'loose', which means it is past the best date for picking.

Growing vegetables under glass

Winter crops

You will need a heated greenhouse for these. Growing winter crops not only demands a lot of experience but also runs up large bills – the latter often so big that a hobby gardener's wallet will not really stretch to it. We will not be paying very much attention to winter vegetables in this book, but will concentrate on the easier plants, which do not demand especially high temperatures.

Broccoli, especially Chinese, is a good alternative to cauliflower. Grow as described for cauliflower; you can even sow it earlier.

Cabbage lettuce lends itself perfectly as both an autumn and a winter crop. Special varieties have to be bought for this purpose, like 'Kwiek'. Sow in small peat pots from the end of July for an autumn crop and from the beginning of October for a winter crop. Make sure the germination temperature is no higher than 20°C (68°F). When raising the seedlings, a minimum of 12°C (55°F) will be enough.

Carrots can be sown in rows from October. A suitable variety is 'Amsterdam Forcing'. The infamous root fly should give you no trouble in the winter. Grow in a cool environment, allow plenty of air and pick in May.

Cauliflower takes up a very large amount

A cold frame for vegetables that need a bit of protection.

Half-walled wooden greenhouse, not ideal for vegetable growing, but well suited to raising seedlings.

of space, but if you have room it can be sown in the last week of September, an example being 'Alpha'. Germination temperature 15°C (60°F). Plant out in December and then keep the temperature to 12°C (55°F). Can be picked at the beginning of May.

Corn salad can be sown in the greenhouse from September onwards, best in rows. Little warmth is required; pick in spring.

Courgettes can be sown in July as an autumn crop, best in small pots. They can then be put in the greenhouse as soon as August. Start the heating in October, keeping it to at least 12°C (55°F), and preferably a little higher. You will have fresh courgettes at the end of October or beginning of November.

Endives can be sown in September, in small pots for example. Temperature: 20°C (68°F). Plant out in the greenhouse at the end of October and keep them at least 12°C (55°F). 'Broad-leaved Batavian' is a good variety to grow under glass.

Leeks can be sown in pots in November, at temperatures between 18–22°C (65–72°F). They will not take up much space. Plant out at the beginning of March and grow at a minimum of 12°C (55°F) until the young leeks can be harvested in May.

Radishes can be sown either very late (up to the middle of October) or very early

(from the middle of December). No heating is needed.

Spinach can be sown in the greenhouse from October onwards. Two good varieties are 'Jovita' and 'Sigmaleaf'. Spinach does not need a lot of warmth and will survive a touch of frost.

Spring cabbage thrives under glass. Sow early in October, preferably in small pots, at 15°C (60°F). Plant out in December and grow to maturity at a minimum of 12°C (55°F). Ready to pick in April.

Turnip tops can be sown direct in the greenhouse from September onwards. They do not need a high temperature, but must be kept frost-free.

Spring crops

From the end of January the greenhouse does not need to be heated, although it helps if some heating is provided during really freezing weather, otherwise the ground will be too hard for you to work. In those conditions it is very important to have your greenhouse well insulated. With spring crops we work on the principle that the plants will be left in the greenhouse until they are eaten. You will also need to use the greenhouse to nurse seedlings in trays or pots for later planting out in the garden. Think about how much room you have before you start, or the greenhouse will become very crowded. Needless to say, some of the vegetables listed above as 'winter crops', such as cabbage lettuce, spinach, etc., can also be grown later.

Aubergine is a typical greenhouse vegetable, and can be sown from February onwards if heating is provided. Germination temperature: 20–25°c (68–77°F); afterwards grow to maturity in a very warm greenhouse – at least 18°c (65°F).

Beetroot is sown in small pots in February at a temperature of 15–20°c (60–68°F). Plant out at the end of March and continue growing at a minimum of 10°c (50°F). Pick in May/June. 'Boltardy' is good for growing under glass.

Black radishes can be sown in March, grow very quickly and can be picked as soon as May. 'Black Spanish Round' is a suitable variety.

Chinese cabbage can be sown in January at 20°c (68°F), with the growing later completed at 16–18°c (60–65°F). Pick in May. A good variety is 'Sampan'.

Courgettes are sown in a heated greenhouse, at 20–25°c (68–78°F), from the beginning of February. Grow to maturity at a minimum of 18°c (65°F) and harvest from May.

Cucumbers are not sown until April, with a temperature of 20–25°c (68–78°F); they are then grown on wires in the greenhouse. 'Petita' takes up relatively little space.

Florence fennel can be sown in pots in February with heating. Grow to maturity at 16–18°c (60–65°F). If the temperature is too high the plants will shoot too quickly. 'Sirio' is a good variety.

French beans can be raised in individual pots at 20–22°c (68–72°F) at the end of March. After 10 days, plant out and grow at 15°c (60°F) or above. Climbing varieties are best, like 'Garrafal Oro' or bush beans will do. The time to start picking is July.

Kohl-rabi grows very quickly: sow in pots from February, at 18°c (65°F), and grow to maturity at a minimum of 12°c (55°F). 'White Vienna' is a good variety. Eat in May.

Melons take up a very large amount of space, but if you have the room it is best to sow them with heating, around the end of March. They are ready to pick in

July/August. Choose a variety with small fruits, such as 'Ogen'.

Peppers (sweet) must be sown in pots at the beginning of March: 20–25°c (68–78°F). Plant out at the end of April and keep above 18°c (65°F). You can start picking them in July.

Seedlings can be raised in small pots in the attic, as long as it is well lit.

Purslane can be broadcast-sown directly into the soil from April. At high temperatures this vegetable grows extremely quickly.

Self-blanching celery can be sown in pots from January onwards at about 20°c (68°F) and then matured at a minimum of 16°c (60°F). Pick in May. 'Golden Self-blanching' is recommended.

Sugar peas (mange-tout) require a lot of space, but can be grown very early. They germinate most quickly in pots at 20°c (68°F). Plant out in the greenhouse, with a minimum temperature of 12°c (55°F). Eat in April. Choose bush varieties only, such as 'Sugarbon'.

Tomatoes should be sown in pots at the end of February at a high temperature, 20–25°c (68–77°F). After germination reduce the heating, prick out the seedlings then plant out in April. The temperature can be high, the night-time temperature not below 17°c (62°F). Your first small tomatoes will be ready by the end of July.

The cheapest greenhouses are made from plastic sheeting.

Plant protection

So much has been written already about spraying with poisonous pesticides and the results this can have on your health and the environment that we will cover this subject quite briefly.

We are definitely against pesticides harmful to man or the environment, and for this reason we always try to find other ways of protecting vegetables against attack. A kitchen garden without protection and at the same time without disease does not exist.

The pesticide industry has come up with a term: 'plant protection'. It sounds better. We have adopted it here, because it often covers the sense better, at least as far as this book is concerned. We certainly want to protect our plants against attack, but preferably without using pesticides!

As you can read on pages 25–26 under 'Complementary Crops' and on page 27 under 'Netting', there are tried and tested ways of preventing attack.

We are very keen on insect netting which you can use to build insect-proof cages round the plants. There is also a sure way of avoiding soil fungi, such as club root: grow your vegetables in large plastic pots filled with disease-free proprietary potting compost.

Besides this, you can avoid a good many diseases by sowing or picking at the right time. You will find precise details for each plant.

An attractive scarecrow gives the kitchen garden some decoration, but does it actually do any good in practice?

Red currants need protecting against birds with a net. Better still is a special net cage.

To deal with the remaining pests and diseases you can spray or dust the plants. You can use chemical or organic products as you choose. The chemical ones are by far in the majority. They work, but their drawbacks are well known. Only the safer ones are permitted for private use, but this does not guarantee that private gardeners won't use one of the more dangerous ones. Anyone who steps inside a gardening or agricultural store can walk out with anything on sale to the professionals!

Few organic products are on sale under commercial brand names. They are only approved for sale if they are really effective, and sadly this is very rarely the case. This leaves us with the treatments you can make for yourself, such as soap spirit, nettle manure, etc. Here are the recipes.

Treatments you can make for yourself. The old country remedies are often far from being as silly as they sound. The effect is usually short-term, but in many cases sufficient, at least provided the treatment is repeated from time to time.

* Chamomile tea: soak dried chamomile in water, then strain.
* Horsetail tea: boil 300 g (10 oz) of dried stems of *Equisetum arvense* for half an hour in 1 litre (2 pints) of water, strain, and add a little soft soap. Before using dilute to one part tea in 100 parts of water. Use against fungus diseases.
* Nettle manure: soak stinging nettles in water for a week, then add some soft soap and strain. Use against greenfly.
* Quassia: soak 300 g (10 oz) of shavings of quassia wood (*Quassia cortex*) for one day in 2 litres (4 pints) of water and then boil for one hour. Filter, add a small amount of soft soap and use in 1:10 concentration.
* Rhubarb soap: cut 1 kg (2 lb) of rhubarb leaf into small pieces and boil for one hour in 2 litres (4 pints) of water. Allow to cool, add a little soft soap, and strain. Use against insects.
* Tobacco extract: leave pipe tobacco or shag to draw in water, filter, add some soft soap. Use against insects.
* Soap spirit: made by dissolving 5 g (¼ oz) soft soap and 5 g methylated spirit in 1 litre (2 pints) of water. Use against insects.

Fighting pests and diseases

This section gives a summary of all the pests and diseases mentioned in this book. Where possible, we always list both the organic (o) and the chemical (c) treatment. Which you use is up to you.

American gooseberry mildew can also attack other berry plants. A light or dark brown coat of mould is visible on the berries and young shoots, and growth is inhibited. Treatment o: remove affected tips. Spray with horsetail tea. c: dinocap.

Aphids (greenfly, blackfly) can cause damage to a number of plants. They attach themselves to the underside of the leaves. Treatment o: with nettle manure, preparations containing pyrethrum, rhubarb soap and soap spirit. c: any suitable insecticide, like dimethoate.

Asparagus beetles are blue or orange, and eat at the leaves after the longest day, with the result that the tips wither. Treatment o: plant nasturtiums between the rows of asparagus. c: spray, e.g. with derris.

Bean beetles attack beans while they are in storage. Non-disinfected seed may be totally eaten away from inside by larvae. Treatment o: keep seeds for sowing cool

Broad beans frequently suffer the attentions of blackfly.

and stop the insects getting to them (e.g. cover with muslin). c: use seed dressing.

Bean seed flies lay eggs in the beans, and the emerging maggots prevent the seeds from germinating. Asparagus stalks are eaten away, as are the tubers of black radish. Treatment o: do not grow following spinach, brassicas or lettuce varieties. Use insect netting. c: treat seed rows with diazinon.

Bean weevil see pea and bean weevil.

Beet flies or leaf miner lay tiny white eggs on the underside of the leaves. The maggots which emerge eat away the soft tissue between the upper and lower skin of the leaf. Treatment o: insect netting. c: spray, e.g. with malathion.

Big bud mites cause the buds to swell in autumn and winter. Mites, larvae and eggs will be found in them. Black currants especially. Treatment o: as soon as the flower clusters become visible, spray with nettle manure or soap spirit. c: spray with benomyl at the same point.

Blackfly see Aphids.

Blight (rust, leafspot) is a fungus disease that occurs in a variety of forms on a large number of vegetables, including beans, cabbage lettuce and leeks, but also on berry fruits, such as black currants, red currants and raspberries. Visible on leeks, for example, as patches of orange spores on the leaves. Treatment o: spray with horsetail tea. c: spray with copper fungicide.

Blindness in cauliflower means that the plant's heart is missing. The last leaf is sometimes beaker-shaped. The cause is damage to the growing point. Late varieties are especially susceptible. Prevention: ensure that the plants grow evenly during raising and particularly after planting out.

Botrytis (grey mould) attacks strawberries, lettuce and peas and beans, among others, during cold, wet weather. An excess of nitrogen increases susceptibility. Treatment o: spray with horsetail tea or a sulphur preparation. c: spray with benomyl.

Cabbage blackrot in spring cabbage is a condition where, if we cut through the cabbage, we can see a circular, brown-

black discoloration some distance from the heart. Treatment: do not plant the cabbages too close together, and avoid over-luxuriant growth.

Cabbage moths Flying pests that lay eggs from which caterpillars appear and devour the leaves at high speed. Treatment o: insect netting with preparations containing pyrethrum. c: spray with carbaryl or HCH.

Cabbage root flies lay eggs on young brassicas, but also on turnips and radishes. The larvae eat tunnels in the tubers and cause the plants to turn greyish. The plants die off soon afterwards. Treatment o: attach collars to plants, spray with nettle manure, cover beds with insect netting. c: bromophos, diazinon.

Cabbage thrips lay eggs in the heart of the plant. This gives rise to a deformed heart: the heart becomes oddly twisted and no cabbage develops. Treatment o: insect netting. c: permethrin.

Cane spot in raspberries: see Spur Blight.

Carrot flies lay their eggs in young carrots, parsnips and other umbellifers. The milky-white maggots eat tunnels through the carrots. Carrot flies are attracted by the smell of carrots, which is spread when thinning out, for example.

Young turnips are especially attractive to the larvae of the cabbage thrips.

LEFT: Twisted heart in cabbages is caused by cabbage thrips (see page 47).

RIGHT: The larvae of cabbage thrips know their way around radishes and many other members of the brassica family.

Treatment o: spread wood ash, plant complementary onions or related plants (especially garlic), ridge up or water after thinning out or picking, close off bed with insect netting (the best answer). c: bromophos, diazinon.

Caterpillars may come from any number of butterflies and moths. The best known in the kitchen garden are the yellow-green ones belonging to the cabbage white butterfly. Leaf vegetables and sweet corn can also be attacked by caterpillars. The damage usually consists of holes in the leaves, sometimes fairly large. On headed cabbages the caterpillars quickly eat their way into the middle of the plant, where they are difficult to get at. Treatment o: spray with pyrethrum. c: spray with carbaryl or HCH.

Chafer beetles are grey-brown or black with a broad, flat snout. They eat holes in the leaves of strawberries and other plants and their cream-coloured larvae consume the roots. Treatment o: trap under balls of wood-wool. c: HCH or bromophos.

Chocolate spot in beans produces watery patches on the leaves, with a yellowish edge. In dry weather these patches may also turn brown. Glassy patches also appear on the beans, and later turn red. The only treatment (prevention) is to grow resistant varieties and use healthy seed. Chemical treatments are not sufficiently effective.

LEFT: You can't leave caterpillars unchallenged on your cabbages, or this is what will happen!

A mass of eggs at the base of the leaf releases hungry caterpillars, which have already had a swift bite at this spring cabbage.

Club root is a fungus disease that produces a tuber-like thickening of the roots of brassicas. It cannot be treated. Prevent by raising young plants in good soil, e.g. potting compost. Keep the soil pH close to 7, adding extra lime as necessary. Grow the plants to maturity in large plastic pots or bottomless buckets let into the ground. Fill these, also, with club root-free soil and add lime. Further: ensure well-spaced crop rotation, since the fungus can hang around for years in the soil or compost.

Colorado bettles are 1 cm ($\frac{1}{2}$ in) long, light yellow in colour with 10 black stripes. With help from their orangy-red larvae, they eat away the leaves of potatoes. Must be dealt with by law! In the UK must be reported to Ministry of Agriculture.

Cutworms are moth larvae. They are grey, roll themselves up when at rest, and eat the parts of plants under the soil or just above. Treatment O: dig out. C: mix an insecticide such as HCH or bromophos into the soil.

Damping off a seedling disease which causes seedlings to keel over and die. Always sow in fresh seed compost and cover the seeds with fresh silver sand, as shown on page 32. C: soak compost with Cheshunt Compound.

Deficiency diseases come about through the lack of one or other nutrient in the soil. Can be cured by adding the appropriate food as required. Some symptoms are mentioned on page 11.

Downy mildew is a fungus disease that grows into the plant rather than on it, as true mildew does. Beyond this, the symptoms are the same. The fuzz of downy mildew is a greyish violet and more often found on the underside of the leaves. Numerous plants are attacked, including lettuce, spinach, onions, and young brassicas. Treatment O: use resistant varieties, spray with chamomile solution. C: spray with mancozeb or zineb.

Earwigs are brown insects with pincers for a tail. They help us to destroy aphids, but also eat plants themselves, especially strawberries. Treatment O: entice into flower pots filled with damp wood-wool or straw, then destroy, or tip into the compost heap! C: spray with HCH.

Eelworm damage in potatoes (potato sickness) is caused by the potato cyst eelworm. In patches, the potatoes will continue growing. The only remedy for this problem is well-spaced crop rotation.

Eelworms in onions cause deformed, swollen and twisted leaves. The plants remain small and have a bluish colour. The onions are often burst, floury and evil-smelling. Treatment: do not grow onions on the same spot more than once in five years, use disease-free seed.

Flea beetles are small, metallic-looking or striped insects that jump about among young plants and eat holes in the leaves, especially the lower ones. Treatment O: wood ash, lime or spread a piece of wood with syrup and hold it above the insects, so that they jump on to it and get stuck. Spray tobacco extract on them. C: any insect killer, e.g. derris, HCH.

Flowering in cauliflowers is a condition in which the plant looks shaggy because of florets maturing too early. Prevent by avoiding too much nitrogen and water and selecting less-sensitive varieties.

Green capsid bugs are 4–5 mm (0.15–0.2 in) long and grass-green in colour, later turning brownish. The insects suck at the young leaves of turnip-rooted celery and other plants, which turn black and drop off. Treatment O: spray pyrethrum. C: HCH.

Greenfly see Aphids.

A young brassica plant with clubroot, a disease for which there is no remedy.

49

Grey mould see Botrytis.

Halo blight is a bacterium that causes blotches with translucent edges on the leaves of gherkins, beans, brassicas etc. No treatment. Use healthy seed and good crop rotation.

Leaf blotch diseases occur in all sorts of variations. Leeks, celery and onions are among the most commonly attacked plants. As long as fungi are the cause, they can nearly all be treated. o: horsetail tea or sulphur preparations. c: treat with zineb, copper, benomyl.

Leaf hoppers first cause small spots on the upper surface of the leaf, then the whole leaf turns brown and drops off. Treatment o: spray with nettle manure, soap spirit (especially underside of leaf). c: malathion.

Leaf rollers on brassicas in particular: small and very mobile caterpillars eat the leaves and twist them together. Treatment o: derris. c: carbaryl.

Leaf spot on berrying plants produces brown spots (blight) on the leaves, which eventually turn yellow and fall early. Treatment o: horsetail tea. c: zineb or thiram.

Leatherjackets are the larvae of the crane-fly (daddy long-legs), grey in colour and with no legs. They eat at the roots in summer and autumn and can do a great deal of damage, especially in what was previously pasture-land. Treatment o: preparation containing pyrethrum. c: work bromophos or HCH into the soil.

The larvae of the onion fly can also do a lot of damage to leeks.

The mealy aphid (here on a cabbage leaf) can multiply at an unbelievable rate.

Leek moths lay eggs that produce small caterpillars which eat tunnels into the hearts of the plants. They also attack onions. Treatment o: insect netting, spraying with pyrethrum. c: fenitrothion.

Mealy aphid is a greyish aphid partial to turnips and radishes as well as brassicas. Large colonies found on undersides of leaves which curl and turn yellow. Treatment o: insect netting. c: dimethoate.

Onion flies lay their eggs at the base of the stalks of onions, leeks and chives. The white maggots appear very quickly and make a meal of the plants. Seed onions especially are attacked: early-potted onion plants become established too soon for them. Treatment o: complementary planting of African marigolds, spray with nettle manure, cover bed with insect netting (very effective). c: bromophos.

Pea and bean weevils are grey and eat away pieces from the edge of the leaves during the night. The larvae nibble at root tubers. Damage is usually not as bad as it looks, so don't apply treatment too quickly. If damage is serious, treatment is o: preparation containing pyrethrum; c: HCH.

Pea moths lay eggs from which small caterpillars emerge to eat the seeds inside the peas. Treatment o: spray with herb extract made up from onion leaves, marigolds, African marigold, garlic. c: spray with fenitrothion.

Pea thrips cause discoloured and damaged pods. Pods become silvery brown. Treatment o: as soon as the leaves containing the first-stage flower buds begin to part, spray with pyrethrum. c: dimethoate.

Potato blight produces large and small brown spots on the leaves, and the tubers also show brown patches. Caused by a mould which can be combatted to some extent by planting deep and ridging in good time. Treatment o: horsetail tea or a sulphur mixture. c: mancozeb or zineb. Spray repeatedly from the moment the leaves become dense, and particularly after a shower.

Potato scab will cause the skins of your potatoes to turn rough. Cause: lime content too high. Provide a more acid soil.

Powdery midew is a mould which causes white, floury patches on leaves. The white powder can be rubbed off. Treatment o: horsetail tea or sulphur preparation. c: benomyl.

Potato blight starts as brown patches on the leaves.

Raspberry beetles are small and grey-brown. They demolish the flower shoots and blossom and lay eggs which develop into tiny worms that picnic on and in the fruits. Treatment o: spray with derris as soon as the insects begin to eat. c: malathion.

Redberry mites cause the fruits of blackberries to ripen unevenly – part of the fruit stays bright red. The affected fruit shrivels. Treatment o: spray with sulphur when the fruit-bearing shoots are 15 cm (6 in) long. Second spraying immediately before flowering. c: ditto.

Red spider mite is a small insect, too small, in fact, for the naked eye. They suck at the underside of the leaves, producing pale mottling, especially in warm, dry weather. Treatment o: keep plants damp, soap spirit, nettle manure. c: spray with dimethoate.

Rings in lettuce are caused by cold, dry winds.

Root aphids do not appear until late in the season, usually in August. They suck the sap out of vegetables like endives, lettuce and chicory, especially in areas where there are a lot of poplar trees. There are two types: woolly and non-woolly root aphids. Treatment o: grow marigolds or African marigolds among the vegetables. c: treat soil with diazinon.

Root eelworms cause short, stumpy roots in scorzonera. Treatment o: plant African marigolds.

Rust see Blight.

Sawflies lay eggs from which light green, black-speckled caterpillars appear. These eat the leaves of berry plants, usually starting in the heart of the bush. Treatment o: derris. c: dimethoate.

Scab produces corky areas on the roots of beet. There is no known treatment. It could be an indication of a poor soil structure. On celeriac the outer leaves turn yellow and grey-brown patches appear on the roots. These go corky and can later turn rotten. No treatment is known for this.

Sclerotinia (barkrot) on the stalks of beans is visible as a thick, white, fluffy mould with black sclerotia in it. Mostly in damp weather and when plants are too closely spaced. Treatment o: do not sow too closely and do not grow after potatoes, endives, cucumbers, lettuce or chicory. c: spray with benomyl.

Slugs and snails hide during the day and come out at night to eat the leaves on numerous plants. Treatment o: trap at night – bury pots full of beer, encircle the garden with strips of corrugated plastic: 10 cm (4 in) is high enough. c: slug pellets.

Springtails are small wingless insects which jump on contact. Only the white sort cause damage. They prefer to live in damp soil and eat germinating plants particularly. Treatment o: spray with soap spirit or nicotine extract. c: malathion.

Spur blight and cane spot in raspberries cause the canes to die back. Treatment: spray with copper, first in April, second spraying after picking.

Strawberry mites cause very pale mottling on the leaves, while they are still folded. They cause the young leaf to turn bronze-yellow to brown and grow deformed. Treatment o: nettle manure, soap spirit, insect netting. c: dimethoate.

Strawberry seed beetle is a small, black insect which eats the seeds from the ripening fruits. Treatment o: use insect netting. c: methiocarb pellets.

Thrips are very small, brown and black insects. The skinny larvae are yellow in colour. The whole family settles on the underside of the leaves and spends its time nibbling and can be spotted by the silvery patches that appear on the upper side. Treatment o: spray with derris. c: dimethoate.

Virus diseases exist in any number. They are carried by affected plant stock and by aphids, among other things. On potatoes we meet quite a variety of virus diseases, of which leaf curl is the best known. The lowest leaves roll up and feel hard to the touch. Ring disease produces dark rings in the flesh. Beans are attacked by, for example, the mosaic virus, which produces colourful, sharply-defined areas on the leaves. Some viruses will infect

A slug trap: fill it with beer, and the unwanted pests will clamber inside and drown.

Mosaic virus (see page 51) is quite common on bean plants. No direct treatment is possible.

gladioli, and these are best not grown too near.

Gherkins, cucumbers and lettuce can also be badly attacked by viruses.

A direct cure for virus attack is not possible. As far as possible, grow resistant varieties and virus-free plants (potatoes, strawberries, etc).

Whiptail in a cauliflower indicates a lack of molybdenum, a trace element. The head becomes pinched tight, while the leaves develop abnormally and turn knobbly. Treatment o: avoid too much nitrogen. Spray plants with foliar fertiliser.

White rot is a fungus disease which stops onion plants germinating. Later in the season, plants may go limp and begin to rot. Prevention: well-spaced-out crop rotation as sclerotina can live in the soil for a number of years.

Woodlice can eat germinating seeds. Treatment o: trap in balls of wood-wool, then destroy. c: methiocarb pellets.

Leaf and stalk vegetables

General information

In this section we discuss the vegetables whose parts growing above the ground – the leaves and stalks – are destined for consumption. It is a very important group of vegetables, and in particular no garden should be without one or more sorts of lettuce, spinach, endives and some rhubarb.

Leaf and stalk vegetables will also produce flowers, but in general that is not desirable. 'Bolting', as it is called, is usually brought about by sowing at the wrong time or using the wrong variety. Follow the instructions we have given in each description, and you will have no trouble in this area.

To ensure good leaf production the plants need to be well provided with nitrogen. For this reason you will find all the leaf vegetables in group A for the purposes of crop rotation. They are very demanding. Too much nitrogen, however, can lead to the formation of unwanted nitrites in the leaves. The extra nitrogen usually cannot be used up quickly enough by the growing plant and ends up in the leaves in a poisonous form. So leaf vegetables need to be manured well, but not over-well.

The juicier and softer the leaves, the more attractive they are, not only to us, but to sucking insects such as aphids. We can therefore expect to come across these particular pests quite often on our leafy plants, especially if they have had a generous dose of manure. In general, spraying with a relatively innocent mixture, such as soap spirit or nettle manure (see page 46), is sufficient to kill off these bandits.

Plants with soft leaves, such as cabbage lettuce, prefer to grow in a sheltered spot. Sharp winds do hardly any vegetable any good, but protection from the wind is especially important for leaf crops.

Among the vegetables described in this chapter you will meet a number that are comparatively unknown and which are hardly ever to be found at the greengrocer's. New Zealand spinach, winter purslane, foliage of swede: these are exclusive vegetables, which you can only really get hold of by growing them for yourself. This is fun for its own sake. But you will have even more satisfaction when you experience the taste. For ourselves, we are constantly amazed that such wonderful delicacies remain unknown.

Cabbage lettuce

Lactuca sativa var. *capitata*

Cabbage lettuce is a variant of the leaf vegetable which forms a fine, round head without encouragement. Just why this particular type of lettuce has become the most popular is something of a mystery, since the taste is hardly different from any of the other kinds, such as leaf lettuce and non-hearting lettuce. It's probably a result of the shape, which makes it easy to handle.

At all events, cabbage lettuce should be given space in everyone's garden. It is easy to grow, and usually eaten raw. It offers no great problems to the gardener.

Varieties. There is an enormous range of lettuce varieties, of which we will list only the best. Seed growers cultivate varieties for their suitability to a particular season, for their shape, for the tenderness of their leaves, for their colour (red lettuce) and finally for taste, although it's very difficult to spot any difference.

Varieties suited to growing under glass are: 'Dandie', 'Kwiek', 'May Queen'.

For the early crop in the open: 'Dolly', 'Fortune', 'Hilde', 'Tom Thumb', 'Unrivalled'.

For the summer crop in the open: 'Avondefiance,' 'Continuity', 'Sigmahead', 'Sigmaball'.

For the autumn crop: 'Avondefiance', 'Lilian', 'Sabine'.

For all seasons: 'All the Year Round'.

Soil type. Lettuce can grow on any type of soil, as long as it retains moisture well enough. This is important because a lot of water is needed during growth, and this moisture must always be readily available.

Stagnant water, on the other hand, is bad for the plants, but this applies to nearly all vegetables. Besides a good

ON PAGE 53: An attractive bed sown with cabbage lettuce 'Little Gem'.

OPPOSITE FAR LEFT: A patch of the kitchen garden where leaf and stalk vegetables are very prominent.

OPPOSITE ABOVE LEFT: Freshly sown cabbage lettuce before thinning out, and LEFT, the thinning out process itself.

supply of organic material, the soil must contain lime: a pH of 6.5 to 7.5 is ideal. As well as this, all the usual nutrients must be present, especially nitrogen. If you supply too much nitrogen, the growth will be magnificent, but the taste will suffer. Try to keep to a happy mean.

When to sow. Under glass, you can sow the whole year round. In the open, sowing begins in March, preferably under cloches. Sowing can continue up to mid-August; the crop will then mature under cloches up to the end of November.

A special crop is the 'over-wintering crop', sown in trays in October. When raised, the plants are pricked out in a cold frame and protected against winter frosts, for example with reed mats. After the winter the lettuce is planted out. For the 'early crop', the seeds are sown under glass, gently heated, in January/February; the plants are then pricked out and grown in cold frames, or sometimes in the open.

A decorative red lettuce. Red lettuce has softer leaves, so it is juicier than most green varieties.

Some cabbage lettuce can be grown equally well at any time of year.

As the last of the spinach is cut, cabbage lettuce is planted between the rows.

Several cabbage lettuce are particularly suited for an autumn crop.

How to sow. Lettuce seed germinates very poorly at a soil temperature above 20°c (68°F), and this is precisely the reason why many summer sowings fail. You can make sure the soil stays cool by making it wet immediately after (or before) sowing. You can also keep the bed cool with paper. If you are sowing in a separate seed bed, make sure it lies in the shade.

However, it is not advisable to make too much use of seed beds, since lettuces bolt earlier if they are pricked out. It is a better idea to sow straight into neat lines about 25 cm (10 in) apart. Sow as thinly as possible in drills about 1 cm ($\frac{1}{2}$ in) deep. When seedlings appear they must be thinned out. Do this, if possible, in stages. The final aim is plants spaced about 25 cm (10 in) apart, as otherwise they will not have the space they need to form a good head.

Do not sow too much lettuce at any one time: it is better to sow a couple of rows every week, then you will have fresh lettuce throughout the entire season. Lettuce seed retains its germinating power for three to four years.

Growing tips. To begin with, choose a variety that suits the season. Then make sure that the soil does not dry out too much, since lettuce plants have a small root system which does not go far below

the surface. Water in the mornings if you can, so that the lettuce has dried out by evening. If the plants stay wet overnight there is a greater risk of fungus diseases.

Time to maturity. From sowing to picking takes between 60 to 80 days, depending on the state of the weather. In the summer the plants will grow faster.

Pests and diseases. If you see a single aphid or slug on your lettuce, this is usually proof that the plant has been grown without any unpleasant poisons. If the attack becomes too much, you can go on the offensive. Keep the slugs away or put out slug pellets. Aphids can be kept in check very easily with relatively

tame treatments (see pages 46 and 47).

Root aphids are less common, but more difficult to keep down: you can try using a tobacco extract.

Birds also enjoy a juicy lettuce leaf. If they get too bold, stretch thin black threads above the plants or cover them with a net.

Mildew and other fungus diseases may occur after a long spell of cold, wet weather. Fortunately, many varieties are more or less resistant to these diseases. Virus diseases, which can be spotted by veining of the leaf or mosaic-like patches, cannot be cured. Keep well weeded and kill the aphids (which carry the virus). Ring spot is a disease which produces broad, brown rings in the heads, especially during biting weather. Provide a windbreak and grow varieties less susceptible to the disease.

Picking. You can start picking as soon as you have to thin out the young plants. These thinnings are fine to eat. Once you have grown a beautiful, full head, it's not worth leaving it in the ground, as it will get no better for it. Cut through the stalk well below the head with a sharp knife.

Successional and complementary planting. For crop rotation, cabbage lettuce belongs to group A. Suitable vegetables for an early crop are peas and beans, because they will add some nitrogen to the soil. Kohl-rabi is another good early crop. We have found favourable complementary mixes to include: asparagus, beans, beetroot, brassicas, broad beans, carrots, celeriac, chervil, cress, cucumbers, dill, Florence fennel, gherkins, kohl-rabi, leeks, sweet corn, onions, peas, mint, radishes and black radishes, rhubarb, scorzonera, strawberries and tomatoes.

The only unsuitable combinations we have discovered are parsley and celery.

After the lettuce is finished you can still grow: aubergines, beans, beetroot, broccoli, cauliflower, courgettes, Florence fennel, gherkins, kohl-rabi, late brassicas, leeks, melons, peppers, sprouts or tomatoes.

Iceberg lettuce

Lactuca sativa var. *capitata*

Iceberg lettuce can be recognized by its hard, crackly leaves and its firm head. This type of lettuce is especially popular in the United States, and is slowly catching on in Europe as well. The heavy heads keep longer than ordinary lettuce.

Varieties. 'Avoncrisp', 'Great Lakes', 'Iceberg', 'Lakeland', 'Lake Nyah', 'Minetto', 'Saladin', 'Webb's Wonderful', 'Windermere'.

Soil type. The same requirements as given for cabbage lettuce (see page 55).

When to sow. The spring crop should be started in March/April, preferably under sheeting. Summer crop from May to beginning of June. Autumn crop from June to end of July.

How to sow. As for cabbage lettuce, but distance between rows a little wider, 30–40 cm (12–16 in). The distance between each plant in the row after thinning out should also be 30–40 cm.

Growing tips. The plants do not bolt as quickly as ordinary cabbage lettuce. Extend the growing season in the autumn by placing cloches over the lettuce.

Time to maturity. It takes 10–15 days longer than with ordinary lettuce before good heads are formed.

Pests and diseases. 'Iceberg' lettuce is sensitive to ring spot; mildew or downy mildew can occur in the autumn. Viruses may attack the plant exactly as with cabbage lettuce. Aphids and slugs are less partial to this lettuce.

Picking. You don't necessarily have to wait until a full head has been formed: just pick the outer leaves, and let the rest continue to grow.

Successional and complementary planting. As for cabbage lettuce (see opposite).

Young 'Iceberg' lettuce which has just started forming a head. The leaves are thick, stiff and crackly.

A fully grown head of 'Lakeland', a variety bred for the British climate. The heads will keep for a long time.

Non-hearting lettuce

Lactuca sativa var. *crispa*

Non-hearting lettuce forms a short stalk on which fairly large, crinkled leaves grow. The idea is to pick the leaves off one by one and eat them raw or stewed.
Varieties. The variety 'Salad Bowl' has serrated leaves and is also called oak-leaf lettuce in restaurants. A red 'Salad Bowl' is also available.
Soil type. See cabbage lettuce (page 55).
When to sow. Greenhouse sowing can be done as early as December; in cold frames from February, and in the open from April.
How to sow. Best sown in the open, 30 cm (1 ft) between rows, after shoots appear thin out to 30 cm (1 ft), since the plants will grow very large. For a very early crop, the plants can be sown in individual pots and re-planted in the open later, preferably under cloches.
Growing tips. Don't wait too long before thinning out. Always provide

Non-hearting lettuce 'Salad Bowl', usually called 'oak-leaf lettuce' in restaurants. There is also a red variety of this lettuce.

plenty of water, and be generous with the manuring. If you follow these rules, the leaves will turn out good and juicy.
Time to maturity. You can start picking after about 25 days.
Pests and diseases. Generally speaking the same diseases as for cabbage lettuce; but in the main the plants are healthy. If left too close together, a risk of smoulder and mildew.
Picking. Start picking when the plant is 10 cm (4 in) high. Always choose the lowest leaves. If you don't take too much, you can keep on picking for a long time.
Successional and complementary planting. See cabbage lettuce (page 56).

Young lettuce can be picked very soon after sowing.

Young lettuce

Lactuca sativa

Young lettuce or 'thinnings' should not be wasted and can be used in salads. The leaves are of course very tender. Any type of lettuce can be used in the seedling stage.
Soil type. See cabbage lettuce (page 55).
When to sow. Young lettuce is first and foremost a spring vegetable. You can sow as early as January under glass or in plastic cloches, and in the open from March. In our experience, an autumn crop also offers attractive prospects: plants sown at the beginning of September have matured under cloches up to November.
How to sow. Broadcast sowing is possible, but a better idea is sowing in rows 10–15 cm (4–6 in) apart. Don't sow too densely within the rows. Thin out a little when the shoots appear, and you can eat these thinnings too.
Growing tips. Young lettuce grown under glass or plastic is juicier than the same plant grown in the open.
Time to maturity. The most attractive thing about young lettuce is of course the short time it takes to grow it: after only a few weeks you can already pick some small leaves. All the leaves must be picked before they get too large and hard: the aim is not to be able to keep on picking, as with non-hearting lettuce.
Pests and diseases. Once again the standard problems as listed under cabbage lettuce. Look out for fungus diseases resulting from over-close planting.
Picking. Don't let the leaves grow longer than 10 cm (4 in) and they will be sweet and juicy. If you take care that the growing point remains intact, you can look forward to a second harvest.
Successional and complementary planting. See under cabbage lettuce (page 56).

It is possible to buy mixed lettuce seed. Pick early and eat as young lettuce.

Cos lettuce

Lactuca sativa var. *longifolia*

Cos lettuce grows upright, with long, sturdy leaves, forming a sort of head, but a tall, stretched-out one. In the past the leaves grew apart more, and had to be tied together with twine to keep the inner leaves good and juicy. Present-day varieties no longer need this attention. It is a typical stewing vegetable, and tastes very like endives, but without the bitter side. However, nothing is stopping you from eating the very hard leaves raw.

Varieties. Cos lettuce comes with completely green leaves and also with paler, so-called 'white' leaves. Good varieties are 'Barcarolle', 'Little Gem', 'Lobjoit's Green', 'Paris White', 'Winter Density'.

Soil type. Cos lettuce can grow on any type of soil, as long as it retains moisture well enough. This is important because a lot of water is needed during growth, and this moisture must always be readily available. Besides a good supply of organic material, the soil must contain lime: a pH of 6.5 to 7.5 is ideal. As well as this, all the usual nutrients must be present, especially nitrogen. However, do not supply too much nitrogen, or the taste will suffer.

When to sow. Grown primarily in the spring, under glass from January; young plants can be planted out in the open from mid-March. You can also sow in the open from March onwards.

How to sow. In rows, 30 cm (1 ft) apart. After shoots appear, thin out until the distance in the row is also 30 cm (1 ft).

Growing tips. No particular problems. If you don't think the heads look tight enough, you can fasten them up with twine or elastic.

Time to maturity. About 60 days.

Pests and diseases. See under cabbage lettuce (see page 56). Cos lettuce is especially sensitive to ring spot, especially the green variety.

Picking. Cut the whole plant.

Cos lettuce is an old-fashioned stewing vegetable that turns white and soft from the inside if the tall heads are tied up with twine at an early stage. Self-closing varieties do not need to be tied.

Successional and complementary planting. For crop rotation, cos lettuce belongs to group A. Suitable vegetables for an early crop are peas and beans, because they will add some nitrogen to the soil. Kohl-rabi is another good early crop. We have found favourable complementary mixes to include: asparagus, beans, beetroot, brassicas, broad beans, carrots, celeriac, chervil, cress, cucumbers, dill, Florence fennel, gherkins, kohl-rabi, leeks, sweet corn, onions, peas, mint, radishes and black radishes, rhubarb, scorzonera, strawberries and tomatoes.

The only unsuitable combinations we have discovered are parsley and celery.

After the lettuce is finished you can still grow: aubergines, beans, beetroot, broccoli, cauliflower, courgettes, Florence fennel, gherkins, kohl-rabi, late brassicas, leeks, melons, peppers, sprouts or tomatoes.

The pith from the stalk of Cos lettuce can be eaten. The picture shows a stalk cut in half lengthwise.

Corn salad

Valerianella locusta (syn. *V. olitoria*)

Also known as lamb's lettuce, this is a plant growing wild in Europe which has no connection with the other types of lettuce discussed above, but which we include here because the plant is eaten as a salad vegetable, nearly always in its raw form.

Corn salad is particularly resistant to frost, and this makes it an ideal salad plant to grow as an early or late crop, when other salads are completely beaten.

Varieties. Listed in catalogues as 'Large-leaved' or 'Broad-leaved English'.

Soil type. Practically any soil will do. Make sure there is enough lime and adequate drainage.

When to sow. Spring crop in the open from March onwards. A more important crop is the autumn one, which starts in mid-August. You can continue sowing until the end of September.

How to sow. Preferably in rows 15–20 cm (6–8 in) apart. Thin out until the plants are 10–15 cm (4–6 in) apart. Do not sow deeper than 1.5 cm ($\frac{1}{2}$ in).

The seeds retain their germinative power for three to five years.

Growing tips. The seed doesn't always germinate as easily as it might: it helps if you cover the ground with a plastic sheet immediately after sowing. As the plants grow, you can replace this with plastic cloches: this will prevent the leaves becoming too tough and enable you to pick them for longer (especially in the autumn). In the spring, given a spell of warm, dry weather, corn salad can easily bolt. Extra watering will help here.

Time to maturity. The first leaves can be picked about 25 days after sowing.

Pests and diseases. As with lettuces, planting too close and cold, damp weather can give rise to fungus diseases, as well as mildew and smoulder. Otherwise, a strong plant that does not suffer much attack.

Picking. The best way is always to pick a few of the oldest leaves: that way you can carry on picking for a long time – sometimes right through the winter with an autumn crop. Another way to do it is to cut off the whole plant as low down as possible. You can then leave the plant whole and present it in a salad as it stands: delicious!

Successional and complementary planting. Corn salad is nearly always planted as a late crop. It doesn't make a lot of difference what you have in the soil before it, as long as it is out of the way by September. As regards complementary crops and combinations to avoid, we have no information.

Corn salad under a plastic tunnel cloche. The plant is already highly resistant to frost; and with this protection it can be picked even later.

Endive

Cichorium endivia

Endive is related to chicory, as the fairly bitter taste confirms. If endive is blanched, however, it loses some of its bitterness. Endive is generally cooked, but it is perfectly possible to eat it raw.

Common endive has entire leaves, while those of curled endive are indented and crinkly. This last type, the var. *crispum*, is the one most commonly eaten in salads.

Endive is mainly grown as an autumn or winter crop, because the plants are very resistant to cold.

Varieties. 'Batavian Green', broad-leaved; 'Green Curled' and 'Moss Curled', crinkly.

For an autumn crop: those listed above.

For the winter crop, 'Batavian Green'.

Soil Type. Endive requires a humus soil loosened to a good depth, containing plenty of lime and not too heavily manured.

When to sow. An early crop to be grown under glass can be sown as early as February. More common is autumn cropping: sow from mid-June to mid-July.

For the winter crop, also, sow no later than mid-July, but the plants will take longer this time.

How to sow. If possible, sow in a seed bed, from which the plants will later be pricked out in rows 30 cm (1 ft) apart. Spacing within the row after transplanting or thinning out should likewise be 30 cm (1 ft). The seed retains its germinative power for four to five years.

Growing tips. Plants raised under glass are planted out in early May. If the correct variety is not chosen for this crop there is a high risk of bolting. Don't plant the young endive too deep, and avoid breaking off leaves. In dry weather new growth will be slow, so water well and provide some shade. Endive sown later – after mid-June – will show less or no tendency to bolt.

If you want to grow large plants which will remain in the ground for longer, allow more space between them. Planting closely has the advantage that the plants will grow cheek-by-jowl, and this will blanch them a little.

If you want your endive to be more thoroughly blanched – and therefore more tender – tie them up firmly with twine or elastic bands when they are 80 days old. This must be done in dry weather, to prevent the hearts from going rotten. Curled endives need more warmth than common endives, so aim to grow this type under glass.

Time to maturity. The first endive can be picked after 60 days, but in autumn at least, the plant can be left in the ground much longer without any sacrifice in quality.

Pests and diseases. Slugs and aphids certainly won't turn up their noses at endives. A more tiresome pest is the root aphid, whose attentions slow down growth. Round, brown spots on the leaves are the signs of a leaf spot disease. Especially common in damp weather. Brown discoloration and rot in the leaves particularly occurs late in the year, when air humidity is high. We know of no remedy for these 'rings'.

Endive 'Batavian Green'. The heads have not been tied up.

Tying up the heads makes the inside whiter and tastier. Only do this in dry weather; otherwise rot will quickly take over inside the head.

Picking. Endive is resistant to frost to
−5°C (23°F), so the harvest can continue
well into December, especially if the
plants are protected with sheeting in
good time. Blanched endive cannot be
picked for as long as unblanched plants.
**Successional and complementary plant-
ing.** For crop rotation, endive belongs
to group A. Suitable for an early crop are
dwarf beans, kohl-rabi, potatoes and
peas, as well as early brassicas and
summer carrots. Complementary planting of beans, brassicas, carrots, cucumbers, kohl-rabi, leeks, lettuce, peas,
tomatoes and Florence fennel is helpful.
The endives will gain a special taste by
the complementary planting of herbs
such as chervil, hemp and sage.

Bad combinations are those with garlic or onions.

Spinach

Spinacia oleracea

A particularly attractive and easily
grown leaf vegetable, which – as long as
a good variety is selected – can be grown
almost the whole year round; but which
is also well suited to freezing. Young
spinach is the tastiest. The leaves, including a short stem, can be eaten raw,
but it is usually boiled (briefly).
Varieties. We can divide spinach into
round-seeded and prickly-seeded
varieties. The latter is mostly used for
early or late crops, when it is cold in the
open. Besides this, the selection takes
account of size, shape and colour of
leaves, length of stem, etc.

Summer varieties (round-seeded):
'Bloomsdale', 'Cleanleaf', 'King of
Denmark', 'Long Standing Round',
'Norvak', 'Sigmaleaf', 'Symphony'.

Winter varieties (most are prickly-
seeded): 'Broad-leaved Prickly', 'Green-
market', 'Monnopa', 'Sigmaleaf'.
Soil type. Spinach demands a moisture-retaining, humus-rich soil with a
good helping of lime (pH between 6.5
and 7.5). The nitrogen requirement is a
large one, which tempts many gardeners
into adding too much nitrogen, as a
result of which the taste is lost and there
is a danger that the leaves will contain a
dangerous amount of nitrite. We have
found a good dose of stable manure or
dried blood to be best.

On clay the growth can be too slow
and the plants may bolt (run to flower) as
a result.
When to sow. Depends on the variety.
The most common is the early crop,
sown from January onwards, as soon as
the soil is workable. If a later frost
occurs, this is usually no problem. With
modern varieties, growing spinach in the
summer is no trouble either. The autumn crop can be frozen with excellent
results.
How to sow. Broadcast or in rows,
whichever is preferred. The seed should
lie 1 to 2 cm (½ to ¾ in) below the surface.
In broadcast sowing, use 25 g per m²
(1 oz per sq yd). The rows should be
25 cm (10 in) apart, with seeds not sown
too densely within the row, which avoids
the need to thin out. The birds will be
happy to pick out the seeds so use plastic
sheeting as a counter-measure. So that
you have fresh spinach ready for the
table whenever you want it, you can sow
a small patch every fortnight. The seeds

Curled endive tastes the same as ordinary
endive, but is decorative and so is mostly
eaten raw (in salads).

Sowing spinach in rows.

retain their germinating power for four or five years.

Growing tips. The length of the day and the temperature have a powerful effect on the growth of spinach. In general, short days and low temperatures are best for the plant; however, selection has succeeded in producing fine summer varieties, too. All the same, these are best grown in the shade. Bolting (premature flowering) is caused by too high a temperature, long days, dryness and above all the wrong choice of variety.

Spinach reacts very unkindly to consolidated soil so hoe regularly between the rows.

Time to maturity. In winter up to 12 weeks, in summer four weeks.

Pests and diseases. Leaf rot or smoulder as a result of sowing too densely. Yellowish leaves: too little potassium. Small plants which bolt very quickly: too little nitrogen or other nutrient deficiency. Fungus diseases such as mildew, from sowing too densely, from over-watering or using non-resistant varieties.

Picking. Most people consider young spinach to be the tastiest. You can cut off the entire plant at one go, which is easiest with a bread-knife or a small serrated kitchen knife. Avoid cutting too low, since this will give you more stalk than you want. Picking leaf by leaf is more labour-intensive, but has the advantage that you can then expect a second harvest.

Successional and complementary planting. The crop rotation group is A. As a crop to grow before late spinach you can consider any vegetable which is out of the way by mid-August or mid-September, according to the variety. Before sowing spinach apply some nitrogen fertilizer, except perhaps after peas or beans.

The benefits of complementary planting with beetroots are disputed. Recommended: brassicas, carrots, kohl-rabi, potatoes, runner beans, strawberries, radishes and black radishes, rhubarb and tomatoes. Bad combination: cauliflower.

There is an enormous number of plants you can grow after early spinach, including: kohl-rabi, potatoes, Florence fennel and brassicas such as cauliflower, broccoli and sprouts.

TOP: Fresh shoots of young spinach. The seed envelopes are still on the leaf tips.

ABOVE: A bonny harvest of broadcast-sown summer spinach.

Spinach 'Sigmaleaf' is a very well-known variety, well suited to a very early crop in the greenhouse.

New Zealand spinach

Tetragonia tetragonioides

An annual plant, sensitive to frost, which is not related to ordinary spinach but rather to purslane.

The method of preparation for the table matches, however: the large, juicy leaves are picked individually and briefly boiled.

Varieties. There are no named varieties on sale.

Soil type. The plant prospers best in warm, fertile soil with a good humus content.

When to sow. From March onwards under glass, from the beginning of April under plastic or in tunnel cloches, and from mid-May in the open.

How to sow. The hard seeds germinate better if you let them soak overnight in

New Zealand spinach, from which the young tops are eaten.

water. Under glass they are usually sown in individual pots; in the open they are sown in threes about 1 cm ($\frac{1}{2}$ in) deep. When the shoots appear the two weaker plants of each group are removed. The final spacing between plants must be at least 50×50 cm (20×20 in), and as much as 100×100 cm (36×36 in) is often advised.

The seeds retain their germinative power for three to five years.

Growing tips. Ensure a warm, sheltered situation in full sun and protect the

Turnips grown for their leaves or 'tops' are usually sown broadcast for optimum use of space.

plants against night frost. Stop the growing plants several times to gain more side-shoots, and thus more leaves. Hoe frequently, especially early on. Apart from this, New Zealand spinach is not difficult to grow.

Time to maturity. About eight weeks to the first harvest. See also 'Picking' below.

Pests and diseases. In wet weather or if the plants are too close, mildew can occur. Leaf spot may also appear.

Picking. Since only a number of leaves are picked you can continue picking until November, especially if the plants are protected against night frost in September by plastic sheeting. Young leaves are the most tasty.

Successional and complementary planting. Include in group A for crop rotation. We know very little about complementary crops – perhaps early inter-cropping of quick-growing vegetables such as cabbage lettuce, radishes and summer spinach.

Turnip tops

Brassica species

Turnip tops are the young leaves of ordinary turnips (see page 79). Because turnip tops are a typical leaf vegetable, we are dealing with them here rather than in the root-crops section. Turnip tops can be eaten raw or lightly boiled, especially in bubble-and-squeak.

Varieties. 'Green Globe' is considered the best variety for turnip tops.

Soil type. Few demands are made of the soil except that it should be reason-ably fertile and not too dry.

When to sow. In the greenhouse you can sow throughout the winter, starting in October. In the open, growing begins in February, preferably under cloches, and can go through to April.

How to sow. Sow broadcast if you want to get as much as possible per square foot (in the frame). Otherwise in rows, 10–15 cm (4–6 in) apart. The seeds retain their germinative power for three to five years.

Growing tips. Water copiously if necessary, otherwise the plant will flop.

Time to maturity. About 40 days.

Pests and diseases. Rot can occur if the planting is too close. Small yellow leaves indicate nitrogen deficiency.

Picking. Do not allow the plants to grow taller than 10 cm (4 in). Often a second crop can be taken a few weeks after cutting.

Successional and complementary planting. For crop rotation, turnip tops are members of group A. No early crop is really possible. Good complementary plants are broad beans, dwarf beans, peas and strawberries. Tomatoes are a bad combination. After turnip tops you can grow practically any vegetable that needs to be in the ground after mid-May.

Purslane

Portulaca oleracea ssp. *sativa*

A less well-known leaf vegetable with a somewhat sour taste. Occasionally seen in the shops, but if you have a kitchen garden you can get as much fresh purslane as you want.

Varieties. Generally listed in seed catalogues is the green type.

Soil type. Purslane grows best on sandy soil with plenty of humus, and not to dry.

When to sow. Can be sown under glass or in cloches from April. In the open from the end of May until August.

How to sow. Always sown broadcast. As the seed is so fine, mixing beforehand with moist sand will make sowing easier.

Growing tips. Purslane needs a very warm and sheltered position. Under glass or plastic the plant usually grows well, but during wet, cold summers it often fails in the open.

Time to maturity. About 20 days; in warm weather or under cloches, 15 days.

Pests and diseases. Be cautious when watering: if the plants are too close they will quickly show signs of smoulder (fungus disease) when damp, and that will make short work of your crop.

Picking. You are interested in the thick, juicy leaves, which should not be too old. A length of stalk is usually picked with them. They can be cooked or eaten raw in salads.

Successional and complementary planting. Group A for crop rotation. Do not grow after other leaf plants, such as spinach. Complementary combinations are hardly possible, on account of the special temperature needs. For late crops you can choose any plant which still has enough growing time in front of it, but avoid leaf plants if possible.

Purslane needs plenty of warmth, so the plant grows best in a cold frame.

Purslane closely sown and at a very good stage for picking.

Winter purslane; it is no cause for concern if there are already flowers when it is picked.

Winter purslane

Montia perfoliata

Winter purslane is a leaf vegetable with diamond-shaped lower leaves and cup-shaped upper leaves. Eaten cooked. This plant occurs wild in many places.

Varieties. We know of no special varieties.

Soil type. As for ordinary purslane: sandy soil with a reasonable amount of humus, not too dry.

When to sow. Usually in August, but also quite possible from the beginning of March.

How to sow. Usually broadcast, but also in rows 15 cm (6 in) apart.

Growing tips. Winter purslane demands much less warmth than ordinary purslane. The plants can go on growing far into the autumn, but as frost turns the leaves brown it is a good idea to cover them with cloches in late September. Do not over-supply with nitrogen.

Time to maturity. From 30 days.

Pests and diseases. Smoulder as a result of over-close planting and too much moisture.

Picking. You can pick only the young leaves; but if the plants grow for longer and come into flower there is no need to worry. If the plants are not cut too low down, a second harvest is sometimes possible.

Successional and complementary planting. Little is known on this. See purslane for some information.

Rhubarb

Rheum rhaponticum

Rhubarb is a perennial which makes few demands and which you can eat for years on end. The parts eaten are the young, generally red stalks, which are stewed or made into jam. The leaves contain too much oxalic acid to be eaten.

It is possible to force rhubarb during the winter, so that it can be picked much earlier.

Varieties. For the main crop, 'Hawke's Champagne', 'Prince Albert', 'Sutton' and 'Victoria'. For forcing we can recommend 'Timperley Early'.

Soil type. Rhubarb prefers a fairly acid soil, pH 5.5–6.0. Apply a little soil conditioner when planting, for example old cow manure or bonemeal, and add manure regularly. However, this is not a terribly critical point.

When to sow. Rhubarb is one of the few vegetables you don't have to sow. The characteristics of the variety are only maintained if vegetative propagation (i.e. division) is carried out.

Young plants can be bought in a garden centre or by mail order.

Propagation. Divide and plant out preferably in autumn. Older plants are dug up and divided with a sharp spade. As far

as possible, each part must have two 'noses': these are the growing points. The noses lie a few centimetres (an inch or so) under the surface.

Distance between plants is 90 × 90 cm (3 × 3 ft).

Growing tips. Rhubarb does not mind slight shade. Water in dry weather and nip out the flower buds in the summer, along with the top two young leaves, as flower production will cost the plant quite a lot of energy.

Forcing. This can be done in two different ways. First, you can cover the plants from mid-January, for example with a large plastic bucket or barrel. This is packed well on the outside with straw, leaves or old blankets, and the whole lot wrapped in plastic to keep it dry. You can then look forward to your first sticks of rhubarb in late February.

If this is not early enough for you there is a second method. For this, older plants are lifted in late October or early November. They are left lying in the open for a few weeks so that the frost can get to work on them. Then they are placed close together in boxes and covered with a thin layer of soil. Water well. The boxes are then kept in complete darkness, for example by placing

another, taller box over them and covering everything with black plastic. Keep in a heated room, with a temperature of 14–16°C (57–61°F). After about four weeks you can start picking from the plants. Forced plants are useless after this and are best thrown away.

Time to maturity. It is best not to pick from plants set out or divided in the autumn for at least one year. In the second year take one stick, carefully; then from the third year on you can pick several sticks.

Pests and diseases. Rhubarb is a sturdy plant and does not have many problems. Bugs may well eat a few holes in the leaves, but the plants can easily cope with that.

Picking. Not when the plants are too young – see under Time to maturity. Young shoots are the tastiest. Take just a few sticks from each plant by pulling them off with a twisting motion. The harvest must come to an end in mid-July, otherwise the plants will become exhausted.

Successional and complementary planting. Rhubarb is not usually grown in a complementary mix, but will fit well in the flower garden, for example among the perennials in the border.

Rhubarb is one of the few perennials in the kitchen garden. Every year a few more of the red stalks can be harvested, through to about mid-July.

LEFT TO RIGHT: forcing rhubarb under a large plastic bucket. Pack with straw and finally cover with plastic to retain the soil warmth. Right: the result – bright red, very juicy stalks.

Leaf beet

Beta vulgaris ssp. *vulgaris* var. *flavescens*

A rather old-fashioned vegetable, little grown these days, which can be eaten in two ways. First, the leaves of young plants can be treated like spinach. Second, the stalks of rather older plants can be cooked like asparagus. The intended method of preparation needs to be taken into account when sowing.

Leaf beet also looks very good in the kitchen garden; the type with red stalks is particularly decorative.

Varieties. Swiss Chard, white leaf stalks and veins; Ruby Chard, red leaf stalks, a very decorative plant, ideal for the flower border. Perpetual spinach or spinach beet is similar in appearance to spinach and is all green.

Soil type. Normal, reasonably fertile soil is fine.

When to sow. March and April. Again in July for a second crop. Leaf beet sown even at the beginning of September provides a fair crop.

Red beet (beetroot) in autumn: despite a sharp frost, still good for picking.

How to sow. If you are interested in the young leaves, sow in rows 15–20 cm (6–8 in) apart. Thin out to 5 cm (2 in). If you want to pick the stalks the rows must be kept 40 cm (16 in) apart and thinned to 30 cm (12 in). Do not sow deeper than 2 cm (¾ in). The seeds retain their germinative power for four years.

Growing tips. Leaf beet is very resistant to frost and can thus be grown very early or very late without much protection. The plants show no inclination to bolt in the first year, which is an important advantage over spinach.

Time to maturity. About 50 days for young leaves. Stalks from 80 days.

Pests and diseases. Risk of fungus diseases, such as downy mildew, only if planted too close. Otherwise very sturdy.

Picking. The young leaves are picked as soon as they are 10–15 cm (4–6 in) tall. Do not cut too low as the plants may sprout again and give a second crop. The stalks are harvested by cutting off a few of the thickest (those on the outside) each time. The plant will then continue growing.

Successional and complementary planting. Leaf beet is in crop rotation group A. When sowing early a prior crop is not really possible. If it is sown later it benefits from following peas, beans, etc. Good complementary plants are brassicas, carrots, dwarf beans, radishes and black radishes. After early leaf beet a large number of vegetables can still be grown, preferably after some nitrogen fertilizer.

Garden cress

Lepidium sativum

A leaf vegetable which is also counted among the garden herbs. Super-simple to grow, and the seeds will even produce edible plants in an artificial growing medium. However, cress grown in cartons always strikes me as tasting synthetic: cress from the garden unquestionably has the edge. Garden cress is always eaten raw.

Varieties. Available as curled, 'Extra Double Curled', 'Super Salad'.

Soil type. Not important.

When to sow. In the open from March to September. Indoors, any time of year.

How to sow. Broadcast or in rows 15 cm (6 in) apart. Children enjoy seeing their names sown in cress.

Growing tips. For growing cress indoors we recommend that the trays or boxes should be filled with real soil. A mixture of potting compost and sharp sand works very well. Soil from the garden is also very good if it is light.

Time to maturity. Only seven days at room temperature. In the open, at lower temperatures, up to 20 days.

Pests and diseases. Generally speaking, no diseases

Picking. Cut off when the cress is 5 cm (2 in) high.

Successional and complementary planting. Can be grown practically anywhere between other crops. Seems to be particularly happy among carrots, radishes and black radishes. The taste is improved!

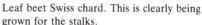

Leaf beet Swiss chard. This is clearly being grown for the stalks.

Garden cress, the simplest vegetable there is to grow, *and* ready to eat very soon after sowing.

Mustard

Sinapsis alba ssp. *alba*

Mustard plants are usually grown for their seeds. The condiment is then prepared from these seeds in a variety of ways. Young mustard plants are very good to eat and are often combined with cress in sandwiches and salads. Their use is comparable to that of garden cress. Growing is equally simple: sow (in rows or broadcast) and eat shortly afterwards. See opposite under garden cress for more detail.

RIGHT: Mustard, here sown in rows, can be picked even a little earlier than cress. Indoor growing, in boxes or trays, is equally problem-free.

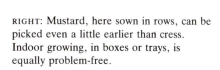

Watercress

Nasturtium officinalis

Currently a very exclusive vegetable – or should we say herb? In the better restaurants there's always a sprig of watercress lying beside the tournedos, and there's no getting rid of the watercress from high-class greengrocers either. The leaves of this wild plant are always eaten raw.

Varieties. We know of none.

Soil type. The name says it all: this is a true water plant, which needs a really wet soil. Besides this, the ground must be fertile. We recommend that watercress is grown in large plastic pots or tubs full of potting compost. Place these in a large bowl or other container, which is kept constantly filled with fresh, clean water. Later, the whole pot can be stood in a pond.

When to sow. From March to July.

How to sow. The seeds must have really wet soil, or they will not germinate. But watercress can also be propagated with ease by taking cuttings.

LEFT: Watercress is very easy to grow if you do it this way. The bowl must always be kept full of water.

Take just one small sprig home from that expensive restaurant and put it in a glass of water. In no time at all roots will appear, and then you can set the plant in wet soil.

Growing tips. Actually grows best in running water, but in our experience it works out fine in a small pond. The growth is so strong that the plant completely disregards the pot and spreads happily over the wet bank. According to the books, watercress is nothing if not hardy; but our plants give up the ghost at the first hint of a hard winter.

Time to maturity. After 30 days the first sprigs can be picked.

Pests and diseases. The plants are not really susceptible to any disease. However, avoid eating watercress from polluted water.

Picking. Young tops 5–10 cm (2–4 in) in length are the tastiest. If the plant flowers, the leaves become too hard and lose their taste. So cut often and follow the flower through to seed, then sow again.

Successional and complementary planting. Not applicable. If you wish, watercress can be grown alongside other waterside plants in the pond.

American cress

Barbarea vulgaris

Also known as land cress. Rather like watercress, but the taste is more on the bitter side. Grows on land, but must be kept damp. Also eaten raw.

Varieties. We know of none.

Soil type. Any soil is suitable, as long as it is moist to wet.

When to sow. From March to September.

How to sow. In rows 30 cm (1 ft) apart, 1.5 cm ($\frac{1}{2}$ in) deep. Thin out seedlings to 15 cm (6 in).

Growing tips. The plants are perennial, but quite sensitive to frost, so it is easier to sow each season. Use cloches to prolong the harvest in the autumn.

Time to maturity. 70 days.

Pests and diseases. Not susceptible.

Picking. The leaves must be picked before the plants flower.

Successional and complementary planting. No information.

Swede tops

Brassica napus

Young leaves of swedes can be eaten raw or lightly stewed, exactly as for turnip tops, which also belong to the brassica family (see page 64).

Varieties. Well known are 'Western Perfection', 'Marian', 'Acme' and 'Best of All'.

Soil type. Any soil is suited, provided it is neither too acid nor too wet.

When to sow. From late January to late August.

How to sow. In rows 15 cm (6 in) apart, or broadcast.

Growing tips. A sturdy vegetable, especially suited to very early or very late growing. Not sensitive to the light frost that can occur at these times.

Time to maturity. 60–90 days; less under plastic sheeting.

Pests and diseases. In dry weather flea beetles sometimes appear on the leaves.

Picking. Swede tops must above all be picked when young: older ones turn hard and tough.

Successional and complementary planting. For crop rotation best classed with group A. There is not really any scope for complementary planting so early in the season; for the summer crop see brassicas.

American cress or land cress is very like watercress and is put to similar use. The taste is a little more bitter.

Swede tops must be harvested when young, and can be eaten raw or lightly stewed. This is a hardy crop that will tolerate light frost.

Roots and tubers

General information

In this section you will find the vegetables from which we eat the swollen underground roots. There is one exception: with Florence fennel it is the swollen stem we are interested in.

Beyond this, tuber plants and root crops are not too closely connected, because they belong to completely separate families. Thus, carrots, celeriac, fennel, parsnips and Hamburg parsley belong to the umbellifers (with their flowers in umbrella-shaped clusters), beetroot to the chenopods (named after their goose-foot-shaped leaves), radishes and black radish to the crucifers (with cross-shaped petals), scorzonera and Jerusalem artichokes to the composites and potatoes to the nightshades.

Underground tubers are usually white, because the light does not get to them. The exceptions are beetroot and carrots, which have a good deal of colouring matter. Among the other plants, the skin of the root is often coloured, but the inside stays white. In some cases, tubers and roots that show above the ground are green or grey-green; and it is decidedly bad if potatoes are not properly earthed up when they are planted, since poisonous substances are then formed. Beets growing above ground become corky.

Florence fennel has no problems with this: there is nothing wrong with letting the swollen stem take on a bit of colour, but you can also keep the stems white by earthing them up.

Roots and tubers are actually the plants' energy reserves. As soon as it gets too cold or too dry above the ground, all the green growth will die off, but the root will live on to throw out new shoots in the next growing season. We usually don't pay any attention to this, because sprouting or even flowering root plants are not nice to eat. It is only potatoes that we can cheerfully allow to flower, as this does not affect the taste.

Given this perennial character of roots and tubers, it goes without saying that they need storing in cool, damp sand. In fact, this works very well with many of these vegetables. As long as the temperature stays low, so that the roots do not shoot, we can keep the quality up to the mark for several months.

Winter carrots will keep well in boxes of sharp sand, which should be set aside in a cool, frost-free place.

The same goes for beetroot. Storing in the ground is also a possibility, but in this case it must not freeze too hard.

In general, root plants have less of a need for nitrogen than leaf plants. For this reason they are assigned to group B for the purposes of crop rotation: this means that they can be grown where leaf plants were grown the year before (if we are using a three-year rotation scheme). Potatoes and celeriac, however, demand rather more nitrogen; so they are in group A.

As with most vegetables, roots and tubers are tastiest if they are eaten young. This especially applies to beets, radishes, summer carrots and turnips. Winter carrots, of course, are suitable for storing, as are scorzonera, celeriac and, above all, potatoes, our staple diet.

You might think that underground organs would be well out of the way of creeping parasites. Nothing could be further from the truth: there is an extensive assortment of vermin dedicated to depositing their eggs in the neck of the root. From these eggs maggots quickly appear and feast on the root or tuber at breakneck speed, undaunted by the hungry stares of the birds, which almost without exception regard maggots as a delicacy. You, too, will often notice only too late what is going on down there in the dark. Carrots especially, and also radishes, turnips and Hamburg parsley are often pretty well gobbled away before you spot what is going on. There are plenty of suitable answers to this destructive behaviour that you can buy, both chemical and biological. We shall discuss them in depth under each individual vegetable.

72

Carrots

Daucus carota ssp. *sativus*

A biennial plant with a swollen main root, eaten for its pleasant taste. The carrots, which also occur in the wild, do not produce flowers until the second year, but we eat the roots in the first year because that is when they are tastier.

We can divide carrots into early or summer carrots, and maincrop carrots which are ideal for winter storage.

Summer carrots can be sown very early: they are a typical summer vegetable, with a relatively short growing period. The roots are eaten (raw or cooked) while they are young and tender.

Maincrop carrots need much more time to grow, and the roots get much larger. It is a typical storing vegetable, which can be eaten right through the winter, likewise cooked or raw.

Varieties. Summer carrots: 'Amster-

The maincrop carrot 'Juwarot' has a very high vitamin A content, and is known for this reason as the 'health carrot'

BELOW LEFT: The well-known variety 'Amsterdam Forcing' of which there are numerous selections.

BELOW RIGHT: Neat round carrots of the variety 'Early French Frame'.

dam Forcing – Amstel', 'Early Scarlet Horn', 'Early French Frame' (round roots), 'Early French Frame – Rondo' (round roots), 'Early Nantes', 'Nandor', 'Nantes – Champion Scarlet Horn', 'Nantes Express', 'Parmex' (round roots), and 'Tiana'. The round-rooted varieties are highly recommended for shallow or poor soils.

Maincrop carrots: 'Autumn King – Early Giant', 'Autumn King – Vita Longa', 'Berlicum – Berjo', 'Campestra' (very highly coloured), 'Camus' (very highly coloured), 'Chantenay Red Cored – Concord', 'Favourite', 'Figaro', 'James' Scarlet Intermediate', 'Juwarot'

(contains double the normal amount of vitamin A), 'New Red Intermediate', 'Regulus Imperial', and 'St Valery'.

Soil type. Carrots grow best in a loose, fertile soil with plenty of lime. The ideal pH is 6.5–7.5. Water must always be able to drain away easily. Fertilizing with horse manure or lime must be done at least a year before planting, and dried blood or bonemeal, or at a pinch artificial fertilizer, can usefully be added just before the start of the season. The soil must be loosened to a good depth, because the longer carrots above all will only grow well in a very loose soil. If the deeper levels are rather firm, grow the

shorter or round-rooted carrots, such as 'Parmex'.

When to sow. Summer carrots can be sown from March onwards, preferably in a cold frame or under a cloche. From mid-April in the open. Sowing can be continued through to the end of June, and the last sowing will then be ready to pull in November.

Maincrop carrots must be sown at the beginning of May in order for them to grow decent-sized roots by autumn. Sowing too early will risk bolting, besides which early-sown maincrop carrots store less well.

How to sow. The art of sowing carrots is to sow them thinly enough so that no thinning out is needed later.

You should not use more than 1 gram of seed per m² (1/30 oz per sq yd). The plants are usually sown in rows, but if the soil is relatively free of weed seeds, so that hardly any weeding needs to be done, broadcast sowing can be recommended. This makes the yield per square metre much greater. Rows should be 15 cm (6 in) apart, and the seeds about 1 cm ($\frac{1}{2}$ in) deep in the spring, to a maximum of 3 cm ($1\frac{1}{4}$ in) in summer – deeper than in spring, because the ground will dry out quicker. The summer carrots should end up some 3–5 cm ($1\frac{1}{4}$ to 2 in) apart.

Maincrop carrots are nearly always sown in rows, with a spacing of 25–30 cm (10–12 in). Plants in each row should finish 5–7 cm (2–2¾ in) apart.

Carrot seeds retain their germinative power for two to three years.

Growing tips. Carrots should receive as much sun as possible, especially in the spring. In summer, a little shade can help germination. Place the carrots where the wind can reach them as well. In dry weather keep well watered otherwise the carrots will not be tender. If the plants need thinning out (avoid this if you can!) do it in the evening and give the remaining plants a good watering. Try to avoid snapping any leaves.

If the tips of the carrots show above the ground earth them up, otherwise they will turn green.

Time to maturity. Summer carrots: 80 to 100 days. Winter carrots: at least 150 days.

Pests and diseases. There are a good 20 diseases known to afflict carrots, but we will not bore you with them. We will make an exception, though, for enemy number one: the carrot fly. This evil creature is attracted by the smell of carrots, spread by thinning out, hoeing too energetically, or broken leaves. It tries to find a way into the ground next to the carrot and lays its eggs in it. After a while, milk-white maggots emerge and munch away with a will, so that there is eventually nothing much left of your beautiful carrots. Now you see why thinning out should be done in the evening and followed by watering: this reduces the smell, and the chinks in the ground are closed up.

Great efforts are made by professional growers to combat the carrot fly: for example, the soil is treated with diazinon or bromophos, and maincrop carrots are given a second spraying three months later. Organic gardeners usually seek the answer in the careful methods mentioned above and in complementary crops. Some wood ash may also be spread on the surface.

We had a lot of trouble with carrot flies in our garden, too, until we covered the plants with fine insect netting. If you fix it up properly, not a single fly will get through.

Picking. Carrots must be picked through a few times so as to make sure the mature ones are always pulled. The rest can be allowed to continue growing. Pull the plants in the evening and then water the ground well. Late-sown summer carrots can be pulled until far into the autumn, if you can provide some protection against frost. The same goes for maincrop carrots. If you don't want to run the risk of frost, store the carrots in boxes of sharp sand and put in a cool, but frost-free place. This will allow you to store the carrots until March or April.

Successional and complementary planting. For crop rotation, we include carrots in group B. An early crop of peas, kohl-rabi or early cabbage (or other brassica) is possible if you sow the carrots fairly late or if we are talking of maincrop carrots. Favourable combinations for complementary planting involve: beans, brassicas, celery, chicory, chives, cress, dill, endive, garlic, leaf beet, leeks, lettuces, onions, parsnips, peas, radishes and black radishes, scorzonera, spinach, strawberries and tomatoes. The only unfavourable mix reported involves beetroot. After summer carrots there is room for a catch crop of cauliflower, endive, kohl-rabi or other late brassicas.

Maincrop carrots given hard soil to grow in: the roots have forked. The heads are a little green from being exposed to light.

Unforked maincrop carrots which have been grown under insect netting.

Beetroot

Beta vulgaris ssp. *vulgaris* var. *conditiva*

A biennial which produces in its first season a globe-shaped, sometimes pointed root of a red, white or yellow colour. The root can be eaten raw or cooked.

Varieties. For the early crop, the decisive characteristic is resistance to bolting.

For the summer crop, suitable varieties are the globe-shaped ones, such as: 'Globe', 'Monodet', 'Replata'.

Long beetroot varieties are 'Forono', 'Cheltenham Green Top', 'Cylindra'.

A yellow beet for the summer crop (botanical name: var. *lutea*), is 'Burpees Golden'.

Suitable for the autumn crop: 'Boltardy', and selections of 'Detroit' such as 'Little Ball'.

Soil type. Medium-heavy to heavy soil, acidity between 6.5 and 7.5, well drained, plenty of humus. The soil should not be freshly manured.

When to sow. Beets can be sown any time from the end of February so long as a non-bolting variety is used. A cold frame or cloche will be needed if sowing is done this early. From early April sowing can be done in the open. It is also possible to raise young plants in the greenhouse and transplant them outside later. For a late crop, sowing can be done in the open up to the end of June.

How to sow. The seeds usually come in clusters of 'druplets' called 'seed balls', containing two to five seeds. Nowadays you can also get cleaned seeds; and there are also balls containing only one seed ('Monodet'). It is a good idea to soak the balls for an hour or so before sowing. Below 7°C (45°F) beet seed germinates poorly, and this also increases the risk of bolting.

Sow in rows 20–30 cm (8–12 in) apart. Thin out seedlings to 5–10 cm (2–4 in). Sowing depth is 1 cm ($\frac{1}{2}$ in) in the spring and up to 3 cm ($1\frac{1}{4}$ in) in the summer.

The seeds retain their germinative power for four or five years.

Sowing in the greenhouse is done at a temperature of 18–20°C (65–68°F). After germination the heating can be reduced to 12°C (52°F).

Growing tips. Water in dry weather. To guard against weeds hoe cautiously

A summer globe-shaped beetroot, not too large and all the tastier for it.

A yellow beet: 'Burpees Golden'.

between the rows so that you do not damage the beets.

Time to maturity. 100–150 days.

Pests and diseases. The beet fly burrows into the leaves; if heart rot strikes, the heart of the plant turns black and rots. This indicates a deficiency of boron. If there is a shortage of potassium the leaves turn knobbly and wavy and darker than normal in colour. Scab produces corky patches on the beets. If too much of the beet appears above the ground, birds and mice will pick at them. Earth them up well.

Picking. Beetroot must not be left in the ground too long, or white rings will form in the root. Pull the plants and twist off the tops; never cut them. The beets must be up before the first frost; a cloche will help against night frost. Beetroot can be stored in a box of sand and kept through to the spring at around 3–4°C (37–39°F).

Successional and complementary planting. Beetroot belongs to group B for crop rotation. Kohl-rabi is a good early crop. The benefits of complementary planting of leeks or potatoes are disputed, so best avoided. The good complementary plants appear to be dill, dwarf beans, gherkins, kohl-rabi, lettuce, onions, peas and strawberries. Bad for beetroot are asparagus, carrots, sweet corn and spinach. After early beetroot you should be able to grow some late dwarf beans, or kohl-rabi, late brassicas or corn salad.

Radishes

Raphanus sativus var. *sativus*

A popular, easily-grown root vegetable with a short growing time. There are red, white and two-colour radishes, in round, oval and long shapes. A typical spring vegetable, but there are now also good summer varieties.

Radishes are always eaten raw.

Varieties. There are special varieties for the spring, summer and autumn crop, as well as a glass or forcing radish for growing in the greenhouse or cold frame.

Growing under glass: 'Saxerre', 'Robino'.

Spring crop: 'Scarlet Globe', 'Crystal Ball', 'Sparkler', 'French Breakfast – Succulent'.

Summer crop: 'Cherry Belle', 'Prinz Rotin'.

There are also half red, half white varieties, such as 'French Breakfast Crimson', 'Saxa'. A totally white radish is the long-bodied 'Minowase Summer No. 2'. A variety that forms very large but still firm roots is 'Long White Icicle'.

Soil type. A fertile, loose soil which holds plenty of humus and maintains a good level of moisture is desirable. Fresh manuring is not a good idea; and too much fertilizer produces heavy foliage and tasteless radishes.

Radishes can be sown either in rows or broadcast. After the seeds have sprouted, thinning out must leave the plants 2–3 cm (¾–1¼ in) apart.

ABOVE: Radish 'Crystal Ball', a variety suited to the spring crop, at the right stage for eating.

BELOW: White radishes can be pulled early when they are small and their flower is still mild.

When to sow. Special varieties can be sown in the greenhouse from December onwards. More usual, however, is the spring crop, sown from early March to mid-April. Covering with plastic sheets brings the harvest forward. Special summer varieties can produce high-quality radishes between May and mid-August. After this the autumn crop take over: both spring varieties and special autumn types can be used for this.

How to sow. Radishes are mostly sown in rows 10–20 cm (4–8 in) apart. Broadcast sowing is equally successful. Sow no deeper than 1 cm (½ in). Thin out to 2–3 cm (¾–1¼ in). The seed retains its germinative power for four to six years.

Growing tips. Radishes grow best given comparatively low temperatures and a short day. This means you will have more trouble with germination in the summer. Sponginess is caused by too much evaporation through the leaves. Early and late in the year, radishes need to be grown in an open position, but during the summer it is better to choose a cooler spot with a little shade. The right choice of variety is very important for a good result.

Time to maturity 40–45 days in spring, 20–30 days in summer.

Pests and diseases In general not prone to attack, but flea beetles can cause damage.

Picking. Radishes must on no account be left to grow old: if they do their taste will suffer and they will go 'woody'. Far better to pick them while they are on the small side. Pull up the biggest ones and leave the rest in the soil. If you leave them lying, cut off the leaves, otherwise the roots will dry out.

Successional and complementary planting. For crop rotation, include radishes in group B. For an early crop you can really grow any vegetable that does not need to be in the soil later than mid-August, except for brassicas and radishes themselves. Cucumbers are a disputed complementary crop, but good ones are beans, brassicas, carrots, cher-

Many radishes can reach a respectable size.

vil (for the taste), cress (taste again), kohl-rabi, leaf beet, leeks, lettuce, onions, parsley, peas, spinach, strawberries and tomatoes. Avoid gherkins and hyssop. Very good to grow after radishes are: aubergines, celery, gherkins, sweet corn, melons, peppers, potatoes, tomatoes and Florence fennel.

White radishes can also be allowed to develop fully. Then their flavour will be strong and quite hot, more like that of a black radish.

Black radish

Raphanus sativus var. *niger*

An annual or biennial plant which is not too popular in Britain. The root, which can run to 30 cm (1 ft) in length in some varieties, has a black skin. It is eaten raw; sliced thinly or grated in a salad.

Varieties. In Britain we only grow the winter variety 'Black Spanish Round' with round roots.

Soil type. If possible, medium heavy soil with plenty of humus. Not straight after liming. Does not need a lot of fertilizer; do not use fresh horse manure. Soil must not be too wet.

When to sow. Winter crop from the end of June to mid-August.

How to sow. Usually in rows 3 cm (1¼ in) deep. Thin out to 15–20 cm (6–8 in).

The seed retains its germinative power for four or five years.

Growing tips. Warm and dry conditions do not suit the plant. The longer the day, the greater the risk of bolting. Low temperatures also encourage shooting.

Time to maturity. About 70 days.

Pests and diseases. Flea beetles plague the young plants; the mealy aphid and the bean fly leave the plant worm-eaten; downy mildew is caused by planting too close. Deformed roots are brought on by too much lime or by fresh horse manure.

Picking. Roots can be kept (safe from frost) in boxes of sharp sand.

Successional and complementary planting. For crop rotation, black radishes belong to group A. Any vegetable which is clear of the soil by mid-August is suitable as an early crop, except for brassicas, radishes and black radish itself. It prospers with complementary crops of beans, beets, brassicas, carrots, cress, kohl-rabi, leaf beet, lettuce, parsley, peas, spinach, strawberries or tomatoes. Not with gherkins or onions.

Scorzonera

Scorzonera hispanica

A plant that also grows in the wild: has a long, black finger root, which is eaten cooked. Because skinning the root is no small job and makes your hands good and sticky, scorzonera used to be known as 'the scullerymaid's bane'. There is also a white scorzonera, *Tragopogon porrifolius*, better known as salsify or 'oyster plant': as far as the gardener and the cook are concerned, this is much the same as the black scorzonera.

Varieties. Black: 'Habil', 'Russian Giant', 'Long Black'. White: 'Mammoth', 'Sandwich Island', 'Giant'.

Soil type. The roots can grow as long as 50 cm (20 in); 30 cm (1 ft) is a good size, however. Loose, deeply dug sandy or loamy soil is needed to prevent the roots forking. Digging in manure encourages this forking and should therefore be avoided. On the other hand, the food

requirements are not very high. pH between 6.0 and 7.5

When to sow. From March onwards, preferably in April or May: bolting is very common after early sowing.

How to sow. Rows 25–30 cm (10–12 in) apart. Sowing depth 1–2 cm ($\frac{1}{2}$–$\frac{3}{4}$ in). Thin out to 8–10 cm (3–4 in). The seed does not retain its germinative power for long, so always use fresh seed.

Growing tips. Hoe with care so as not to damage the roots. If the plants bolt, don't worry: bolting does not spoil the quality or taste of the roots of the black scorzonera. Make sure the plant is kept well watered. Mulching helps keep weeds at bay.

Time to maturity. About 180 days.

Pests and diseases. On the whole, very few diseases. During damp summers mildew may form on the leaves. Root

Scorzonera should be dug out very carefully with a spade.

eelworms may cause odd-shaped roots.

Picking. No earlier than October as the plant will go on growing for a long time. The plants are winter hardy, so long as you can still dig the ground you can keep on pulling them right through to March. The long roots will break very easily if you don't dig them up carefully. If kept at a low temperature they can be stored for months in damp sand.

Successional and complementary planting. Scorzonera belongs to group B for crop rotation. Since they take up the whole season there is not a lot to be said as regards successional planting. Helpful complementary crops that have been reported include beans, brassicas, carrots, celeriac, endive, kohl-rabi, leeks, lettuce, onions and spinach. We do not know of any specific plants not to choose.

Scorzonera is winter hardy: the leaves may die off after a sharp frost, but the roots survive.

Turnips

Brassica rapa var. *rapa*

A winter hardy vegetable with a multitude of uses. It is eaten cooked; larger turnips taste sweeter than the miniature varieties.

Turnip tops – the young leaves of the plant – are dealt with on page 64.

Varieties. Separate varieties have been developed for different purposes. The larger varieties grown for eating often have yellow flesh: examples are 'Arca', 'Golden Ball', 'Green Globe', 'Manchester Market – Green Top Stone', 'Model White', 'Veitch's Red Globe'.

The miniature varieties are divided into flat and round types. Flat varieties include: 'Milan White Forcing', 'Purple Top Milan'. Both are suitable for an early crop. Those rounder in shape include 'Snowball – Early White Stone' for the summer and autumn crop.

Soil type. Not too critical. Preferably not too acid, fairly fertile soil, pH 6.0–7.0

When to sow. Spring turnips from March on, best under cloches. Maincrop preferably in early June. Autumn crop from July to mid-August.

How to sow. Mostly in rows, which should be 50 cm (20 in) apart for the

ABOVE: Turnips of the 'Milan White Forcing' variety. Those at the top are good for size, while the flat shape can be seen from the lower ones.

larger varieties. After germination thin out until the plants are 35–40 cm (14–16 in) apart. Can also be raised in a seed bed, then planted out later.

For the very much smaller varieties, a distance between rows of 25 cm (10 in) is ample. Thin out quickly as soon as the shoots appear until the young plants are 10 cm (4 in) apart, otherwise root formation will be restricted. Sow to a depth of 1–2 cm ($\frac{1}{2}$–$\frac{3}{4}$ in).

The seeds will keep their germinative power for three to five years.

Growing tips. Never let the soil dry out, as this will give you less juicy and therefore less tasty vegetables.

LEFT: A 'Snowball' type, here pulled good and small, is suitable for a summer and autumn crop.

Ordinary, large turnips can be kept well in boxes of sharp sand. The temperature must be kept low, or the turnips will sprout.

Time to maturity. Miniature varieties 40–80 days, larger plants 140–170 days.
Pests and diseases. Flea beetles infest young plants most of all.
Picking. Larger turnips are usually pulled no earlier than October–November, and could in fact be left in the ground much longer. However, they would be no tastier for it, but more like the kind used as cattle-fodder. This applies even more to the smaller types: these must not be allowed to grow beyond 5 cm (1 in) in diameter. Frost has a bad effect on the taste of autumn turnips, so use a cloche.

They can also be stored, either in pits (clamps) or in boxes filled with sand.
Successional and complementary planting. For crop rotation turnips belong to group B. Good complementary crops are beans, beets, carrots, celery, chicory, leeks, lettuce, peas, potatoes and spinach. Tomatoes make for a bad combination. After early turnips you can grow beans, peas or chicory.

Parsnips

Pastinaca sativa

A biennial plant which also grows in the wild and has a long, thick, yellowish root, white on the inside. The roots are eaten raw or, more usually, cooked. The growing time for parsnips is particularly long.
Varieties. 'Avonresister' (short root), 'Cobham Improved Marrow', 'Improved Hollow Crown', 'Tender and True', 'The Student', 'White Gem'.
Soil type. Prefers very loose, reasonably fertile soil, which should not be too dry. pH 6.5–7.0.
When to sow. From March, but in that case under a cloche; otherwise mid-April. The seed germinates slowly if it is cold.
How to sow In rows 35–40 cm (14–16 in) apart. Thin out seedlings to 15 cm (6 in). Sowing depth 2 cm ($\frac{3}{4}$ in). Use fresh seed each year.
Growing tip. Hoe regularly but carefully. Mulching is a very good thing provided that the soil is already moist. Water in dry weather. For extra long and well-formed roots you can dig a hole 60–100 cm deep (24–40 in) and fill it with very loose soil.
Time to maturity. Parsnips do not start to grow quickly until autumn, which makes the time needed extremely long: at least 200 days.
Pests and diseases. On the whole very healthy. Sometimes trouble with carrot root fly – see under carrots (page 74). In winter sometimes attacked by mice.

Parsnip canker is a physiological disorder that results in brown patches on the roots. This condition is more prevalent on heavy soils. There is no cure, so choose a resistant variety like 'Avon resister,' or 'Tender and True' and grow your parsnips on a good deep well-cultivated loamy soil.
Picking. Harvesting does not start until October, and can continue until May, if the roots are protected from frost by a little soil or straw. Lift roots carefully, otherwise they will break. In the spring roots can be lifted and stored if the ground is needed for other crops.
Successional and complementary planting. The crop rotation group is B. Early and late crops do not come into the picture, since parsnips occupy the

If parsnips are pulled late they can grow very long, since the growth speeds up in the autumn. An excellent storing vegetable.

ground during the entire season. Good complementary vegetables are beans, beets, brassicas, carrots, sweet corn, onions and peas.

Celeriac

Apium graveolens var. *rapeceum*

A form of celery in which the lower part of the stem and the roots swell up. Also known as 'turnip-rooted celery' for obvious reasons. The stem is eaten raw or cooked. An excellent vegetable for including in soups and stews. Typical winter vegetable with a very long growing time.

Varieties. 'Globus', 'Iram', 'Jose', 'Snow White', 'Tellus'.

Soil type. Celeriac requires a very fertile, humus-rich soil, which should if possible contain some well-rotted horse manure. On no account must the ground dry out.

When to sow. It is a good idea to sow very early, preferably under glass. March is a good time for this. Raise the plants if possible in individual pots and plant them out in the open at the end of May after hardening. This also gives you the chance to grow an early crop before the celeriac. If you sow direct in the garden in April or May, the stems will not grow enough.

How to sow. In seed boxes, at a temperature of 18–20°C (65–68°F). After about five weeks prick out in pots and continue the growing at 12–16°C (54–60°F). The seeds retain their germinative power for three to six years.

Growing tips. Plants should be spaced 50 × 50 cm (20 × 20 in). Do not plant too deeply.

Always water generously and apply fertilizer in the summer: dried blood, bonemeal or similar. In dry soil it can help to plant the vegetables in furrows 15 cm (6 in) deep: the water will then soak towards the roots.

Time to maturity. Very long: a good 200 days.

Pests and diseases. Aphids are responsible for crinkly leaves which fall prematurely. Aphids can also carry virus diseases. Root fly larvae can eat tunnels in the stems. See under Carrots. Scab turns the outer leaves yellow, and produces grey-brown patches on the root: these go corky and later rot.

Picking. The roots are not dug until October. If the leaves are cut off, the stems can be kept in boxes of sand right through the winter (safe from frost, of course). They can also be left in the ground, but will then need protecting from sharp frosts.

Successional and complementary planting. Celeriac belongs to group A for crop rotation. Suitable early crops are cauliflower (winter crop), early lettuce, kohl-rabi and spinach. Good complementary crops are beans, brassicas, carrots, leeks, lettuce, peas, sage, scorzonera, tomatoes and onions. Late crops do not come under consideration.

Young celeriac plants can be raised in small pots and planted out later.

Celeriac is dug in autumn. If covered against frost, it can be left where it has grown.

Jerusalem artichokes and Chinese artichokes

Helianthus tuberosus and *Stachys affinis* var. *tubifera*

Little-known perennial vegetables. The Jerusalem artichoke belongs to the same family as sunflower, and the plants, which can grow to 3 m (10 ft), are similar to sunflowers except that the golden flowers are much smaller. They also come into bloom later.

The kitchen gardener is interested in the underground tubers, which have long been known to the American Indians. They contain a lot of fructose and consequently taste sweet. They are eaten cooked.

The Chinese artichoke is not related but offers the same possibilities.

Varieties. The Jerusalem artichoke comes in varieties with white or purple tubers.

Soil type. Not too critical, but the soil must not get too wet. Too much manuring is undesirable.

When to sow. In this case, it is when to plant, since we always start from tubers grown the previous season. They can be put in the ground in March or April.

How to sow (how to plant). Jerusalem artichokes: in rows 90 cm (3 ft) apart. Distant apart within the row should be 30 cm (1 ft). The Chinese artichoke, which does not grow anything like as tall, should have 50 cm (20 in) between rows and 25 cm (10 in) in the row. Both types are planted 15 cm (6 in) deep.

Growing tips. The Jerusalem artichoke usually needs some support. In summer it is a good idea to earth up the plants in the same way as potatoes. Water in dry weather or the tubers will not grow.

Time to maturity. About 180 days.

Pests and diseases. Practically free of diseases.

Picking. From October. Jerusalem artichoke tubers are winter hardy and best left in the ground until you want them, since they dry out very quickly once they are dug up. Chinese artichokes should be covered with straw or leaves, as their tubers are less resistant to frost. Harvesting can continue

Jerusalem artichokes are strange, white tubers which grow to tall 'sunflowers'.

through to March.

Successional and complementary planting. Little is known about this aspect. Usually the plants go wild: they stay where they are put until they are removed root and branch. You can try beans, cucumbers and sweet corn as complementary crops, but this is not terribly practical. Catch crops are out of the question with a settled plant of this sort.

Picking. From October onwards. Roots can be left in the ground (cover during sharp frosts) or stored free from frost in boxes of sand.

Successional and complementary planting. The crop rotation group is B. Do not grow after carrots, celery or ordinary parsley. Good complementary crops are beans, peas, horse-radish, radishes, sage and lettuce. Late crops do not apply.

Hamburg parsley

Petroselinum crispum ssp. *tuberosum*

Also known as turnip-rooted parsley. Same family as ordinary parsley (page 177), and the leaves are used in the same way. But this variety also forms white, fleshy roots which look like parsnips and can be put to the same use.

Varieties. In British seed catalogues it is simply listed as Hamburg parsley.

Soil type. Humus-rich and moisture-retaining.

When to sow. From late March.

How to sow. In rows 30 cm (1 ft) apart, thinned out to 6–10 cm (2¼–4 in) in the row. The seeds germinate extremely slowly, so could be raised in moist sand beforehand. They retain their germinative power for two to three years.

Growing tips. Always provide plenty of water, hoe etc. Can be grown in pots or trays.

Time to maturity. About 180 days.

Pests and diseases. Sometimes troubled by fungus diseases or root fly.

Hamburg parsley can be eaten either raw or cooked.

Florence fennel

Foeniculum vulgare ssp. *vulgare*
var. *azoricum*

A vegetable which is being eaten more and more in Britain. Can be grown with great success in a sheltered garden or under a cloche.

The part we are interested in is the bottom of the plant, which swells up to form a pseudo-cabbage tasting of aniseed, which can be eaten both raw and cooked.

Varieties. 'Perfection', 'Sirio', 'Sweet Florence', 'Zefa Fino'.

Soil type. Loose soil rich in humus and nutrients, with plenty of lime. Clay is not suitable.

When to sow. From May onwards. If sown too early there is a good risk of bolting. This results from the cold. It is also possible to raise plants in the greenhouse in peat or plastic pots. If they are kept warm they will not germinate. We have sown as early as March, with great success! Final sowings late June to mid-July.

How to sow. In the open, in rows 40–50 cm (16–20 in) apart. Thin out to 20–25 cm (8–10 in) in the row.

Growing tips. Florence fennel needs plenty of warmth, so the use of cloches is worthwhile. The plants cannot take more than a light night frost. Always hoe thoroughly and water well if it is dry. In the course of the summer the pseudo-tubers should be earthed up: you can also blanch them with cardboard or plastic collars.

Time to maturity. 80–90 days.

Pests and diseases. Few problems in

the main. Keep slugs and snails away, and look out for aphids, cutworms and root fly. Plants grown for too long in over-fertile soil will soon rot.

Picking. From mid-August. Late-sown plants can be put under cloches in autumn and harvested until late November.

Successional and complementary planting. Florence fennel belongs to group B for crop rotation. Early crops: peas, radishes, spinach, kohl-rabi or early lettuce. Good complementary crops are cabbage lettuce, chicory, corn salad, cucumbers, endive, peas and sage. Bad: beans or tomatoes. For catch crops following early fennel try: endive, unblanched chicory, late brassicas, radishes, late dwarf beans, corn salad or summer spinach.

ABOVE: Florence fennel 'Zefa Fino', a young plant which needs to be allowed further growth after earthing up.

FAR LEFT: Once shoots appear the plants are thinned out until they are 20–25 cm (8–10 in) apart.

LEFT: A full-grown stem of 'Zefa Fino', ready for eating.

Potatoes

Solanum tuberosum

Potatoes form our staple diet. Since their introduction to Europe (1565) they have mainly been eaten cooked, and nowadays increasingly in the shape of chips, crisps, croquettes, or one of the hundreds of other ways potatoes can be prepared. Always well cooked, never raw. Potatoes are prodigious producers of starch.

Needless to say, every right-minded amateur grower will want to include potatoes in the garden. However, it's not that simple: growing these creamy-yellow tubers is woven around with a fine web of laws and regulations, which even the unversed amateur will come up against. Thus, for example, potatoes may not be grown more than once in four years on the same piece of ground. If you don't keep to this rule your crops are liable to suffer from all kinds of diseases and soil-borne pests. Nonsense, is the opinion of Alwin Seifert, champion of organic market gardening. He has grown potatoes for *seventeen* years in succession on the same spot without once being troubled by disease. His secret: he kept the soil fertile with compost made from . . . potato leaves. And an old proverb

Potatoes in a tray of peat, kept at 15°c (60°F) and not too dark. The shoots pictured here are of a good length.

This home-made dibber frame makes two holes: the left-hand stump keeps them at the right distance.

says that lazy farmers grow the best potatoes. In other words, farmers who forget to clear up the leaves. We have tried this out, but after five or six years we were getting pretty miserable potatoes.

There are a thousand anecdotes, tips and mysteries of this sort surrounding the cultivation of this important foodstuff. We won't bore you with them any further.

Varieties. There is a vast number of potato varieties, which can be classified in different ways. Some of the most important criteria are: yield when dug early, regularity of shape, eating quality and resistance to specific diseases. We can also classify according to the time of the crop: first earlies, second earlies and maincrop. A further distinction is made between eating and manufacturing potatoes (grown for potato flour and such like) and between potatoes for home use. We shall concern ourselves here

Potatoes can also be very successfully planted with a garden line and a hand planter. Working along a straight line makes hoeing easier.

At this stage the potatoes must be earthed up to prevent the tubers turning green.

horse-manure, compost, blood, hoof and horn, or bonemeal will always work well. Or, if desired, with a composite artificial fertilizer.

When to sow. Traditionally potatoes are never sown, always planted. However, there is a trend towards raising the crop from seed, and this may become more widely practised in the future. But here we will stick to the traditional method. The planting stock consists of seed potatoes, which are small tubers kept from the previous year. It is a good idea to buy in seed potatoes each year, because a good supplier will always deliver virus-free stock. If you want to keep your own seed potatoes, only do this for one year, otherwise your yield will fall off very quickly.

It is very common to start seed potatoes into growth before planting out, a procedure known as 'chitting'. The tubers are packed together on end in shallow trays with the end showing most eyes or buds at the top. The bottom of the tray is covered with a thin layer of peat. The trays are then placed in good light and kept at a temperature of 15°C (60°F). If the seed potatoes are kept too much in the dark, the result will be long, weak shoots which will easily break off during planting. What we are looking for are short, squat, sturdy shoots.

with eating potatoes for Britain.

First early varieties: 'Arran Pilot', 'Duke of York', 'Epicure', 'Maris Bard', 'Pentland Javelin', 'Ulster Chieftain', 'Ulster Sceptre', 'Vanessa'.

Second earlies: 'Catriona', 'Craig's Royal', 'Estima', 'Maris Peer', 'Pentland Dell', 'Wilja'.

Maincrop: 'Desiree', 'Drayton', 'King Edward', 'Majestic', 'Maris Piper', 'Pentland Crown', 'Pentland Dell', 'Romano'.

Soil type. Potatoes can be grown on various soils, as long as the right variety is chosen. There are typical clay-soil potatoes, for example, as well as varieties which are better suited to sandy soil. The soil must be good and fertile and not too dry, but certainly not too wet. Low-lying land is not really suitable for potato growing. Not much lime is needed, and may in fact encourage the appearance of scab. The best pH is between 5.0 and 6.0. Fertilizing with old

LEFT: Bad potatoes must be removed before storing.

RIGHT: Early potatoes can be lifted from late June onwards.

BELOW LEFT: Potato tubers green from poor earthing up.

We want to plant our potatoes so that there is no longer risk of night frost by the time the shoots appear above ground. In Britain we can expect night frosts up to about the end of May. Chitted potatoes will break through the soil within a couple of weeks, given reasonably warm weather, so you can calculate from this that the best time to plant is mid-May, although they can be planted in late April, and often are. Chitting takes some five weeks, so you should start in early April.

If you don't intend to do any chitting, you can plant in mid-April.

For a very early crop you can raise and plant a bit earlier, so long as you can protect the plants from frost, with plastic sheeting, for example. Usually only a small surface area is involved, so it should not be too much trouble to set up a cloche.

How to sow. Or, in this case, how to plant. The spacing recommended varies from 30 × 30 cm (12 × 12 in) to 45 × 45 cm (18 × 18 in). The planting depth is 10–15 cm (4–6 in), and you can make the planting holes most easily with a hollow planter, but also with the shaft of a rake or hoe. Close up the holes again after planting. It is a good idea to work in straight lines, as this makes maintenance (hoeing, ridging) much easier.

Growing tips. As we have said, potato shoots are easily harmed by night frost. It is not a total disaster if this happens: the tubers have a few more eyes, still dormant, which will produce shoots if the first ones are killed off. But we should try to avoid this. Covering with plastic sheet has already been mentioned. Another way of preventing freezing is by spraying with water. You will have to keep this up as long as the night frosts last, which can make your potato patch quite a messy place.

Once the potatoes have thrown up good shoots you can start the hoeing. Do this very carefully: besides the shoot you can see there will be more about to appear, and you can easily destroy these with the hoe. The hoeing can be a sizeable job, especially on fresh or previously unused land where there are a lot of weeds, and even more so if you get a lot of rain. But persevere: the potatoes will thank you for it.

If the weather is very dry it is worth watering sandy soil now and then. The early crop especially will give a better yield for it.

It is usual to earth up potatoes no later than mid-June. This means piling extra soil around the plants. The advantage of this is that the tubers will not peep above the ground, which would turn them green. Besides this, earthing up in-creases the yield and is a good way of fighting weeds. However, do not do this before hoeing the weeds well out of the way, because once you have done it there will be practically no more chance for hoeing. You can earth up each plant separately with a shovel, to a height of 20–30 cm (8–12 in). Using a ridging tool (see photos on pages 37 and 85) makes it easier, as you can do a whole row in a sweep.

Time to maturity. From 60 days for the very earliest varieties to 150 days for late potatoes.

Pests and diseases. There are about 50 known diseases, deficiency conditions and other ills which can spoil our potato crop. Of these, a full dozen are virus diseases.

To start with the last: there is not a lot that the amateur can do about these. The best remedy is always to start with well-selected seed potatoes. There is an increasing number of varieties resistant to the most dangerous viruses.

Eelworm is an extremely small 'worm' which lives off the roots. It is increasingly common to use varieties resistant to this pest.

Crop rotation is a proven way of keeping the eelworm population small. Also as mentioned earlier, it is recommended that potatoes should not be grown in the same spot more than one year in four.

Potato blight produces irregular, large and small brown patches on the leaves. The skin of the tubers affected is pitted here and there, and the flesh is partly brown. To prevent this annoying disease preventive spraying is advisable, using a fungicide such as zineb or maneb. Damp weather in July encourages the disease. Here again, resistant varieties are available.

Common scab is a disease that occurs principally in dry summers. The skin is rough, with small wart-like spots. The affected areas later sink inwards.

We will spare you a summary of all the other diseases in this book. Manure well, keep to a proper crop rotation, and you should have a reasonable harvest.

Picking. The first, still tiny tubers of the earliest varieties can be lifted from the ground at the end of June. They taste delicious, but many people prefer to wait a few more weeks until they are a bit bigger. At all events, once the flowers are completely open it is time to lift the early varieties. Second-early potatoes are lifted in August and the maincrops at the end of September, or in some cases in October.

You can use a special potato fork for the purpose, with blunt prongs. This way, the tubers will come to least harm. In dry, frost-free weather the potatoes can be left lying for one day to dry off, then they must be kept in the dark again to prevent them from turning green. Make sure they have fully dried out first, otherwise they will soon go rotten.

Second-early and maincrop potatoes will keep well. Storage in 'clamps' (see

ABOVE: A late variety with sizeable tubers.

LEFT: Red potatoes: note the useful potato fork with blunt prongs.

pictures) is one way of doing it, but in general preference should be given to a cool, frost-free shed or a dry cellar. Check the store regularly for rotting potatoes.

In late February most potatoes will start producing shoots, at which point the quality will quickly deteriorate.

The yield from a well-kept potato patch should run to about 250–300 kg per 100 m² (500–600 lb per 120 sq yd).

Successional and complementary planting. Potatoes belong to group A for crop rotation. Suitable early crops are cress, radishes and spinach. Complementary crops of disputed value are beetroot, peas and tomatoes; good ones include beans, broad beans, dill, early brassicas, horse-radish, kohl-rabi, sweet corn, spinach and turnips. African mari-

A traditional way of keeping potatoes involves making a 'clamp' or pit. This only works on high, dry ground. The floor of the clamp is first lined with straw, and a layer of potatoes placed on top.

golds help combat eelworms; hemp is said to be effective against potato blight. Generally speaking, proper complementary planting is not very practical, but you could always try it out. But on no account grow potatoes together with celery, cucumbers, gherkins or sunflowers.

Plants suited to a late crop are: dwarf beans, endive, late brassicas such as cauliflower, broccoli and sprouts, lettuce and strawberries.

ABOVE RIGHT: The potatoes are surrounded with straw to avoid contact with the wet soil.

RIGHT: After packing with straw, a layer of soil 20–30 cm (8–12 in) thick forms a cover for the clamp.

Onions and their relatives

General information

All the plants in this chapter belong not only to one family, the *Liliaceae* (lily family), but also to the same genus: *Allium*, the onions.

Many onion-type plants form an underground bulb, which is a stalk with thickened leaves. The leaves fit very tightly together and each closes round the next.

Bulb-producing plants of this sort mostly occur in areas where it is extremely dry in the summer – so dry that most green plants give up. Bulb-producing plants do so too, soon enough, but without grumbling, because they have prepared themselves for it: there are enough reserves of food stored away in the bulbs to keep them alive until things improve (i.e. until next spring). The bulbs then break into flower, and several new bulbs develop from axillary buds at the base of the old bulb: this is the brood. The old plant then dies off and history repeats itself.

Shallots, garlic and onions themselves quite clearly follow this pattern, even in our own climate, where August is the wettest month. Your onions will begin to die off at this time of year however much it rains and however much you water them. They have finished growing, and are ready to eat.

With leeks, the bulb shape is somewhat different: it consists of tall, stretched-out, firmly closed leaf bases, which open out at the top, however, into long green leaves. We can lengthen the shank, that is, the lower part of the plant, by earthing it up, which is really a blanching process.

Onions and related plants are for a large part storing or winter plants. Seed-grown onions, especially, can be kept for a long time, as long as the frost stays away. It is only in spring that the bulbs put out shoots, and then the quality quickly goes downhill. Onions and shallots that have been planted do not keep for as long. Leeks are a winter vegetable little harmed by frost, and can be left in the ground until the early spring.

Although onions and particularly garlic deter numerous pests by their smell

and can thus profitably be planted among carrots, for example, they are also prone to attack themselves. The onion fly, which also turns up on leeks, clearly finds the strong scent attractive and deposits its eggs at the base of the stalk. Its progeny then makes short work of the young onion plants.

There are quite a few flies and beetles which feed on onions and the like in this way, so you must always be on the alert to prevent too much damage coming about.

We have included some lesser-known members of the onion group in this book, such as garlic, Welsh onions, Egyptian or tree onions and winter onions. Garlic seems to grow well in our climate, so long as you have the right stock. It is not subject to any kind of attack from pest or disease. The tree onion is interesting for the small bulblets produced high on its stalk. Some varieties of garlic also show this phenomenon. The Japanese overwintering onions are becoming increasingly popular, because this winter-hardy type allows you to have fresh onions early in the spring, an important plus. For details see under the individual type.

Onions and shallots

Allium cepa

The onion is a bulb plant of which countless types have been grown as food since time immemorial. There are also decorative onions with attractive bowl-shaped flowers, which we can use in the flower garden.

In most cases, the bulb is the part of the onion that is eaten, either raw or boiled (or baked), but it can also be the stalk (usually the lowest part) that is meant for the table.

Onions can be eaten very young and fresh, but by far the majority of the onions we grow are the typical storing vegetable, which can bring tears to our eyes the whole winter through. Home-grown onions are particularly liable to make you cry, we have noticed – probably because the essential oil that starts you off is more concentrated than in the market gardener's onions, grown with a generous dose of nitrogen.

In this section we discuss seed onions, planting onions ('sets') and shallots, the onions that form clusters of small bulb-lets in a short time.

The other types will be dealt with in their own sections.

Varieties. Onions have undergone a good deal of hybridization in recent years, the result being onions that are more consistent in shape and often more resistant to disease. We will divide them into seed onions, onion sets and shallots (also planted).

Seed onions: 'Ailsa Craig', 'Bedford-shire Champion', 'Brunswick', 'Buf-falo', 'Hygro', 'Hyduro', 'Lancastrian', 'North Holland Blood Red', 'Rijns-burger', 'Rijnsburger – Balstora', 'Rijnsburger–Bola', 'Rijnsburger–Wi-jbo', 'Solidity', and 'Southport Red Globe'. These are considered among the finest seed onions available in the UK.

Sets: 'Ailsa Craig', 'Dobies All-rounder', 'Marshall's Giant Fen Globe', 'Rocardo', 'Stuttgarter Giant', 'Sturon', 'Turbo'. These are supplied by our well-known seed companies.

Shallots: 'Dobies Long Keeping Yel-low', 'Dutch Yellow', 'Giant Red', 'Giant Yellow', 'Hative de Niort', 'Santé'. Again these are supplied by seed companies.

Soil type. In commercial farming,

ABOVE LEFT: Sets being planted between carrots sown earlier. As a complementary crop, this keeps the carrot fly away.
ABOVE RIGHT: Shallots some time after planting the bulbs.

Red set onions are very decorative. They are red inside as well, so are often used raw in salads.

onions are usually grown in clay soil, and not without reason. This is because onions like a pH reading above 6.5, ample potash and not too much nitro-gen. Organic material (such as compost or manure) must be worked well under, preferably before the winter.

Mind you, you can grow onions very

successfully on other soils, too, espec-ially if you keep the above needs in mind. At all events, we have grown super onions on sandy soil.

When to sow. Onions can be sown in a heated greenhouse as early as January. The temperature should be kept be-tween 10 and 16°c (50 and 60°F). When

Spring onions are early onions, sown close together and harvested before they are fully grown.

Shallot 'Santé' provides an early yield of high quality.

the seedlings are large enough to be pricked out they are transplanted to their own individual peat or plastic pots. Harden off by degrees, then plant out at the beginning of April.

What is more usual is to sow under cloches in late February or early March. The seed only begins to germinate when the mercury gets above 7°c (45°F). Sowing in the open can take place from the end of March.

Instead of sowing, we can also plant onions. For this we can buy 'sets', that is, onions grown from seed by the grower the previous season. These are pressed 4 cm (1½ in) deep in the soil during April. You can produce your own sets, in which case you must sow at the beginning of April.

Good sets are no more than 2 cm (¾ in) in diameter.

Shallots can be planted by February. You should be careful not to start too early with onion sets and shallots, as there is then a very great risk of bolting. This can be prevented by keeping the planting stock at 20°c (68°F) for one month. Usually, the supplier will have done this for you already.

How to sow. Onions are sown or planted in rows, 25 cm (10 in) apart. Sowing depth is 1.5 cm (½ in). Seed onions are thinned out and sets are planted so that there is 6–10 cm (2½–4 in) between them.

If you are sowing to grow sets, then only thin them out by the merest amount, if at all, because you want the onions to stay small. Onion seed retains its germinative power for two to three years.

Growing tips. Onions grow best in a sheltered, sunny position. If it turns extremely dry in the middle of the summer the onions will stop growing and the leaves will die. The result is small onions. To prevent this you will need to step in quickly with the watering can in dry spells.

Time to maturity. 150 days from seed. Sets can be harvested after only 60 days, but usually they are also left for 150 days.

Pests and disease. Quite a number of diseases threaten the health of our onions. A very unpleasant condition results from attacks by the onion fly. The pest lays its eggs at the base of the young plant at the end of May. The larvae, which appear after a while, eat the onion. The leaves turn prematurely yellow and die.

Onions grown from sets generally have less trouble with the onion fly. Stalk eelworms cause deformed, swollen and twisted leaves. The bulbs are floury, often burst and smell bad. Grow no more onions on affected soil for five years. Some pesticides made for the onion fly also work against the stalk eelworm.

Downy mildew (the white sort) makes itself visible to begin with by light green to yellow coloured spots on the leaves. Later, grey and purply-black mould appears. In wet weather spray with fungicides.

White rot principally attacks germinating plants, which turn yellow and limp and then rot. No further onions should be grown on affected soil.

Picking. Onions not fully grown can be harvested early as 'spring onions'. For this you choose, from the earliest shallots and onions grown from sets, those that are on the large side (because it is these that are in greatest danger of bolting). After this, July sees the start of harvesting time for early-planted shallots. Small shallots can be saved as planting stock for the following year. At the same time, of course, you can dig up a half-grown onion to use along with them. However, most of your onions will

Ordinary onions grown from sets, as they should look by late June.

not be fully matured until the end of August. You can judge the right time by watching for the leaves to die. Some people recommend pushing over the leaves during a wet August, when the leaves refuse to turn brown: this is understood to help the onion to ripen. Others are against this. In any event, the onions must be taken out of the soil towards the end of August and left for a while on the ground to dry out: unless it rains, when they will have to dry under shelter.

After this the withered leaves are cut off and the onions are moved to an airy store-room to dry further. We simply hang them up under the roof of a shed, where they stay until the first frost arrives; then they are transferred to a cool, dry and frost-free room (such as an attic). If you wish, you can leave the leaves on the onions and plait a string of them, as is often done with garlic. It looks very attractive, but the strings usually fall apart after a month or so as the leaves dry out even more and start to shrink.

The best onions for storage are those grown from seed; sets grow faster, but are less suited to keeping. If the onions are kept cool enough they will keep till the end of March, after which they usually sprout. The brown skin must always be left on the onions: this helps them to keep.

Successional and complementary planting. For crop rotation onions are members of group B. An early crop is difficult to fit in, because both seeds and sets need to be in the ground early. Good complementary crops are beetroot, carrots, celeriac, chicory, courgettes, cucumbers, dill, gherkins, leeks, parsley, parsnips, radishes, spring turnips, scorzonera, strawberries, summer savory and tomatoes. Bad ones are asparagus, beans, black radish, brassicas, peas and potatoes. After the onions you can sow a little spinach or corn salad.

Welsh onions

Allium fistulosum

At an early stage Welsh onions look very much like spring onions, but there is a big difference. Spring onions are ordinary onions or shallots, picked while still young. Welsh onions, however, never form a bulb, and the thickened stalk is much more like a leek. And just as with leeks, earthing up can keep a large part of the stalk white.

Welsh onions are eaten raw or briefly cooked (baked).
Varieties. Not usually sold as named varieties in Britain.
Soil type. See onions (page 91).

When to sow. From January under heated glass for a spring crop, to the beginning of June for an autumn crop.
How to sow. Early sowing in seed trays at a germinating temperature of 20°C (68°F). After germination the temperature can be allowed to drop to 15°C (60°F). Later in the season sowing can also be done in the open.
Growing tips. Early-sown plants can be planted out in the open after about three months. Distance between rows 25–30 cm (10–12 in), in the row 10 cm (4 in). It is a good idea to plant your Welsh onions in furrows 10–15 cm (4–6 in) deep. These dips can then be gradually filled up with soil as the plants grow, which will help the stalks to turn out white. When sowing in the open the rows should be 30 cm (1 ft) apart, and seedlings are thinned out to 10 cm (4 in). The plants can be earthed up a little while they are growing.
Time to maturity. For the spring crop, 180 days; for the summer and autumn crops, 120 days upward.
Pests and diseases. Little is known about this: see onions (page 92).
Picking. Welsh onions can be pulled at any stage of growth. If you wait too long there is a risk of bolting. Late crops can be left for a fair time, as these onions will bear a few degrees of frost.
Successional and complementary planting. See onions (page 93).

Welsh onion can be eaten raw or briefly cooked. Not widely grown in Britain.

Silverskin onions

Allium cepa

Silverskin onions are small, round, white onions specially grown for pickling. Most are grown in southerly countries, but they can be grown successfully here as well.

Varieties. All are derived from ordinary onions. 'The Queen', 'Paris Silver Skin'.

Soil type. Will grow on any soil which is sufficiently loosened and contains enough lime and potash. If there is too much nitrogen in the soil the onions will grow too hard, with the result that they will not be round, but more bottle-shaped.

When to sow. From late March onwards in the open.

How to sow. In rows 5 cm (1 in) apart. Within the row you will need to sow fairly thickly: the plants should grow close to each other, otherwise the onions will grow too big. Sowing depth 2·5 cm (1 in). The seeds retain their germinating power for two to three years.

Growing tips. If the onions should show above the soil, earth them up a little, otherwise they will turn green.

Time to maturity. About 100 days.

Pests and diseases. See onions (page 92).

Picking. As soon as the leaves begin to die off the onions are ready to be taken up. If you leave them in the soil there is a risk that they will bud again, and this means a loss of quality.

Successional and complementary planting. See onions (page 93).

Silverskin onions, here a little on the large side.

Tree onions or Egyptian onions

Allium cepa var. *viviparum*

The tree onion is a perennial plant that forms bulbs not only under the ground but also on its stems. These small bulblets are eaten raw or baked. They can also be used for planting. Compare this way of growing with some lilies, which also produce bulblets on their stems.

Varieties. We know of no named varieties.

The tree onion or Egyptian onion is an odd plant: the tiny bulbs grow up on the stalks.

Soil type. See onions (page 91).

When to sow. Because tree onions do not flower here, no seed is formed. No problem: we can also start from the stem bulblets. These can be set in the soil as early as March.

How to sow. Plant in rows 40 cm (16 in) apart, with 30 cm (12 in) in the row.

Planting depth 5 cm (2 in).

Growing tips. These sturdy plants can also bear slight shade. No special treatment needed: hoe regularly. The plants will last for years.

Time to maturity. Tree onions throw shoots early in the spring. The first bulblets can be picked late in May.

Pests and diseases. See onions (page 92). In general, however, more sturdy: not many problems with diseases.

Picking. Part of the pickings can be used for propagation. Stem bulblets left on the ground will look after themselves, and very soon produce roots. Bulblets that have been picked will keep very well in a cool, dry place.

Successional and complementary planting. See onions (page 93).

Winter or Japanese onions

Allium cepa

These are extremely winter-hardy selections which can be sown before the winter begins. With luck and a little covering they will survive in the soil and develop very quickly in the spring. In this way you can have fresh onions as early as May, which is an attractive proposition in spite of the long growing time.

Winter onions have been given a new lease of life by the introduction of Japanese varieties that mature extra early. For this reason, these onions are also known as Japanese onions.

Varieties. 'Buffalo', 'Express Yellow', 'Extra Early Kaizuka', 'Imai Early Yellow', and 'Senshyu Semi-globe Yellow'.

Soil type. See onions (page 91).

Winter onions are sown in August and can be pulled from mid-May. This is the variety 'Senshyu Semi-globe Yellow'.

When to sow. It is important to sow at the right time. If you sow too late the onions will be too small when winter comes; if you sow too early they will bolt in the spring. The best time is August.

How to sow. In rows 20–25 cm (8–10 in) apart. In the rows, the seeds should lie about 2 cm ($\frac{3}{4}$ in) apart.

Growing tips. In dry weather give plenty of water after sowing. After 10 days the plants should show above the ground. There is no need to thin out, but the onions should show vigorous growth, so that they reach a height of 15–20 cm (6–8 in) towards the end of October.

Protection against the winter should not be necessary under normal circumstances, but if the frosts are bad we would be inclined to cover them with plastic.

Time to maturity. About 300 days, as the onions can be taken up in mid-June.

Pests and diseases. The great advantage of winter onions is that not many pests are active at the time they are

This is how winter onions must look in October to come through the winter successfully.

growing. It is only in the spring that you need to reckon with attacks, which are in general the same as those given for onions on page 92.

Picking. In March (but not before) the winter onions should be thinned out until they are about 10 cm (4 in) apart. The thinnings, incidentally, are good to eat. From mid-May you can harvest when you need to, but winter onions are not full-grown until June. Laying the leaves on one side, so that the sun can shine strongly on the bulbs, encourages ripening. Winter onions cannot be kept for very long, and are designed to be eaten within two months.

Successional and complementary planting. See onions. The possibilities for a late crop are a bit better, because winter onions are clear of the ground earlier.

Garlic

Allium sativum

Garlic is more of a spice than a vegetable because the 'cloves' are used in cooking in very moderate amounts. It is infamous for its smell, but because healing properties are ascribed to it and because many people do like the taste, this bulb plant is widely used.

Garlic requires a warm climate, and in wet summers it will not give a very high yield in this part of the world. Nevertheless, it deserves to be given a try in the kitchen garden or, failing that, in a tray or pot on the balcony.

Varieties. Little is known about specific varieties: even the EEC varieties list has nothing on the subject. And yet distinctly different growing types exist. In our experience, garlic ordered from Dutch seed dealers has given very poor results. On the other hand, a string of imported French garlic, bought at the greengrocer's, grew into formidable and very productive plants with large, juicy bulbs. Once you have a good variety in your hands, part of the crop can be replanted every year in the spring.

Soil type. See onions (page 91).

When to sow. In fact, garlic is always planted and not sown. This can be done very early, from February onwards. With a good variety the leaves will appear incredibly quickly and it shows good resistance to night frosts.

How to sow. Plant in rows 15–20 cm (6–8 in) apart. Space in the row 10 cm

In our climate, French or Spanish garlic will usually grow satisfactorily.

Garlic can be lifted quite early, as soon as the leaves begin to die off.

(4 in). Planting depth should be 3 cm (1¼ in): make sure the pointed end is at the top.

Growing tips. Garlic has a firm preference for a warm, and therefore well-sheltered location. Early in the spring cloches can help. In dry periods water from time to time to prevent premature ripening. This would stop the cloves from growing fully.

Some varieties of garlic will produce stem bulblets even in their first year, and these can be used for propagation. Oddly enough, these bulblets do not produce cloves – at least, not in the first year. The taste is less strong, too.

Time to maturity. About 120 days.

Pests and diseases. See onions (page 92). In general, no diseases.

Picking. Can be lifted as soon as the leaves start to die off, which is usually in late June. Of course, this doesn't stop you pulling a fresh bulb before that. The garlic should be pulled from the ground and, in sunny weather, left lying for a few days. Then, if you are nifty with your fingers, you can plait strings, which can be dried out further in an airy, dry place. In winter the garlic must be taken indoors to prevent it freezing. The cloves will not sprout quickly, so a string can be left hanging in a warm kitchen without concern. If the garlic does throw shoots it will also be more or less time for planting again.

Successional and complementary planting. Garlic's strong odour will keep away all kinds of nibbling insects, especially the carrot fly. For this reason garlic

is often planted between rows of carrots. In our experience, however, this does not help enough by itself. See also under onions (page 93).

Leeks

Allium porrum

Leeks belong to the same genus as onions, as can be clearly seen from the unfinished, stretched-out bulb shape of the lower part of the stalk. The edible part is white, and can be made even longer by earthing up.

Leeks are biennial, but in the second growing season they become too hard to eat, so they are always grown on the basis of a single year. Because leeks are very winter hardy they can be left in the soil right through the winter. They then become a typical winter vegetable, which can be eaten up to March or April. Leeks are always eaten well-cooked (or at least *al dente*), never raw.

Varieties. We can divide leeks into three groups: early, mid-season and late. The earliest can be ready in late summer or early autumn, the mid-season in autumn and winter, and the late varieties in late winter.

Early: 'Early Market', 'Lyon-Prizetaker'.

Mid-season: 'Giant Winter–Catalina', 'Musselburgh,' 'Walton Mammoth'.

Late: 'Giant Winter–Wila', 'Royal Favourite', 'Winter Crop'.

Soil type. Leeks require a fertile, loose soil with a pH between 6.5 and 7.5. Heavy, wet soils are far less suitable. Adding rotted manure or compost is helpful.

When to sow. For early leeks, sowing must be done in a heated greenhouse by January, in trays of seed compost. Temperature 18–20°c (65–68°F).

Mid-season leeks are sown under cold glass from the end of February.

Late leeks can be sown in the open in April.

How to sow. Leeks are always sown broadcast, usually in trays in the greenhouse or cold frame, or in a separate seed bed in the open. Use a proprietary seed compost when sowing in trays.

When raising leeks in the greenhouse the temperature can be allowed to fall gradually as they grow, so that they are well hardened off by the time the plants are to be planted out, which is from mid-March onwards. As it can still be perishing cold and raw outside at that time of year, it is advisable to protect these leeks with tunnel cloches or growing sheets immediately they have been planted.

Leeks sown under cold glass must be well hardened, too, before they are planted out, although this is a bit later, generally early May.

Leeks must be transplanted from seed beds before late June.

Leeks are transplanted only when the seedlings have become as thick as a pencil.

Growing then continues in rows, with 30 cm (1 ft) between. Plants in the row should be 15 cm (6 in) apart. A hole is made with a dibber, the plant is put in it, then the hole is closed up with water. That way, the roots make better contact with the soil, and the risk of drying out is reduced.

There is nothing wrong with planting your leeks in the usual way, but the white bottom part of the stalk will then turn out very short. If you want a long blanched stalk to your leeks, it makes sense to plant them in furrows 20 cm (8 in) deep. After planting the furrow is generously watered, but not so well that it completely fills up. The idea is for it to fill gradually as the leeks grow, and the rain should take care of that.

Leek seeds retain their germinative power for one to two years.

Growing tips. Always make sure the plants have plenty of water, especially immediately after planting out, but also watch that the ground does become compacted after all the watering, because the roots need oxygen to grow properly. Mulching is a good way of keeping the soil moist and keeping weeds down.

If the tips of the leaves turn brown this may indicate a shortage of nitrogen. Water with a manure solution.

Leeks can be sown very early in trays. Plant out no later than late June.

Leeks can be encouraged to make reasonably long blanched stalks.

If the furrows become completely silted up or if you did not make any in the first place, the leeks can be blanched (even more) by earthing up the plants. Do this in stages.

Time to maturity. From about 90 days for young leeks, up to almost a year for late-maturing leeks.

Pests and diseases. There is a number of leaf-spot diseases producing long, white or brown patches. Some diseases are carried by the seeds. These diseases can be controlled with fungicides.

The leek moth lays eggs from which emerge tiny caterpillars which eat tunnels into the leaves. Spray with a treatment against caterpillars.

The onion fly can also attack leeks: the white maggots can be found in and around the base of the plant.

Picking. The earliest can be lifted from the end of June. The harvest continues until all the early leeks have been lifted at the end of September. Then the mid-season leeks take over: they can be

By earthing up leeks more of the stalk can be blanched.

Late leeks are extremely winter hardy and not lifted until spring.

taken up until Christmas. The late winter leeks stay in the ground right through the winter (in the event of a sharp frost, earth up well or provide some other protection) and are harvested in late winter and early in the spring. If they are in the way you can always lift them and store in a clamp. This will also prevent the plants from flowering (bolting). Leeks that have flowered are not so tasty: they become tough.

When lifting leeks you would be advised to use a spade, otherwise you will risk pulling up the leek in two halves. Cut off the roots and unwanted leaves at once, and pull off the dirty outer leaves, then it won't make such a mess in the kitchen.

Successional and complementary planting. For crop rotation adopt group A. Before the leeks go into the ground you can grow early cauliflower or winter cauliflower on the same spot, or broad beans, early lettuce, kohl-rabi, radishes, peas or spinach. Early potatoes would also be a possibility. Complementary planting of carrots, beans, beetroot, brassicas, kohl-rabi or lettuce is disputed, and so best left alone. Good complementary crops are celery, celeriac, chicory, endive, lettuce, onions, scorzonera, strawberries and tomatoes. Peas are bad. After early leeks you should be able to grow some late brassicas. Endive or green chicory could also be tried, but only after a fresh nitrogen manuring.

Brassicas

LEFT TO RIGHT: Growing brassicas in bottomless tubs.

Digging holes for the tubs; the tub without its bottom; adding extra lime to the potting

compost in the tub; the brassica plants, already raised in pots, are planted out; the

General information

All the different brassicas belong to the *Cruciferae* – that is, the family with cross-shaped flowers, which are clearly visible when a brassica bolts and the huge cluster of yellow flowers appears. In seed production, which turns the fields of France such a magnificent yellow, this may be intentional, but if it happens in our kitchen gardens it's definitely a mistake. If our brassicas burst into flower we have done something wrong.

The vegetable that comes closest to flowering is broccoli. The part of this plant that we eat consists of the flower buds, just before they open. The piece of stalk below the bud is just as tasty. If we wait too long before harvesting broccoli, the right moment, when the flower buds are still hard, is past and the yellow flowers quickly appear.

After the main bud has been picked the axillary buds will readily grow, so a second harvest can soon be made.

With cauliflower we also eat the flower buds; but here they are packed closer together. The whole cauliflower is harvested at one go, and that's the end of it. Cauliflower does not bolt so readily, but it is still important to pick this vegetable at the right time.

In the case of Brussels sprouts we pick buds that appear in the leaf-axils of the tall stem. In the second year these large buds will shoot, but we do not leave them long enough for that to happen.

Then there are the cabbages, such as white cabbage, red cabbage and savoy cabbage. These plants produce a huge bud, whose leaves are curled hard round each other. Usually they are smooth and firm, but savoy cabbages have wrinkled leaves. Pointed cabbage is a white cabbage of different shape.

A cabbage which is not round but tall and erect is the Chinese cabbage, a type that very quickly bolts (forms flowers). Because of this it is not grown until after the longest day.

A well-known leaf cabbage is kale or borecole, though not with crisp leaves; it is easy to grow.

Finally, the swollen-base brassicas. There are two types, with their swollen stems or roots above or below ground.

An underground root is the turnip, also a popular animal foodstuff and only really tasty when very young. This vegetable was dealt with among the root and tuber plants on page 79.

A swollen stem growing above ground is found in kohl-rabi, a less well-known vegetable, but tasty if harvested young.

So much for the wealth of variety in the genus *Brassica*. Now something about growing these vegetables.

Growing brassicas is not as simple as it seems. Most allotment gardeners know the plants as difficult charges, prone to fall incurably ill. A number of common parasites plague brassicas and can cause the harvest to come horribly to grief.

After a good deal of experimenting in our garden, where all our brassicas were a fiasco to start with, we have found a way of growing healthy brassicas without spraying.

First there is the threat of club root, a fungus which spreads through the soil and cannot really be dealt with by the amateur. We have admitted defeat on this and grow our brassicas – from the moment of sowing through to harvest – in potting compost, straight from the bag, with a little extra lime added. This is because a high pH quickly sees off the club root fungus. You can see from the photographs how we go about this.

Secondly, protection against pests such as cabbage white butterfly, cabbage thrips, etc. Insect netting is the magic cure for these, if you do not want to spray your plants. The pests cannot get past it, and the vegetables stay hale and hearty.

Finally, a last tip: begin growing your brassicas as early as possible – you can happily start sowing in February. Only with Chinese cabbage and some types of broccoli do you need to sow late, otherwise flowering will take place.

Brassicas are greedy: they nearly all fall into group A for crop rotation. On poor soil you will need to add fertilizer while they are growing.

roots stay inside the tub and do not penetrate the soil, which may be infected

with club root disease (see page 49).

White cabbage and pointed cabbage

Brassica oleracea var. *capitata capitata*

These are the most widely grown sorts of brassica in professional market gardening. Commercially white cabbage is mostly grown for the production of sauerkraut. For fresh vegetables for the table the amateur generally prefers the earlier, quicker-growing pointed cabbage.

White cabbage and pointed cabbage can be eaten both raw and cooked.

Varieties. Early white cabbage: 'Derby Day'. For the summer crop: 'Golden Acre – May Express', 'June Star', 'Primo', 'Quickstep', 'Vela'. For the late crop: 'Celtic', 'Christmas Drumhead', 'January King', 'Minicole', 'Rearguard', 'Wiam'.

White cabbage varieties suitable for making sauerkraut: 'Holland Late Winter', 'Holland Winter White, Extra Late', 'Polinius'.

Pointed cabbage for the early crop: 'April', 'Durham Early', 'Harbinger', 'Spring Hero'. Summer crop: 'Greyhound', 'Hispi', 'Winnigstadt'.

Soil type. A good soil is a nutritious, humus-rich and above all well-limed soil (pH around 7.0). In summer plenty of water is needed if the weather is dry. Clay soil is very good for white cabbage, while pointed cabbages will grow well on lighter soils.

When to sow. Early varieties in January, under glass. Medium early cabbage varieties: March, under glass. Late cabbage varieties: April, in the open.

Pointed cabbage for the early crop (spring) is sown at the end of September. The young plants are overwintered in pots and planted out in March. The summer crop is sown very early, in January, under gently heated glass.

How to sow. We have discovered the great importance of raising cabbages free of club root. The easiest way of ensuring this is to grow the plants in ordinary potting compost from the garden shop, with a little extra lime added. The seeds will germinate in a seed tray at temperatures of 10°c (50°F) by day and

Young pointed cabbage, a variety that can be grown very early in the year.

Pointed cabbage ready to cut.

6°c (43°F) at night, but it is better if the temperature is a little higher, up to 18°c (65°F). As soon as they can be pricked out the plants are set in 9 × 9 cm (3½ × 3½ in) pots, again in potting compost with some added lime. Now transfer to the greenhouse or cold frame, where the temperature does not need to be so high. Given reasonably frost-free weather the plants can be planted out in the beds in March – a touch of frost will do them no harm. If the weather is too cold, however, this can lead to bolting. For this reason we recommend you to place tunnel cloches over your cabbages.

If you sow cabbages in the open in a seed bed you must make sure that there is no club root lurking in the soil, otherwise failure is guaranteed. Work some extra lime into the soil.

Pointed cabbages sown for the early crop are planted out at the beginning of October.

By far the easiest way is to start from bought-in plants rather than sowing for yourself.

Cabbage seeds retain their germinative power for four or five years if stored well.

White cabbage is perhaps not so popular as pointed varieties.

Growing tips. It is important to plant out cabbages early. In March and April there are not many insects flying about, and this gives you a head start. But for the summer crop of pointed cabbage you can of course plant out in early summer.

White cabbage is planted out at a minimum spacing of 50 × 50 cm (20 × 20 in), or even 70 × 70 cm (28 × 28 in) in well-manured soil. Pointed cabbage is set out at 40 × 40 cm (16 × 16 in).

If there is no club root in your soil you can plant straight in the ground. Add a little lime round the roots for safety's sake, and firm the plants well. Then water well in. Keep the soil loose and keep weeds away. Once the plants are growing well you can add some chemical or organic manure, e.g. dried blood.

If growth is too fast or dry weather sets in pointed cabbages are particularly prone to burst, so keep your eyes open for this.

Time to maturity. From 100 days for quick-growing pointed cabbage to 250 days for white cabbage.

Pests and diseases. A very important factor for cabbages. On page 100 we have described how we keep the worst pests at bay without spraying. We will list all the pests and diseases again here.

Aphids, especially the mealy cabbage aphid, can easily be dealt with.

This also goes for leaf rollers, small but active caterpillars which weave the leaves together.

The mealy aphid can be kept off with insect netting.

Club root is a fungus disease which causes large knobbly growths on the roots of brassicas.

Cabbage moths and butterflies lay eggs, which all produce caterpillars that eat your plants.

Cabbage black rot can be recognized by the brown to black discoloration that becomes visible when the cabbage is cut in half. Usually occurs when the plants

have grown too quickly (too much nitrogen).

Slugs are not averse to cabbage leaves: they eat round holes in them.

Downy mildew turns up during damp weather, and can particularly affect the young plants: yellowish-white spots on the leaves.

Picking. Pointed cabbage must be picked early, certainly before tears appear. It is worth having a look at your crop every day. Summer white cabbage should also be picked in good time, and should not be left to grow as large as it can if you can help it. Only the cabbages to be kept for later should be left in the ground longer: they can stay there until the end of September. Some can stand throughout the winter.

Successional and complementary planting. For crop rotation, nearly all brassicas belong to group A. Before a late cabbage crop you can grow early dwarf beans, carrots, lettuce and peas. However, most white cabbage needs to be in the ground so early that this is not possible.

Disputed complementary vegetables are leeks, peas and potatoes. Good ones: beetroot, dill, dwarf beans, caraway, celery, coriander, cucumbers, endive, gherkins, lettuce, mugwort, peppermint, radishes and black radishes, sage, spinach and tomatoes. Plenty of possibilities here, then, to grow another, quick-maturing plant between the rows of young cabbages.

Bad combinations result from planting garlic, mustard, onions or strawberries. As a late crop to follow early cabbages, you could choose endive or carrots.

Savoy cabbage

Brassica oleracea var. *capitata sabauda*

Savoy is a headed cabbage with a very loose bud and crinkly leaves. There are pointed and globe-shaped varieties and two principal colours: yellow-green and dark green.

Savoys are suited to the early, summer and autumn crops, while some varieties can stay in the ground for the whole winter. This cabbage can be eaten raw as well as cooked.

Varieties. For the late summer crop: 'Spivoy' and 'Savoy King'.

For the autumn crop: 'Taler', and 'Ostara'.

For the winter crop: 'Alexander's No. 1', 'Winter King', 'Wivoy', 'Ormskirk', 'Ormskirk Rearguard'.

Soil type. A good soil is a nutritious, humus-rich and above all well-limed soil (pH around 7.0). In summer plenty of water is needed if the weather is dry for the soil should not be allowed to dry out. Clay soil suits savoy cabbage very well.

When to sow. See white cabbage. Alternatively, sow in heat from January. For the late autumn/winter crop seeds can be sown in the open until mid-May.

How to sow. See under white cabbage (page 101).

Growing tips. Early savoy cabbage is planted out at a spacing of 50 × 50 cm (20 × 20 in) and late savoys at 60 × 60 cm (24 × 24 in). Beyond this, cultivation is as given under white cabbage.

Time to maturity. From 130 days for early savoys to around 200 days for late varieties.

Pests and diseases. See white cabbage (see opposite). There is an extra sensitivity to aphids.

Picking. August and September for late summer crop; October to December for autumn crop; and from December to April for the winter crop.

Successional and complementary planting. See white cabbage (this page).

This is how a typical savoy cabbage looks in section.

A savoy cabbage for the late crop, with typically crinkled leaves.

Savoy cabbage of the green-leaved type.

Red cabbage

Brassica oleracea var. *capitata*

Red cabbage is very like white cabbage, but it is purple in colour (definitely not red!). This headed cabbage contains a lot of colouring matter and grows rather more slowly than white cabbage.

It is a very good storing vegetable, but there are also quick-growing varieties, which can be used for a raw cabbage salad as early as June.

Varieties. For a very early crop we can consider: 'Langedijk Red Medium'.

For a rather later crop: 'Langedijk Early–Norma'.

For the autumn crop: 'Ruby Ball' (a mini-red cabbage) and 'Red Drumhead'.

Soil type. The early varieties are best grown on light soil, while the late red cabbage is more suited to clay soil. But as long as you keep the pH at the right level and make sure the plants are well fed, any soil will really do.

When to sow. The earliest crop starts with a January sowing. For rather later crops, sowing is done in February or March. Under glass in each case, needless to say. For the autumn crop sowing is done up to the end of March, under glass or in the open.

How to sow. See under white cabbage (page 101).

Growing tips. If the spring is very cold your early red cabbage is quite likely to bolt. So keep the plants fairly warm until the weather is better, or use a tunnel which can be removed later. The spacing for early varieties is 50 × 50 cm (20 × 20 in), and for later ones at least 60 × 60 cm (24 × 24 in).

While the plants are growing they will need further manuring, especially late red cabbages.

Time to maturity. From 120 days for the earliest varieties to around 200 days for late varieties.

Pests and diseases. See white cabbage (page 102).

Picking. The earliest varieties can be picked as early as June. It doesn't matter all that much whether the cabbages are fully grown by then: they are just as tasty when they are younger.

Successional and complementary planting. See white cabbage (page 103).

Cabbage collars are a traditional and well-proven way of keeping various pests at bay, particularly cabbage root fly.

ABOVE: Red cabbage is often used for pickling.
RIGHT: 'Ruby Ball'.

Chinese cabbage

Brassica pekinensis

In contrast to the headed cabbages mentioned so far, Chinese cabbage is an annual. A tall, erect head is formed, with no stalk. The plants are usually grown no earlier than the second half of the season, as they will otherwise bolt. A natural late crop.

Chinese cabbage can be eaten raw or cooked.

Varieties. Commonly listed in catalogues of British seed companies are 'Green Rocket', 'Nagaoka 50 Days', 'Pe-Tsai', 'Sampan' and 'Tip Top'.

Soil type. Chinese cabbage grows best on a humus-rich sandy or loamy soil, with a pH around 7.0. The ground must always have plenty of moisture, and a lot of food is needed.

When to sow. Chinese cabbage is usually sown after the longest day, because otherwise there is a great risk of flowering (bolting). The Japanese hybrids are a little less prone to this, but it is still a risk. The best time for sowing is between mid-July and the beginning of August.

How to sow. Because bolting does not depend on the length of day alone, but on temperature as well, you can sow earlier provided you make sure that the temperature you raise the young plants in is not too low. Sowing under glass, at a minimum temperature of 20°C (68°F), and no lower than 16°C (61°F) at night, will usually produce good plants. Sow straight into individual 9 cm (3½ in) pots or pressed peat pots, since pricking out introduces a further risk of bolting.

If sowing in the open, do it in rows 40 cm (16 in) apart, and to a depth of 2 cm (¾ in). Make sure the seed bed is always kept moist.

The seeds retain their germinative power for four or five years.

Growing tips. Chinese cabbage seedlings are thinned out until the plants are 40 cm (16 in) apart. Always water well and add some plant food after the first month. Chinese cabbage which has been left in too dry a soil becomes practically uneatable.

Most varieties are self-closing so you will not need to tie up the heads with twine.

Chinese cabbage.

Chinese cabbage ready for cutting.

Time to maturity. At least 75 days.
Pests and diseases. See under white cabbage (page 102). Chinese cabbage is especially sensitive to club root, so if growing this brassica in infected soil it should likewise be grown in large, bottomless tubs, as explained on pages 100–101. Besides this, any of the other cabbage diseases may occur.
Picking. From the end of September. Chinese cabbage can take a few degrees of frost, so harvesting is sometimes possible up to the end of November. The vegetable will often keep until January in a cool place of storage.
Successional and complementary planting. For crop rotation, keep to group A. Because this type of cabbage is sown so late, a good range of early crops can be fitted in, such as carrots, dwarf beans, lettuce, peas and early potatoes.

For good complementary crops and combinations to be avoided see under white cabbage. There is no scope for a late crop.

Curly kale or borecole: one of the modern uniform-shaped hybrids.

Borecole or kale

Brassica oleracea var. *acephala sabellica*

Curly kale or borecole is the simplest of all the brassicas. It is noticeably less susceptible to disease than the others, and the plants will grow in practically any soil.

Borecole is widely eaten in Britain, often in bubble-and-squeak, and thus always cooked.

It also makes a good vegetable on its own. This leaf brassica is practically unknown in other countries, and even in star-rated restaurants it is very rare to see it on the menu. This seems unfair to us.
Varieties. We can divide the varieties between those bred for the autumn crop and those for the winter crop. There is also a difference in the height of the plants: sometimes a tall stem, and sometimes none.

Well-known varieties include 'Dwarf Green Curled, a dwarf variety as the name suggests, 'Tall Green Curled', which is taller, and the old 'Cottagers', which is also tall and at its best in spring. Newer varieties include the dwarf, hardy, 'Frosty', 'Westland Autumn', dwarf and very frost resistant, and 'Fribor', also very hardy.
Soil type. Not critical. Kale will grow equally well on sand or on clay. Because it is effectively always a late catch crop, you will need to provide some extra manure, especially on sandy soils. A pH around 7.0 should be aimed for, as with all brassicas.
When to sow. Kale must be sown from the beginning of May to mid-June.
How to sow. Usually in a separate seed bed, so that the main crop can be left in

the ground a little longer. Do not sow too densely, and water well. The seeds retain their germinative power for four or five years.

Growing tips. Varieties for autumn cropping must be planted by mid-July and for winter by mid-August. The less-tall varieties should be spaced out at 50×50 cm (20×20 in), the taller plants at 60×60 cm (24×24 in). Water generously immediately after planting. Hoeing is also needed.

Time to maturity. About 150 days for the autumn varieties, and for winter varieties, not harvested until after Christmas, 240 days.

Pests and diseases. The usual cabbage diseases strike kale far less than other brassicas, but in poor conditions they can nevertheless occur. Caterpillars of the cabbage white butterfly are the most common brassica pests encountered on kale.

Kale left standing for a long time is gratefully consumed by birds, not forgetting rabbits. The plants can be protected from these raiders by fences or nets.

Picking. The old saying has it that kale is tastier 'when the frost has been and gone'. In any event, it is sweeter after the frosts, because the frost raises the level of sugar in the leaves. With true autumn varieties, however, you should not wait this long, because there will then be a great risk of freezing the kale. Very hardy kale can be left in the ground until March, but the taste will then deteriorate.

Successional and complementary planting. Crop rotation is not something you need to bother with. Kale can be grown after any early vegetable. Obvious choices would be carrots, dwarf beans, lettuce, peas, early potatoes, etc.

Complementary planting is possible using beetroot, late dwarf beans, endive, kohl-rabi, lettuce and late spinach. Late crops can be disregarded.

Brussels sprouts

Brassica oleracea var. *oleracea gemmifera*

This brassica, discovered in Belgium only in the 18th century, is one of the most important winter vegetables. As with kale, many varieties are extremely winter hardy, so that the sprouts can be left in the ground through to the spring. The plants are biennial: in the second year the sprouts produce flowers. If we intend eating the sprouts, we don't let things go that far.

In general, sprouts are eaten cooked.

Varieties. Commercial market gardeners prefer the modern hybrid varieties, which produce sprouts very regularly distributed along the stalk. They all become ready for picking at the same time, which means that harvesting can be done by a machine. As your toolshed probably doesn't run to a sprout harvester, you might just as well grow one of

Brussels sprout 'Roodnerf' in August. An old variety, whose sprouts do not all ripen together.

the older varieties, where the sprouts do not all mature at once. This is even an advantage.

The best-known of the older varieties are 'Bedford–Fillbasket', 'Bedford–Winter Harvest', 'Cambridge No. 5', 'Early Half Tall', 'Huizer's Late' and 'Roodnerf'. Good hybrid varieties include (listed from early to late maturing) 'Peer Gynt', 'Predora', 'Widgeon', 'Welland', 'Wellington', 'Fortress'.

Soil type. Sprouts grow best on heavier soils, such as clay and loam. The sprouts must be allowed to grow steadily, otherwise they will go loose. This happens quite often on light sandy soils with too much fertilizer, especially horse manure. The sprouts best suited to these soils are those that form a low and sturdy plant. A very high pH (around 7.0) is a good protection against club root.

LEFT: 'Fortress' has nice-looking Brussels sprouts with firm heads.

Your sprouts should not look like this – over-fast growth has made the heads too loose.

When to sow. Sprouts have a long growing period, so they must be sown early: from the beginning of March to the end of April.

How to sow. Usually sown in a separate seed bed, best under glass or plastic if this is very early. Add some lime and some manure to the seed bed.

The seeds retain their germinative power for four or five years.

Growing tips. Raising the young plants will occupy some six weeks, so planting out in beds can take place from the end of April to June. Only healthy plants are to be used; the spacing is 60 × 60 cm (2 × 2 ft).

Add fertilizer as necessary during the growing season; it is also common to provide a little extra manure after the first picking in September.

Time to maturity. At least 200 days. If late sprouts are left in the soil this can stretch to almost a year.

Pests and diseases. Brussels sprouts are sensitive to most brassica diseases, as listed under white cabbage (page 102). The mealy aphid is also eager to lay its eggs in sprouts. Leaf spot disease produces round, brown blotches on the leaves, which later turn white. On sandy soil a potash deficiency can occur.

Picking. With hybrids all the sprouts will be ready for picking at the same time. Other varieties must be picked several times, taking the sprouts that are ready. Rotting sprouts can be removed at the same time. The first picking usually begins at the end of September, and winter-hardy varieties can be harvested through to spring. It is not a good idea to pinch out the tips of sprouts, as is often done, as this reduces the winter-hardiness.

As with kale the sugar content of the leaves is increased by frost. Sweeter sprouts are usually considered more tasty. If the sprouts have been frozen hard they will have to be cooked immediately after thawing, since these sprouts will not keep.

Successional and complementary planting. For crop rotation, Brussels are members of group A. Before sprouts you can grow early cabbage, lettuce, peas, spinach and sometimes even very early potatoes. Summer carrots may also have been cleared from the soil by June. For complementary crops and bad combinations see under white cabbage. No scope for a late crop.

Cauliflower

Brassica oleracea var. *botrytis botrytis*

The developing flower buds of cauliflower form a hemispherical growth which can be white, green, purple or orange in colour. Growing cauliflowers is the highest achievement in kitchen gardening: only experienced gardeners can grow this plant without problems – unless, of course, you spray whole cans of pesticides at it, as most professional growers do.

Cauliflower can be eaten either raw or cooked.

Varieties. A good way of classifying cauliflowers is by sowing time. We can divide them into winter cauliflower, which is sown in June, stays in the ground over the winter and is ready to eat in April; the winter crop – sow around 1st October, harvest next spring; the early crop – sow in early spring; the summer crop – sow up to mid-May for summer eating; and finally the autumn crop, which can be sown up to the beginning of July.

Winter cauliflower: 'Walcharen Winter – Armado April', 'Walcheren Winter – Markanta'.

For the 'winter crop': 'Mechelse–Delta'.

For the early crop: 'Alpha', 'Snow Crown'.

Summer crop: 'Dominant'.

Autumn crop: 'All the Year Round', 'Torina', 'Nevada', 'Dok–Elgon', 'Barrier Reef', 'Canberra', 'Snowcap'.

Soil type. Cauliflower requires a very fertile, moisture-retaining soil with a high pH (around 7.0).

When to sow. Varies a good deal, according to the type.

Winter cauliflowers are sown in the last week of June. The best time for the winter crop is the last week of September or the first week of October. Early crop from late January to early March. Summer crop from mid-March to mid-May. Autumn crop from the end of May to no later than the first week of July for the very late varieties.

How to sow. We recommend that you sow all types of cauliflower in seed trays, using seed or potting compost mixed 50:50 with sharp sand. Add a little extra lime to this medium. In the cold season

provide a temperature of at least 12°c (54°F). Prick out seedlings in individual 9 cm (3½ in) pots filled with fresh potting compost mixed with a little lime.

Harden off the cauliflower as necessary before planting out.

Growing tips. Winter cauliflowers will fail at temperatures below −8°c (18°F). If you live inland you could try covering your winter cauliflowers with tunnels. Make sure that the plants are big and strong before winter starts. In the spring they will then first burst out in leaf, then produce cauliflowers.

The winter crop is also a fairly bothersome business. After planting in the autumn, the plants spend the whole winter under glass, and are planted out in March.

An easier job is provided by the early crop in which the young plants raised in mild warmth are transferred to the garden in April. They should not be too large at this point, because this can lead to disturbed growth and bring about

Cauliflower 'All the Year Round', an English variety which, as its name suggests, can be grown at any time.

premature formation of the head, known as bolting. Planting out without disturbing the roots and the ball of soil around them, and a quick watering, can prevent this evil.

Space plants out to at least 50 × 50 cm (20 × 20 in).

For the summer crop you can, if you wish, sow in the open in a seed bed, but we are more given to raising in pots, as described under *How to sow*. Within four weeks you can be setting young plants in the beds, spaced out 50 × 60 cm (20 × 24 in).

The same goes for autumn cauliflower, which can be given a little more space, up to 70 × 70 cm (28 × 28 in).

As the cauliflower grows you must continually ensure it has plenty of water. Adding manure in the form of a little dried blood or other nitrogen fertilizer

Cauliflower of the 'Alpha' type.

Successional and complementary planting. Cauliflower is in group A of the crop rotation scheme. Early and late crops vary widely, according to the time you sow the cauliflower. Before taking the ground for autumn cauliflower you can use the space for early potatoes, or for early dwarf beans, peas or carrots. A good complementary plant is celery, beyond which very few complementary plantings have been tried. It does not seem to work out with spinach.

After early cauliflower there is a whole world of autumn vegetables to be grown, and even more to follow the winter crop. Late dwarf beans, celeriac and leeks are a few examples.

can be very useful. Once the head is formed, two of the leaves are usually broken so that they protect it from sunlight. If this is not done discoloration can occur.

During its growth cauliflower must enjoy complete protection from insects, whether by spraying or by the use of insect netting. This last material is a perfect godsend for organic gardeners. Growing cauliflowers over winter has the great advantage that there are no pests active during the growing period, so that protection is less of a concern.

Time to maturity. The shortest for the summer crop is 120 days. The longest for winter cauliflower: 300 days.

Pests and diseases. All the problems listed under white cabbage (page 102) can strike cauliflower, along with: blindness, a total lack of head resulting from damage to the growing point in the plant's youth. Especially common in autumn cauliflowers. Whiptail (a poorly developed heart and strap-like, often crinkled leaves) is caused by molybdenum deficiency, especially in the 'Alpha' varieties. A loose, open curd is due to the flower buds having formed too early. The curd or head has a lumpy surface and quickly turns grey.

Picking. Cauliflower is ready as soon as the leaves round the edges start to become slightly loose. They should then be cut at once, since especially at higher temperatures the cauliflower will quickly go over-ripe. Harvested cauliflowers can be kept for a short time in a cool place.

To avoid the cauliflower becoming discoloured, a leaf is usually broken over the head. The curd then stays beautifully white.

Sprouting broccoli

Brassica oleracea var. *botrytis italica*

Sprouting broccoli is very similar to cauliflower, but the flower buds grow far more quickly, with the result that this brassica also bolts far more quickly, especially in the warmer weather. The groups of flower buds are often spread around the plant, and are picked with some of the stem attached. After the main flowers have been picked broccoli will produce new heads from the axillary buds.

Broccoli can be eaten either raw or cooked.

Varieties. Purple and white sprouting broccoli remain in the ground over the winter to produce a multitude of small heads in the spring. Green sprouting broccoli, also known as calabrese, is picked in summer or autumn, often with a large main head.

Good varieties of green-sprouting broccoli are 'Corvet', 'Express Corona', 'El Centro', and 'Romanesco Precoce'.

Soil type. See cauliflower.

When to sow. Purple and white is sown as early as April or May. Green sprouting broccoli can be sown from the end of January to the end of May.

How to sow. Purple and white sprouting broccoli is usually raised in a seed bed, but there is no reason why this should not be done in a seed tray. The latter is certainly advisable for green-sprouting broccoli, because a little extra warmth will hasten germination. But don't grow young plants above 25°c (77°F) as they will grow too tall. Con-

Purple sprouting broccoli, a winter type.

BELOW LEFT: 'Romanesco Precoce' is a new variety of uniform habit.

BELOW: Green spouting broccoli is also known as calabrese.

tinuing the growth in pots, as for other brassicas, excludes any risk of early infection by club root.

The seeds retain their germinative power for four years.

Growing tips. Early sown plants of green broccoli can be transferred to the beds at the end of March or beginning of April after hardening off. A light night frost will do little harm. Plants sown later and purple and white sprouting broccoli are large enough to plant out after some four or five weeks. Do this no later than the end of July.

Spacing should be 50 × 50 cm (20 × 20 in) for green-sprouting broccoli and 60 × 60 cm (24 × 24 in) for purple and white sprouting broccoli.

Time to maturity. From 90 days for green broccoli and up to 360 days for purple and white broccoli.

Pests and diseases. Here again all the infamous brassica diseases, albeit to a rather smaller extent than with cauliflower. The broccoli grown early has a definite advantage in that there are less villains flying about at that time. But pesticides and insect netting are not a luxury. For details, see under white cabbage (page 102).

Picking. A tricky matter: calabrese, especially, is often picked too late. The flower buds have then swollen too much, and the heads become too loose. In warm weather it can be a matter of half a day! So walk round your broccoli every day and pick what is ready.

When cutting off the head a decent section of stalk should be included. If this is too hard to eat, it is pared down.

The broccoli collected in this way can be kept in the fridge until you have enough for a meal. In autumn and spring (purple and white sprouting broccoli), things fortunately don't happen so fast, and this gives you a bit more time to make your selection.

With purple and white broccoli the central head is picked first, and after that a number of smaller heads will develop from the axillary buds. You can carry on in the same way for quite a while.

Successional and complementary planting. Grow as group A for crop rotation. Before purple and white sprouting broccoli are planted out the same bed can support early dwarf beans, peas, cabbage lettuce, summer carrots, early leeks or spinach. For complementary vegetables see under cauliflower. After very early broccoli there is time for a later crop of spinach or corn salad.

Broccoli 'Express Corona', an excellent summer variety.

Kohl-rabi

Brassica oleracea var. *acephala gongylodes*

A giant kohl-rabi variety that does not go woody quickly. Smaller varieties are more commonly grown.

Kohl-rabi is the odd man out among the brassicas. The plant produces a massive swollen stem, quite a different product from the head-shaped leaves offered by most other related varieties. But kohl-rabi should not be confused with the turnip (see page 79).

The white, light green or purple stems are eaten raw or cooked, and the leaves are sometimes used for food as well.

Varieties. Available varieties include 'Lanro', 'Purple Vienna', 'Rowel' and 'White Vienna'.

Soil type. Can be grown successfully on lighter soils, as long as the pH is right (around 7.0). If some horse manure or other organic material is mixed in, this is excellent.

When to sow. From the end of January for a greenhouse crop to mid-July for an autumn crop grown outdoors.

How to sow. Preferably in seed trays, as described for other brassicas. Continue growing in pots. When sowing in the greenhouse a temperature of 18–20°c (65–68°F) is desirable during germination, later around 16°c (61°F). The mercury should not fall below 12°c (54°F) at night either, since there is otherwise a risk of bolting.

The risk of bolting is still a serious one when sowing later, hardening off and planting out. For this reason, as far as possible, grow this early crop under plastic sheeting.

Growing tips. After hardening off, plant the khol-rabi out at 30 × 30 cm (1 × 1 ft) and make sure the plants continue to grow at a regular rate, otherwise the stems will soon become woody. This means water as necessary and don't worry about a touch too much manuring if the plant is busily growing. Protection from brassica parasites is needed here, too: spray or take whatever other measures you prefer.

Time to maturity. From 90 days in the summer to 150 days in the early spring.

Pests and diseases. See white cabbage (page 102). The mealy aphid can be particularly troublesome, and club root is always on the prowl. When growing under glass botrytis (grey mould) and downy mildew may occur if the air humidity is too high.

Picking. It is tempting to grow large stems, because you will then have more on the table at one picking. Don't: kohl-rabi of about 5 cm (2 in) in diameter is much tastier. Do not keep the stems long once they have been harvested.

Successional and complementary planting. Kohl-rabi can be used as an early or late catch crop, because its growing time is so short. As far as crop rotation is concerned, this vegetable – unlike other brassicas – belongs to group B. For an early crop you can choose any vegetable which will have been picked by the end of July. Tomatoes as a complementary crop are disputed, so don't try them. Reportedly good complementary crops include asparagus, beans, beets, cab-

Kohl-rabi 'Purple Vienna' growing in a pot. A good idea for the balcony.

bage lettuce, celery, gherkins, other brassicas, peas, potatoes, radishes and black radishes, scorzonera and spinach.

Suitable crops for a late crop: aubergines, beans, beets, cabbage lettuce, carrots, celeriac, courgettes endive, gherkins, leeks, melons, peppers, Florence fennel and tomatoes.

Some kohl-rabi varieties produce a nice white stalk, like 'White Vienna'.

Other brassicas

Brassica species

In recent years a veritable flood of new brassicas and brassica varieties has rained on us from the Far East, of which most are quick-growing leaf brassicas. The parts eaten are the leaves, the stalk and sometimes the flowers. Some are still difficult to find in seed catalogues, though. The best known in Britain is probably Pak Choi.

Pak Choi (*Brassica campestris* var. *chinensis*). This looks very like Chinese cabbage, but the head does not close. It is grown for its thick, white stalks, which are picked in an early stage, sometimes together with the leaves. Sad to say it is susceptible to bolting.

Amsoi (*Brassica juncea*). This is a low growing, mustard-like plant with a loose rosette. The leaves, leaf-stalks and flower buds can be eaten. In our climate, unfortunately, the plants bolt very quickly.

Choi-Sum (*Brassica campestris* var. *parachinensis*). This also forms a low, loose rosette, which flowers quickly.

Kai-Lan (*Brassica campestris* var. *alboglabra*). Also called Chinese broccoli, this plant looks not unlike calabrese except that the 'heads' are much looser. The flower buds open very quickly; but that's no problem, as the flowers are eaten too.

Soil type. The best is a well-manured, moisture-retaining soil with a pH around 7.0.

When to sow. Nearly all the types mentioned bolt as a result of low temperatures and short days. Transplanting from a seed bed to the permanent location also frequently brings on bolting. The best chance of success is offered by late sowing (end of July and August). Early sowing is only possible if the plants are raised in a heated greenhouse.

How to sow. Directly into 9 cm ($3\frac{1}{2}$ in) pots if possible. Leave only one plant after shoots appear. When sowing early, 20–25°c (66–77°F) germinating temperature, then grow at 18–20°c (65–68°F).

Growing tips. If sowing early indoors do not plant out until the temperature is at least 18°c (65°F), or use cloches. Spacing for most varieties is 20 × 25 to 30 × 30 cm (8 × 10 to 12 × 12 in).

Time to maturity. The plants grow quickly and should not be harvested too late. Pak-Choi, for example, is ready after only 50 days.

Pests and diseases. There is little known about this as yet. We have noticed that slugs are wild about Pak-Choi. The mealy aphid is also a problem.

Picking. In good time, or at least before the plant has a chance to bolt fully. As a general rule, the plants are ready for eating earlier than you think. Eat at once.

Successional and complementary planting. Little known. Most particulars given for white cabbage (page 103) are likely to apply here too, but this is not confirmed.

Pak Choi is probably the best known and most easily grown exotic stalk vegetable.

Peas and beans

General information

Peas and beans belong to the *Leguminosae* family, along with acacia, broom and laburnum; and more particularly to the sub-family, *Papilionaceae*, or butterfly-flowered plants. And indeed, with their keel, wings and standard, the flowers do look rather like butterflies. The fruits are fleshy pods containing the seeds. Sometimes the pods can be eaten whole; in other cases the seeds have to be shelled from the pods because there is a hard, parchment-like skin on the inside of the pod, which makes it inedible. Often this skin only starts to get hard when the fruits are fully ripe, so that unripe pods are quite edible. A good example of this is the 'haricot vert'.

Peas and beans can be eaten either half-ripe or ripe, but they are always cooked first. Ripe, dried peas and beans can be kept for a very long time: in

PREVIOUS PAGE: The runner bean is naturally a climber with an unusually rich and striking show of flowers: a 'scarlet runner'.

RIGHT: At the top you can see the hard skin that can make the pods inedible.

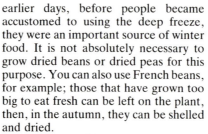

earlier days, before people became accustomed to using the deep freeze, they were an important source of winter food. It is not absolutely necessary to grow dried beans or dried peas for this purpose. You can also use French beans, for example; those that have grown too big to eat fresh can be left on the plant, then, in the autumn, they can be shelled and dried.

Of all vegetables, peas and beans provide far and away the most energy in the form of protein and carbohydrates.

We can divide legumes into two main groups: peas (genus *Pisum*) and beans (genus *Phaseolus*). Alongside these there are a few further legumes, such as broad beans, soy beans, lentils, etc.

Many *Leguminosae* are climbers. Climbing beans have curling stalks: these are left-handed: that is, they spiral anti-clockwise if you look down on them from above. They are supported with canes and for this reason are sometimes called pole beans. Climbing peas put out tendrils, with which they can hold on to any kind of support they come across. Formerly twigs and sticks were used to support the plants.

More and more of the peas and beans grown today are the non-climbing types. Bush beans will more or less stand up by themselves. This saves a lot of work,

especially in mechanised gardening. Bush peas do not develop a particularly strong stalk: the plants remain at ground level, but they are grateful for any support. In general, dwarf varieties will give you a smaller yield than climbing peas or beans, but the growing time is shorter.

The great difference between peas and beans lies in their sensitivity to frost and their germinating temperatures. Peas germinate at low temperatures, and the bush types can stand a few degrees of frost. Beans will only germinate in warm soil, and at the slightest touch of night frost they throw in the towel.

Broad beans, which belong to a different genus (*Vicia*), are not bothered by cold.

Most *Leguminosae* can enrich the soil with nitrogen from the air via their bacterial root nodules. This is a highly profitable process, because it means that the gardener does not need to add any nitrogen himself, unless the soil is espe-

ABOVE LEFT: The string, another inedible part of many legumes.

LEFT: Bean stalks spiral anti-clockwise, the opposite way to the sun.

RIGHT: Peas will grow best if supported by strong netting.

ABOVE LEFT: Bamboo bean poles in sets of four.

ABOVE RIGHT: Bean poles arranged in a long row.

ABOVE: The 'wigwam', an attractive way of supporting climbing beans.

cially poor. As a result, the fertilization needed by legumes is limited to a little phosphate, potash and maybe lime. Trace elements need to be added just once, particularly manganese.

As far as crop rotation is concerned, peas and beans are assigned to group C. It is often recommended that peas are grown on the same spot not just once in three years, but only once every six years.

An early crop of leaf vegetables or very early brassicas is really only possible with beans, because peas often have to be in the ground by February or

LEFT: A plastic plant tie with a buckle is ideal for fastening poles together. It can be re-used each year.

March. Possible late crops, after early-harvested peas or early dwarf beans, would be late brassicas, especially Chinese cabbage, as well as late vegetables such as endive and Florence fennel. For more details, especially on complementary plants, see the individual vegetables.

Just as with other vegetables, legumes suffer from their own set of diseases; however, these can largely be prevented among peas by starting very early with sowings. You will find a summary of the most common diseases under each plant.

Dried beans

Phaseolus vulgaris

Dried beans are so called because they are dried out between being picked and being eaten. They are also called boiling beans. Think of brown beans and plover beans, and you will get the idea. The only exceptions are the 'Flageolet' varieties, which are shelled and eaten before they are ripe. You will find a full run-down on these under Varieties.

Growing dried beans is much less popular than that of soft-shelled beans, such as French beans and runner beans. Usually it is left to the professional growers, and a packet or jar of brown beans is bought in as food for the winter. If you have some spare garden space, though, we would recommend you to give them a try, because home-grown beans will naturally be much tastier.

Dried beans are nearly always dwarf beans. However, some varieties grow taller and will need a pole for support.

All dried beans are eaten cooked and usually need presoaking.

Varieties. The best known are 'Mont D'Or' with black seeds, the yellow seeded 'Kinghorn Wax', and the white-seeded 'Blue Lake'.

Kidney beans, which are imported from the USA in cans, may be available from health-food shops. They are dark red and kidney-shaped.

Finally, the Flageolet varieties, which are quite popular in France. They do not do well in wet or cold weather. 'Chevrier Vert' is an example.

A less-popular type is the tropical soya bean, which we can properly count among the dried beans, even though it belongs to a completely separate genus (*Glycine*). The variety 'Fiskeby V' is still the best for our climate. The yield is usually poor.

Soil type. As a rule, beans will grow easily on any soil that is not too wet. A humus-rich, warm sandy soil is the best. The pH should be on the high side, around 7, so there must be plenty of lime in the ground.

Besides this a good helping of phosphate and potash is important. Nitrogen matters less: bean plants will always produce a certain amount of this nutrient for themselves. Organic manure is recommended.

Dried beans in their pods.

When to sow. Because all beans are sensitive to frost, sowing does not usually begin before early May. Another reason for sowing late is that beans germinate very poorly in cold and wet soil. Sowing in individual pots in the greenhouse, which we strongly recommend, and not only for the tropical beans, can begin in mid-April.

How to sow. Dried beans are usually sown in rows, which should be 40 cm (16 in) apart. Within the row, the bean plants should be spaced out by 5–10 cm (2–4 in). Put in a few extra, because they won't all germinate. Sowing depth is 2–3 cm ($\frac{3}{4}$–$1\frac{1}{4}$ in). If you are sowing in pots, use 9 cm ($3\frac{1}{2}$ in) plastic pots, fill them with ordinary potting compost and put three to five beans in each. The germinating temperature must be at least 10°c (50°F). The seeds will retain their germinating power for four to six years.

Growing tips. All beans like warmth, so look for a sheltered spot for them full in the sun. In dry spells water generously, especially while they are flowering and when the fruit is coming on. Hoe frequently to keep the soil open.

Time to maturity. 140 days. The Flageolet varieties take a little less.

Pests and diseases. Beans germinating in the open may be attacked by the bean fly. The maggots spawned by this nuisance eat out the heart of the germinating plants, and as a result they die.

Usually the seed will have been treated with insecticide so that this cannot happen.

The seed you are given may already have been attacked by the bean beetle, which means that the larvae will have eaten away the inside of the seeds. Here again, seed treatment will help, and will usually have been done.

High air humidity may cause fungus diseases during the growing stage, such as botrytis or sclerotic rot. Take care not to plant too closely and spray with fungicides if necessary.

Little can be done against the most persistent virus diseases: the simplest answer is to choose resistant varieties. Flea beetles first produce tiny spots on the leaves, and later the leaves turn pale brown and drop. You can use a pesticide designed to beat the red spider mite. Finally, aphids: easily combatted chemically, and equally well with environmentally harmless treatments.

Picking. The Flageolet varieties can be picked as soon as a decent bean has been formed. It will not be completely ripe at this stage, but this is when it is shelled and eaten, just as with broad beans.

All the other dried beans are harvested at the end of September, but at all events before the first night frost. The plants are pulled up whole and hung up

After picking, dried beans are hung up for a while like this. They can then be threshed.

Dried beans need warmth and sun to develop well.

in bunches in a dry, airy spot (loft or shed, for example). Once the plant is completely dried out the beans can be beaten out of the pods. They should then be stored dry for winter use.

Successional and complementary planting. Crop rotation class is c. Beans can be preceded in the same year by kohlrabi, lettuce or radishes. Good complementary crops are: beetroot, brassicas, carrots, celeriac, celery, courgettes, cucumbers, dill, endive, gherkins, kohlrabi, lettuce, potatoes, radishes, black radishes, rhubarb, spinach, strawberries, sweet corn and tomatoes.

Bad for complementary planting: chives, fennel, garlic, leeks, onions and Florence fennel.

There is little scope for a late crop as the beans must be left in the soil for so long.

French beans

Phaseolus vulgaris

French beans are soft-shelled beans, which means we are not just interested in the contents of the pods, as with dried beans, but that the pod itself is eaten. French beans are also called green beans or haricot beans. There are two types: climbing varieties which need a cane or some other support, because they are liable to grow very tall – up to 3 m (10 ft) – and dwarf varieties which keep near the ground and so need no support, or at best only a little.

There are flat-podded and pencil-podded varieties. In the former the pods are fairly flat so that the seeds can be clearly seen through the wall of the pod at a very early stage. Pencil-podded varieties are much rounder and so less tightly packed.

The colour of the pods is usually green, but there are also varieties with yellow pods or with a purplish-red skin.

Green beans often have a string to the pod (hence they're also known as 'string beans'), which is generally removed with a knife. The older the beans the thicker and stronger the string. There are string-less varieties, but at high temperatures they are likely to form a string as well.

Another undesirable side to the French bean as far as preparation for the table is concerned is the hard, parchment-like skin formed in the wall of the pod. The older the beans, the tougher

Flowers of the climbing 'Purple Podded' bean. The beans are the same colour, but turn green after cooking.

this skin is. There are now skin-free beans that do not have to be picked so early. Beans of the haricot vert type form a skin very quickly, which is the reason why they are always picked very young.

Green beans are never eaten raw.

Varieties. Flat-podded beans: 'Canadian Wonder' (an old variety not so easily found today in catalogues, but still very good); 'Longbow'; 'Masterpiece'; 'Purple Podded' (purple pods, a climbing variety); 'Sigmacropper'; and 'The Prince'.

Pencil-podded beans: 'Blue Lake' (a climbing variety and a heavy cropper, with white seeds); 'Cordon'; 'Garrafal Oro' (an excellent climbing variety); 'Loch Ness'; 'Phoenix Claudia'; 'Pros Gitana'; 'Remus'; 'Sprite'; and 'Tendergreen'.

Soil type. See dried beans (page 117).

When to sow. As these beans are sensitive to frost, they are not usually sown early, except in greenhouses. The

The dwarf bean 'The Prince', a popular and very tasty variety. The beans can be clearly seen.

beginning of May is early enough. Some dwarf beans can be grown very late: you can still sow in late July.

How to sow. Climbing beans are usually sown at the base of the canes in early May, generally three to five together. If the weather is cold and wet the beans will not germinate, but rot into the ground. To prevent this, we always sow the beans in 9 × 9 cm (3½ × 3½ in) pots filled with potting compost. Again, three to five beans per pot. Germination takes place indoors, in the greenhouse or on a window sill. The minimum germinating temperature is 10°c (50°F). Then harden off a little and plant next to the canes after mid-May.

Dwarf beans are grown in rows 40–60 cm (16–24 in) apart and thinned out in the row to 10 cm (4 in). An alternative is to set five beans together at a spacing of

LEFT: 'Kinghorn Wax' is a yellow dwarf French bean, of the sort known as 'wax beans', which can be eaten fresh or dried.

RIGHT: A modern variety of dwarf pencil-podded French bean.

$40 \times 40\,cm$ ($16 \times 16\,in$). The seeds should be sown 2–3 cm ($\frac{3}{4}$–$1\frac{1}{4}$ in) below the soil. Raising in pots will give you a good start here as well, although it makes more work when you are growing in rows. Early crops can be started under plastic sheeting: set up your tunnels in March to let the soil warm through.

Growing tips. As with all beans, warmth and shelter should be provided. Wet and cold weather gives poor results. Avoid having too much nitrogen in the soil.

Climbing beans must be given strong supports like bamboo canes, which can be re-used for a number of years. These are set up in rows or wigwams. You can also use a tall support made of bean netting or wire, which the beans can be trained on. Whichever way you support your beans, make sure the arrangement can stand a bit of battering, otherwise a summer gale will see the whole lot flat on the ground. All beans are left-handed: if you are going to train them round the canes, do it anti-clockwise.

Time to maturity. About 100–120 days for climbing beans. Dwarf beans are ready earlier, from 40 days for the first 'haricots verts' to 90 days for most other varieties.

Pests and diseases. Beans germinating in the open may be attacked by the bean fly. The maggots spawned by this nuisance eat out the heart of the germinating plants, and as a result they die. Usually the seed will have been treated with insecticide so that this cannot happen.

The seed you are given may already have been attacked by the bean beetle, which means that the larvae will have eaten away the inside of the seeds. Here again, seed treatment will help, and will usually have been done.

High air humidity may cause fungus diseases during the growing stage, such as botrytis or sclerotic rot. Take care not to plant too closely and spray with fungicides if necessary.

Little can be done against the most persistent virus diseases: the simplest answer is to choose resistant varieties. Flea beetles first produce tiny spots on the leaves, and later the leaves turn pale brown and drop. You can use a pesticide designed to beat the red spider mite. Finally, aphids: easy combatted chemically, and equally well with environmentally harmless treatments.

BELOW LEFT: Climbing beans being planted out next to spinach ready for harvesting.

BELOW: Tying up beans.

Dwarf French bean 'Pros Gitana', one of the modern pencil-podded varieties.

The pods of French beans must on no account be allowed to grow large or they will develop a tough skin.

Runner beans

Phaseolus vulgaris ssp. *vulgaris* var. *vulgaris*

In this section we will also discuss scarlet runners, *Phaseolus coccineus*. All of these beans are usually cut up before cooking. That is, we are going by the way the beans are prepared.

Runner beans come in tall (climbers) and dwarf varieties. The pods are long and flat.

Scarlet runners are all climbers. A pleasing side to these is that they exist in both red-flowered and white-flowered varieties. The pods are more filled out and taste every bit as good as those of French beans. The red-flowered varieties decorate the kitchen garden nicely.

Varieties. Dwarf beans: older varieties are very susceptible to virus diseases, so you would be better off trying more resistant selections, such as 'Hammond's Dwarf Scarlet', which is early. Climbing runner beans: the earliest varieties, such as 'Kelvedon Marvel', will produce strings if they are left on the plant too long. Stringless varieties follow later. 'Butler', and 'Mergoles' are recommended.

Scarlet runners: An excellent variety

One particularly disagreeable disease is chocolate spot. Watery patches with a yellowish edge appear on the leaves, but dry up in warm weather. Glassy patches appear on the pods as well. This disease derives from infected seed stock and cannot really be treated, even with chemicals. Fungus diseases can be prevented to some extent by picking the beans very carefully, so that you don't wound them, and by making sure the weather is good and dry when you plant out.

Picking. Some people consider a French bean with good, fat pods to have the most taste, but on the whole it's far better to pick your beans fairly young. If you can, walk down your rows of beans every day, picking only those that have reached the desired size. Usually you will find that far too many beans are ready at the same time, and you will be tempted to leave them on the plant for just another week; but this is not a good idea. Freezing can be one answer to this surplus problem. Or you can leave them on the plant, but then harvest them later for drying. Pick the beans with care: large wounds increase the risk of fungus infections.

Successional and complementary planting. Beans are in group c for crop rotation. For an early crop you can choose kohl-rabi, radishes, black radishes or early lettuce. Late (dwarf) beans can also follow early potatoes or early cauliflower. The good complementary crops are listed for dried beans on page 118, as well as the combinations to avoid. After an early crop of dwarf beans you still have time for endive, late cauliflower, kohl-rabi and a range of brassicas.

Fine young runners. Do not allow the pods to become too large or they will be tough and stringy.

is 'White Emergo' which produces white flowers, as does the variety 'Desiree'. Red-flowered scarlet runners can be bought under the names 'Prizewinner', 'Red Knight' and 'Streamline'.

Soil type. See dried beans (page 117).

When to sow. As these beans are sensitive to frost, they are only sown early under the protection of glass. The beginning of May is early enough and a late May or early June sowing will still give a successful crop.

How to sow. See French beans, page 121.

Growing tips. True runner beans are by far the most sensitive to poor weather conditions. Scarlet runners, on the other hand, are very sturdy, and rarely suffer from disease either. They grow more luxuriantly than ordinary runners, so usually fewer seeds are sown at each cane (three is enough). Scarlet runners have one drawback: in warm weather a lot of the flowers will often fall off, which means there will be less pods. So don't plant them in too sheltered a spot, as we advised for other kinds of beans, and if possible grow a little later (sowing in the open at the end of May), so that the pods can come on in a cooler month. Otherwise, the advice is the same as for green beans.

Time to maturity. 100–120 days.

The ordinary climbing runner bean is long and flat with the beans packed in tightly.

An unusual runner bean, dragon's-tongue wax-bean, which can be difficult to obtain.

Pests and diseases. Scarlet runners are very resistant to disease. However they are very prone to attack by blackfly. See also French beans (page 120).

Picking. On no account leave on the plant too long, because the beans will then develop a skin; scarlet runners, especially, must be eaten young.

Successional and complementary planting. Beans are in group c for crop rotation. For an early crop you can choose kohl-rabi, radishes, black radishes or early lettuce. Late (dwarf) beans can also follow early potatoes or early cauliflower. The good complementary crops are listed for dried beans on page 118, as well as the combinations to avoid. After an early crop of dwarf beans you still have time for endive, late cauliflower, kohl-rabi and a range of brassicas.

LEFT: Modern runner beans like 'Desiree' are stringless and very tender when young.

RIGHT: Red-flowered scarlet runners add a welcome splash of colour to any kitchen garden.

Broad beans

Vicia faba

Also called field beans or Roman beans. The beans are large, broad and flat and grow in huge, fleshy pods, from which they must be shelled before cooking. Because broad beans can take quite a strong frost, they can be grown much earlier than dwarf or climbing beans, to which they are not really related anyway. The Longpod varieties are the hardiest and ideal for early crops, while the shorter-podded Windsor varieties are less hardy and have better flavour.

Varieties. Longpod: 'Aquadulce' (white seeds); 'Imperial Green Longpod' (green seeded); 'Imperial White Longpod' (white seeded); 'Hylon' (white seeded); 'Bunyard's Exhibition' (white seeded); 'Express' (green-white seeds); and 'Red Epicure' (reddish brown seeds which turn yellowish when they are cooked).

Windsor: 'Green Windsor' (green seeded); 'White Windsor' (white seeded).

Dwarf varieties: 'Bonny Lad' (white seeded); and 'The Sutton' (white seeded).

Soil type. Will grow on practically any soil that stays fairly moist.

When to sow. Broad beans are often sown far too late. The young plants will take several degrees of frost so they are best sown in March. Better by far is to sow your broad beans in individual pots in the greenhouse in February; then they can be transferred to the garden at the beginning of April after a little hardening.

How to sow. In the open: in rows 40–60 cm (16–24 in) apart. Thin out to 10 cm (4 in) within the row. Sowing depth 3–5 cm (1½–2 in), minimum germinating temperature 5°C (41°F). If sowing in pots, sow one or two beans per pot, but leave only one after germination. Sowing in boxes or trays is another alternative. The seeds retain their germinative power for four years.

Growing tips. As we have already said, broad beans must above all be raised early. With a late crop there is a risk of virus diseases, less pods and especially attack by the black bean aphid, which can multiply in amazing quantity on broad beans.

A comfortable bed for the seeds of the broad bean, a pod plant that can be grown especially early.

Tall varieties of broad beans need plenty of support from canes and twine.

Time to maturity. Up to 90 days.

Pests and diseases. Inspect the plants every day while growing for the presence of the black bean aphid. It can easily be kept at bay with a soap-spirit solution, in which case spray daily. Because the insects particularly congregate on the juicy tops of the plants, these are often nipped out. However, this reduces the yield a little, so we find it better to fight the aphids. If the plants are sown earlier they are not so juicy or tasty for the little pests, and they often remain free of attack.

After late sowing, virus diseases may also occur in June.

Picking. Young broad beans are tastier than old ones, so you should pick them regularly and not too late. Picking begins at the bottom of the plants, where the fattest pods are found, and gradually moves up the plant. The harvest lasts only a few weeks, then the broad beans are over.

Successional and complementary planting. Broad beans belong to group c for crop rotation. An early crop is hardly ever possible. Good complementary crops are dill and potatoes. There are many possibilities for a late crop, such as endive, kohl-rabi, lettuce and late brassicas.

Broad beans raised in pots are transferred to the garden after hardening off at the beginning of April.

Garden peas

Pisum sativum ssp. *sativum* var. *sativum*

Garden peas are grown for the small seeds hidden inside the pods. They are shelled, cooked and eaten. Quite a job this shelling, especially if you consider the little young peas the tastiest.

There are tall climbing peas which need some support, and dwarf peas which can more or less stand up for themselves.

Besides this, garden peas can be divided into round-seeded peas, a little more bitter in taste, and wrinkle-seeded peas, which taste fairly sweet. Round-seeded varieties are the hardiest, and can be sown earliest.

Varieties. Tall peas, round-seeded: 'Pilot'.

Tall peas, wrinkle-seeded: 'Hurst Green Shaft', 'Onward', 'Senator'.

Dwarf peas, round-seeded: 'Feltham First', 'Meteor', 'Histon Mini', 'Douce Provence'.

Dwarf peas, wrinkle-seeded: 'Bikini', 'Early Onward', 'Hurst Beagle', 'Kelvedon Wonder', 'Little Marvel'.

Soil type. Garden peas will grow on any reasonably fertile, well-loosened soil with a pH preferably between 6 and 7. The plants do not need a lot of

Dwarf garden pea 'Bikini'. If the soil has a generous helping of nitrogen, some support will certainly be needed.

Peas can be supported with twiggy sticks as seen here. It gives a more natural look than netting.

nitrogen, so don't add any fresh manure. A little extra potash and phosphate can do no harm.

When to sow. Peas do not mind the cold, especially the round-seed varieties. The seeds can go in the ground from February onwards. After April you should not sow any more garden peas, because in warmer and drier periods less fruit is formed.

How to sow. Dwarf peas are sown in the open in rows 40–50 cm (16–20 in) apart. Within the rows, thin out the plants until they are 8–10 cm (3–4 in) apart. Tall peas, which can grow to a full 1.5 m (5 ft), should be spaced further apart: up to 1.2 m (4 ft) between rows. Often a double row is sown, with 10–15 cm (4–6 in) between, and then the next row 1.2 m (4 ft) away. Sowing depth: up to 5 cm (2 in).

It is also possible to let your peas germinate in the greenhouse in pots or boxes. The minimum germinating temperature is 5°C (41°F). After hardening off, the plants are transferred to the garden, but best put under cloches if you are aiming for a very early crop. The seeds retain their germinative power for three to six years.

Growing tips. Birds will often attempt to make off with the seeds just after they have been sown. You can prevent this by stretching netting or plastic sheeting over the top. Plastic sheeting will also speed up germination out of doors. As soon as the plants are 5 cm (2 in) high they must be given some sort of support, which can consist of either twiggy sticks or an upright net. Make sure it is strong enough, as the plants will eventually become quite heavy, especially the climbing varieties.

Time to maturity. From 90 days for very early varieties to 120 days for late ones.

Pests and diseases. The pea moth can be a big nuisance. This insect lays its eggs in the flowers, and when the larvae hatch they eat the young peas. By growing early (flowering by mid-June) you will be too quick for the pea moth.

Fungus diseases can be prevented by a well-spaced rotation of the crops.

Picking. Picking early makes for a small yield and a delicious taste. Picking too late will give you a huge quantity of floury bullets.

Successional and complementary planting. Peas take part in crop rotation as members of group C. An early crop is practically impossible. Good complementary crops are beetroot, carrots, courgettes, cucumber, dill, early endive, kohl-rabi, lettuce, radishes and black radishes, Florence fennel, sweet corn and turnips. Disputed plants are beans, brassicas and potatoes. Avoid combination with chives, fennel, garlic, leeks, onions and tomatoes.

As a late crop you can choose between carrots, endive, Florence fennel, lettuce and late brassicas.

Dwarf peas are usually grown along a net as well, as this makes maintenance and picking much easier.

A variety of tall early pea with round seeds.

LEFT: The white butterfly-like flowers of the pea, where the pods will grow later.

LEFT: Large, sweet garden peas, such as this sugar pea, are widely grown and popular.

Sugar peas

Pisum sativum ssp. *sativum*
var. *axiphium*

There is not a great deal of difference
between garden peas and sugar peas, but
sugar peas, or mange-tout, do not have
the hard, parchment-like skin on the
inside of the pod. This makes it possible
to eat sugar peas and young garden peas
at the same time.

Just as with garden peas, we can divide
the varieties into tall peas (climbing
against a support) and dwarf peas (more
or less free-standing).

The pods should be picked when they
are very young and cooked whole.

Varieties. 'Edula' (tall); 'Oregon
Sugar Pod' (tall); 'Sugarbon' (dwarf);
'Sugar Dwarf Sweetgreen' (dwarf);
'Sugar Rae' (dwarf); and Sugar Snap'
(tall).

Soil type.   See garden peas (page 124).

When to sow. See garden peas (page
124).

How to sow. See garden peas (page
124).

Growing tips. See garden peas (page
125). Use netting as protection from
birds, not just for the seeds but also for
the pods.

Time to maturity.   About 90 days.

Pests and diseases. See garden peas
(page 125).

Picking.   Pick sugar peas early at all
costs, as they will get too tough later.
Some, which produce fatter pods, like
'Sugar Snap', can be picked just that

ABOVE: Dwarf sugar peas provide a good
yield very early in the season.

LEFT: For many sugar peas this is the right
stage for picking. No skin has yet formed.

RIGHT: A fatter sugar pea, 'Sugar Snap',
which can be allowed to grow larger.

little bit later, when they will be sweeter.

Successional and complementary planting. Sugar peas take part in crop rotation as members of group c. An early crop is practically impossible. Good complementary crops are beetroot, carrots, courgettes, cucumber, dill, early endive, kohl-rabi, lettuce, radishes and black radishes. Florence fennel, sweet corn and turnips. Disputed plants are beans, brassicas and potatoes. Avoid combination with chives, fennel, garlic, leeks, onions and tomatoes.

As a late crop you can choose between carrots, endive, Florence fennel, lettuce and late brassicas.

Asparagus pea

Lotus edulis

A curious and very little known vegetable with fins running the length of the pods and attractive red flowers. The tiny pods must be picked young and eaten cooked.

Varieties. We know of no specific varieties.

Soil type. Grows well on a reasonably fertile, not too dry soil.

When to sow. In the open, from the end of April.

How to sow. In rows 20–30 cm (8–12 in) apart. Sowing depth 1–2 cm ($\frac{1}{2}$–$\frac{3}{4}$ in). When shoots appear, thin out until the plants are spaced 10 cm (8 in) apart.

Growing tips. These vegetables need a fair bit of warmth to grow well, but once they have started they will mature without problems. The plant is very lax and we support it with bamboo canes and wires, which allows it to grow to a height of about 50 cm (20 in), produce a multitude of flowers and supply a plentiful yield of pods. Flowering lasts for quite a long time, which means that the harvest does, too.

Time to maturity. From 90 days.

Pests and diseases. No information.

Picking. It is very important to pick the pods young. If they grow longer than 5 cm (2 in) they are no longer pleasant to eat. The more you pick, the longer flowering will continue. You can continue picking in this way until the end of August.

Successional and complementary planting. Little known on this aspect: see

other legumes. Examples of an early crop could be early lettuce, kohl-rabi and spinach. Late crop: corn salad. We have no information on complementary crops or combinations to avoid.

The fatter-podded sugar peas are similar to garden peas but without the tough internal skin. They taste pretty good.

The asparagus pea has unusual fins. It has to be eaten very young, so the yield is small.

Dried peas

Pisum sativum ssp. *sativum* var. *sativum*

Dried peas include all the varieties of *Pisum sativum* harvested in their mature state. The purple-podded pea can also be dried if desired. They can be stored dry and will then provide food through the winter. As an example: green peas (for pea soup!).

Home growing of peas for drying is not terribly popular in Britain. But if you have space to spare you could give it a try.

All peas are eaten cooked. If they have been dried, they require steeping in water first.

Soil type. See garden peas (page 124).

When to sow. Peas can be sown early, because the young plants can easily take a few degrees of frost. March is the best month.

How to sow. One can use dwarf peas, and the correct distance between rows for these is 40 cm (16 in). Within the rows seeds should be 5–8 cm (2–3 in) apart. For tall peas, the spacing should be a good 100 cm (40 in), and supports will be necessary.

Growing tips. See garden peas (page 125).

Time to maturity. 110–140 days.

Pests and diseases. On soils with high pH manganese deficiency can arise. The lowest leaves will then turn yellow, although the veins will stay green. The seed germ often dies, and these peas will stay hard when cooked. This syndrome is called 'chlorosis'. Spray with manganese sulphate while the plants are growing, and grow on soils with lower lime content.

Fungus diseases occur in wet weather on soils that have been over-generously supplied with nitrogen fertiliser. The pea thrip lays its eggs in the flower buds, and the maggots then eat out the bud. Other information under garden peas. Most diseases can be avoided by sowing as early as possible.

Picking. All peas destined for drying must be allowed to mature fully. This stage has been reached when the leaves begin to turn yellow. Pull up the plants and leave them lying for a while to dry

ABOVE AND BELOW LEFT: Purple-podded peas being grown for drying.

out, then hang them in a shed or under shelter. Once the peas are completely dry they can be threshed: put them in a sack and beat it with a carpet-beater. After this you can sieve out the peas.

Successional and complementary planting. Dried peas take part in crop rotation as members of group c. An early crop is practically impossible. Good complementary crops are beetroot, carrots, courgettes, cucumber, dill, early endive, kohl-rabi, lettuce, radishes and black radishes. Florence fennel, sweet corn and turnips. Disputed plants are beans, brassicas and potatoes. Avoid combination with chives, fennel, garlic, leeks, onions and tomatoes.

As a late crop you can choose between carrots, endive, Florence fennel, lettuce and late brassicas.

Blanched vegetables

General information

It must have been a tramp, a nature-worshipper, a smallholder or some other figure intimately associated with plants and the soil who first observed that some plants taste much better and are much more tender for having spent some time underground. The discovery probably occurred with salad dandelions, which the Dutch call 'mole lettuce' – the leaves of an ordinary dandelion covered by chance by a molehill thrown up in the construction of a burrow. These leaves are pale, and far less tough than normal leaves.

Or was it wild asparagus, perhaps, which chance covered with earth? However it happened, since the initial surprise the popularity of blanched vegetables has grown and grown, until with asparagus we can now practically talk of an 'asparagus nouveau' cult ('Have you tried this year's asparagus yet?'), while there are whole factories dedicated to growing chicory, without a grain of soil in sight. The third blanched vegetable in the big league is self-blanching celery (or simply celery), another plant grown by millions.

All these blanched vegetables are relatively easy for the amateur to grow, with celery being perhaps the hardest, depending rather on the soil type. Delicious asparagus, fresh chicory and other blanched stalks – all will be discussed.

Blanched vegetables are usually grown over a two- or three-year period. It is not hard to appreciate that a plant growing underground or in the dark cannot carry out the assimilation process because the lack of sunlight puts a stop to photosynthesis (page 7). If there are still enough reserves in the roots the plant is better equipped to carry on growing in the dark for a while. But if the darkness goes on without stopping, any plant will eventually collapse beyond recovery. For this reason, blanching is never done for more than a few months, after which either the plant will die or it must be given the opportunity to produce normal green leaves again, so that it can get back on its feet. As we shall see when we deal with each plant, there are further fine points to master in blanching vegetables, but the principle that less light means

less toughness holds good for all of them.

Because of the separate location given to most blanched vegetables, the possibilities for complementary planting are somewhat limited. Asparagus, for example, takes off like a house on fire, and in the second half of the growing season the plants take on enormous dimensions, so that it gets pretty dark underneath. In principle you could grow a few heads of lettuce underneath, but is that really such a good idea? It's much the same with catch cropping: in principle it's quite possible to grow something before or after, but it's not always easy.

There are surprisingly few diseases encountered with blanched vegetables. Of course, there is always a risk of fungus, especially when forcing chicory, but munching and egg-laying parasites are generally absent.

This chapter, again, has an odd man out: when we come to chicory, which is a blanched vegetable, we shall also discuss green and red chicory. These are clearly close relatives, but they are not blanched. Their taste is very much like that of blanched chicory: a little bitter.

A plant which is sometimes blanched is rhubarb. As blanching is more the exception than the rule in this case, you will find this particular plant in the chapter on leaf and stalk vegetables.

This handy blanching jar has no bottom, and is placed over a plant such as rhubarb or seakale when it begins to shoot. The lid allows you to see how the blanching is progressing.

Asparagus

Asparagus officinalis

Nearly everyone knows the asparagus plant, because certain types, among them *Asparagus densiflorus* and *Asparagus falcatus*, are very sturdy house plants and can be found in nearly every home. Here we are concerned with the winter-hardy *A. officinalis*, that is, 'medicinal' asparagus. The plant is little used as a medicine these days, except perhaps as a tonic for the patient's love life, since it enjoys a firm reputation as an aphrodisiac. Our findings on that subject fall outside the scope of this book: what we want to do here is initiate you into growing this delicious vegetable.

Varieties. An old popular variety is 'Connover's Colossal'. Another to be recommended in 'Martha Washington'. 'Luculus' is new and produces only male plants which are much more vigorous than females. In Britain asparagus is only partially blanched (the lower parts of the stems).

Soil type. A very important point, if only because there is so much misunderstanding on the subject. In nearly every book you will read that asparagus must be grown on light sandy soil. This is quite wrong. Asparagus is a kind of weed: it has remarkable growing power and will grow just as well, or even better, on clay. There are only two conditions: the soil must contain a good measure of lime (pH around 7.0) and the ground water level must not be too high – at least 80–100 cm (32–40 in) below the surface.

It's a different matter when we come to the cover soil. The soil with which we cover the plants, and through which the blanched shoots will be growing, must not be too heavy, because that would make the asparagus bent and unattractive. In commercial growing, of course, it would be far too expensive to transport sand to a clay area, but the amateur who wants to eat home-grown asparagus can always order a few cubic metres of sand, which will last for years.

When to sow. You can sow asparagus, but it is possible to buy plants. Sowing is best done in small pots: in a cold frame this can start at the beginning of March, in a seed bed in the open from April onwards.

One-year-old asparagus is planted in a trench with its roots well spread out.

The raised asparagus bed is smoothed out in the spring.

How to sow. In pots: use potting compost and two seeds per pot. Sowing in a seed bed and then pricking out will also work very well. Germinate at 20 °c (68 °F), then grow at a slightly lower temperature.

The seeds retain their germinative power for three to five years.

Growing tips. If you are sowing your own asparagus it is planted out in rows in a sunny growing bed for the first year, with a spacing of 30 cm (1 ft) between rows and 15–20 cm (6–8 in) in the row. The plants need to grow vigorously, so water well in dry weather and add a little manure in mid-season. Picking the asparagus is out of the question for the first year.

In the second year the asparagus plants are moved to their final location. This is done early in the spring, as soon as the plants get to a reasonable size.

The growing beds are laid out 1.5 m (5 ft) apart and the plants spaced 40 cm (16 in) apart in the row. Usually however, one row of asparagus is enough in a garden.

For this first year the asparagus is planted in a trench cut 25–30 cm (10–12 in) below the surface. Cover the bottom of this trench with a good layer of garden compost, horse manure or other soil improver.

After planting do not fill up the trench completely: just cover the crowns of the plants with about 5 cm (2 in) of soil. The fleshy roots should be well spread out.

This is the stage at which you can use bought plants, in which case you avoid all the sowing and growing on you would have to do during the first year.

As the seasons pass and the plants grow the trench can be gradually filled up with soil. The rain will do a good part of this job for you, and you can give it a hand now and then. Add a little manure in the summer, and leave the asparagus to grow. Again, harvesting is out of the question for this year as well.

In December cut off all the frosted leaves at ground level.

In the very early spring (January or February) of the third year you should then add 30–40 cm (12–16 in) of cover soil on top of these trimmed plants. The bottom of this mound should be 80 cm (32 in) wide, and the top 40 cm (16 in). The soil for this can be taken from between the rows, or you can use separate cover soil. The cover should be given a tapering shape, with a flat top.

At the end of April or the beginning of May the bed is smoothed off neatly again, and then it's just a matter of waiting for the first heads: see further under 'Picking'.

After harvesting, the area of the raised bed is flattened out again. The soil is returned to the trenches between the beds, but not before these are lined with horse manure or compost. If separate cover soil has been used it is simply collected up and saved for the following season.

The asparagus should now set about producing leaves again, so that we have strong roots for the next year. In December cut off the frosted leaves at ground

Asparagus announces its arrival by cracks in the soil.

Cutting the asparagus starts with the removal of a little soil from around the stalk.

If you do not own a special asparagus knife you can use a kitchen knife to cut the spears.

level as before, and in spring build up the beds again.

Asparagus can be grown like this for at least 15 years.

If you are not blanching asparagus (using it green) no cover soil is used.

Time to maturity. Not really applicable to perennials like this. There is a definite time for harvesting, though: see below.

Pests and diseases. While we have been growing asparagus we have not been troubled by any attacks, but this is because there are no commercial asparagus growers in the neighbourhood. If you live in an asparagus-growing area you are more likely to have dealings with the asparagus beetle, which only

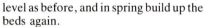

At the end of the season the dead foliage is cut off.

becomes a bother when there are leaves on the plants. That's what they eat.

The asparagus fly, too, will only turn up at the end of June, mainly in beds where there are young plants. Its larvae eat tunnels in the stalks.

Picking. The first year of harvesting (i.e. the third year after sowing) you will only be able to harvest your asparagus for a short time. Do it no later than 1 June. In the second year and beyond you will be able to harvest the crop up to 24 June. One day here or there doesn't matter, of course, but it's a good date to remember.

The moment to dig out the asparagus has arrived as soon as a crack can be seen in the smooth bed. Scratch away some soil with your finger, and chances are you will see the pale head of an asparagus stalk. The blanched shoot now has to be dug out very carefully by hand or with a small trowel, and then cut off at the bottom with a sharp knife. A special asparagus knife has been developed for this purpose so that you don't have to dig down so far. But you can get by perfectly well with a little more work and an ordinary kitchen knife. Don't cut asparagus any longer than the width or height of your pan – we have found 20 cm (8 in) to be a good length.

Check through the beds every day and take out the shoots that are ready. If you don't do this the heads will turn purple. This is not too much of a disaster because it's not likely to affect the taste, but it will look untidy on the plate. Cut asparagus

can be kept in water in the fridge for several days.

After every day's digging, the gaps must be filled up again and the beds smoothed out.

Picking green asparagus is a much simpler matter: just cut them as soon as they are 20 cm (8 in) long. Picking should finish by 24 June for this type as well.

Successional and complementary planting. Successional planting does not apply for a perennial of this sort. Cabbage lettuce, cucumbers, kohl-rabi and tomatoes seem to make good complementary crops, but this does not seem too practical to us. Avoid growing garlic or onions nearby. Neither late crops nor crop rotation apply.

Chicory

Cichorium intybus var. *foliosum*

The form of chicory best known in England is the blanched type, a shoot developed in the dark from roots grown earlier. Green chicory is the same shoot, but grown in the light. And the red chicory (radicchio), familiar to Italians and Swiss, and similar in looks to red lettuce, is yet a third form of chicory, the same plant which provides us with coffee substitute.

The usual scenario involves a large plant grown from seed in the summer, which has its leaves cut off in the autumn. The roots are saved, and the leaves which later grow from this are the starting point. For green chicory, however, the head is grown directly.

Varieties. If we limit ourselves for the moment to blanched chicory, we will see that there is a small range of varieties as well as some for growing without cover soil (see above). 'Normato', 'Prezo R.Z.', and 'Witloof Zoom' (F₁).

Suitable varieties for growing without cover soil include: 'Normato' and 'Witloof Zoom'.

Better known varieties of green chicory are 'Crystal Head', 'Pain de Sucre', 'Snowflake', 'Sugar Loaf', and 'Winter Fare'.

Radicchio varieties include 'Rossa de Verona' and 'Prima Rosa'.

Soil type. It is not good to grow chicory in very rich soil. The poorer the soil the better the roots will develop. In very fertile soil forked roots develop, which makes potting difficult. All this holds good for green and red chicory, too.

When to sow. In view of the risk of bolting as a result of temperatures that are too low, blanching chicory should not be sown before the beginning of May. For a very early crop it can be raised under plastic (which is warmer). If you sow too late, on the other hand, the roots will be too small in the autumn to force well.

Green chicory is best sown in the last week of June. Sowing earlier brings with it a great risk of bolting. Red chicory is sown between the end of May and early August. The least risk of bolting is assured by sowing after the longest day.

How to sow. Directly in the open, 30 cm (1 ft) between rows. Thin seedlings to 15 cm (6 in) apart. Green and red chicory should be 30 cm apart in the row. Sowing depth: 2–3 cm (¾–1¼ in). The seeds retain their germinative power for at least three years.

Growing tips. Growing the leaf plants is simple: hoe and water as necessary. The leaves can stand a few night frosts, except for radicchio, which must be protected with plastic or straw. The plants will usually continue growing until late October.

You can now start forcing the blanching chicory. First of all the roots are dug out, after which they are left lying for a week or so, with the leaves still attached, and out of the sun. Make sure they do not freeze.

Then the leaves are cut off 2 to 3 cm (¾ to 1¼ in) above the root. No lower, because then you might damage the

growing point. The side roots are removed and the main root is usually shortened a little.

For cold forcing, the chicory roots are placed in a pit in the garden, somewhere where drainage is good. The roots are laid close together on the level bottom of the pit and then covered with 20–30 cm

ABOVE: Red chicory, a vegetable which is not so easy to grow here because the roots are sensitive to frost.

Green chicory, easy on the spade and on the palate, can be picked in late October.

(8–12 in) of light soil. Finally, as a protection against frost, the pit is covered with straw. Depending on the temperature, the shoots should now start growing through the cover soil. Around mid-January you could take a look to see whether the heads are big enough.

The warmer the ground is, the sooner the heads will form. So we will turn now to warm forcing, which is the most common method. You can now sit the roots in boxes, also filled with soil. Do not warm them up for the first 10 days; then bring the bottom soil up to temperature, but if possible keep the cover soil roots can stand in it firmly. Do not cover the tops of the roots with soil. The box or bucket must be kept in complete darkness or the heads will be green instead of white, and as a result too bitter to the taste.

The best temperature for this method of forcing is around 16°c (61°F).

Green chicory does not need forcing: the heads can be harvested in October.

Red chicory is sensitive to frost, so it must be dug up in good time. The roots are dealt with in the same way as those of blanching chicory and then placed in a cold but frost-free greenhouse. You can also try growing the red chicory in the open under a tunnel cloche, then the roots would not need to be dug up. The temperature should be no higher than 10°c (50°F), or you will be left with disappointing heads. A soil cover is not necessary for red chicory.

Time to maturity. 180 days for blanched chicory, 120 days upward for green and red chicory. These timings go up to the time of forcing.

Pests and diseases. Chicory is rarely troubled by disease. However, signs of rotting may occur during forcing if the temperature is too high or the soil is too wet.

Picking. The crop is picked when the

cooler. For very early forcing you can warm up to as high as 22°c (72°F), for medium-early to 20°c (68°F) and for a late forced crop to 18°c (65°F). These are maximum temperatures, and you can get good results with a temperature between 7 and 13°c (45 and 55°F).

Chicory roots for late forcing can be kept in a refrigerator at a temperature a little above zero. These roots will not be used until the spring.

Instead of boxes, which are usually not high-sided enough, we can also recommend the use of large plastic buckets, as shown in the photographs. These must be provided with drainage holes.

There are also varieties that form a sturdy head without the need for cover soil. This saves a good deal of work. The roots are again set up in boxes or buckets, or even in cardboard packing cases lined with a black plastic sheet. Soil should be added between the roots. Settle this soil with water, so that the

ABOVE LEFT TO RIGHT: Forcing blanching chicory: dig out the roots, cut off the leaves, but not too low, and on the right potting in a good-sized container.

A good result from forcing chicory.

134

Young plants of red chicory.

Blanching celery

Apium graveolens var. *dulce*

A type of celery that is being eaten more and more in recent years, and which is available more or less all the year round (much of it imported). It is the long, pale leaf stalks that are eaten, both raw and cooked.

Varieties. The traditional varieties need blanching by keeping the stalks in the dark while they are growing. More recently, self-blanching varieties have been developed, which remain more or less blanched without any special measures having to be taken. 'Golden Self-blanching' is very well-known, are are 'Lathom Self-blanching and 'Celebrity.' Even newer are the varieties that stay green, and go stingy less quickly than the self-blanching. Of these, 'American Green' and 'Ivory Tower' are a good choice.

Soil type. The soil must always be good and moist and hold plenty of humus. Dig deep to loosen the soil and if necessary add lime to bring the pH up to around 7.0. The soil must contain a good supply of food to enable the plants to grow easily.

When to sow. Under glass, late March to mid-April.

The soil in the trenches is first improved with potting compost.

How to sow. In seed trays, keeping the compost fairly moist. Prick out seedlings in individual pots. The seed germinates slowly, so begin by soaking them for one night in lukewarm water, or germinate the seed in a tray of moist sharp sand.

Growing tips. Do not plant out until the second half of June. Ordinary varieties are planted in trenches, 15–

heads are the desired length. At low temperatures, the heads can be kept for a time (in the dark). Green chicory is brought in direct from the ground at the end of October.

Successional and complementary planting. The crop rotation sequence is c. Chicory is a main crop and does not really leave any room for other crops in the same year. Good complementary crops are carrots, onions, Florence fennel and tomatoes.

Green and red chicory can be preceded by early crops such as spinach, radishes and other vegetables that are out of the ground by mid-July.

Planting out the celery.

20 cm (6–8 in) deep and 40 cm (16 in) apart. Within the row, the plants are set out at 20 cm (8 in) intervals. Self-blanching celery is planted very close, on the peat, at 30 × 30 cm (1 × 1 ft). The plants must grow firmly against each other. The same goes for green blanching celery. In dry weather always water well. Fill up the trenches slowly over the course of the growing season. Add organic or inorganic fertiliser once or twice for all varieties.

Celery can also be blanched by tying sleeves of paper or black plastic round the stalks.

Time to maturity.　About 180 days.

Pests and diseases.　Brown hearts soon lead to rotting of the plants. The cause is an excess of nitrogen. Aphids and bugs may suck at the plants. Leaf spot can be avoided by buying treated seed. Slugs must be killed or trapped.

Picking.　The plants can be lifted as needed in September. Blanching celery can be kept in a fridge (in a plastic bag) for some days. The plants can also be left standing in the soil if protected from frost by plastic sheeting.

Successional and complementary planting.　For crop rotation blanching celery is a member of group A. Before you plant it you can grow any sort of vegetable that does not need the space after mid-June, such as peas, kohl-rabi, early brassicas (spring cabbage), radishes, black radishes and spinach. Apply a good measure of nitrogen afterwards! Complementary plants don't really matter here since the celery plants need to grow tight up against each other, which enhances the blanching effect and encourages the stalks to grow tall. And there is no room for a late crop.

Other blanched vegetables

There are other vegetables, often perennials, which – on a very limited scale – are also blanched. The best known are cardoon, dandelion and sea-kale.

The blanching effect is generally achieved by covering the parts to be blanched with soil or black plastic. In England we spotted some clever blanching pots made from earthenware. These pots have no bottom, so they can be set over the plants. By lifting the lid you can keep an eye on the plant's growth.

Cardoon (*Cynara cardunculus*). This looks very like an artichoke, and Spanish artichoke is one of its names. Growing is all done within the year: sow in spring, allow it to grow and blanch in September.

The plants can be sown in pots as early as the end of March and germinated at a temperature of 20°c (68°F). In May, after hardening off, they are planted out 80 × 80 cm (32 × 32 in) apart. Blanching can be started in mid-August: wrap the stalks in black plastic so that no light can get at them. After a few weeks the leaf-stalks are picked, given a good long boiling and eaten.

The problem is that cardoon often throws shoots before you want it to, in which case the leaf stalks are no longer tender and sweet. Bolting like this can be prevented by sowing in the warm no

If you look inside a molehill you will often find the blanched stalks of a dandelion.

Blanching cardoon stalks is a job for the autumn. Black plastic sheet keeps the light out.

With its decorative, grey-green leaves, the cardoon is not out of place in the flower garden.

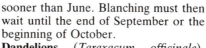

sooner than June. Blanching must then wait until the end of September or the beginning of October.

Dandelions (*Taraxacum officinale*). These familiar 'weeds' are perennial, and very commonly met with on pastureland. If the fresh leaves happen to be covered by a molehill thrown up in the spring, the result is what the Dutch call 'mole lettuce': delicious blanched leaves and leaf stalks.

Special varieties of dandelion have been developed for the kitchen garden, which produce a lot of leaf and less flowers. These are available from British seedsmen as a 'Continental' vegetable.

Sow in the open in the spring, in rows 25 cm (10 in) apart, and thin out the seedlings to 20 cm (8 in). Leave to grow, and dig up and pit late in the year as for chicory.

Dandelions can also be grown without cover soil in a dark room. A bit of extra warmth helps the growth of the roots, but you must not go above 15°c (59°F). As soon as the shoots are 10 cm (4 in) long they are cut off and eaten raw or lightly cooked.

Scorzonera roots left in the ground will throw fresh shoots. The eyes are already developing.

This is how the leaves of scorzonera look after the cover soil is removed.

A sea kale plant in its unblanched state.

Scorzonera (*Scorzonera hispanica*). This plant has already been described among the root vegetables on page 78. This is a winter-hardy perennial which – if it is not dug out – will throw fresh shoots each spring and then flower. Before that happens you can cover the young shoots with soil and they will become pale and tender. The shoots will appear a little quicker under plastic sheeting. After picking the blanched scorzonera leaves, you can either eat the roots as well or (if they are too tough) throw them away.

Sea kale (*Crambe maritima*). This winter-hardy plant is sown in the spring and blanched in its second year.

Sowing is best done in individual pots, under glass from the end of March. Transfer to the open in May and plant 60 × 60 cm (2 × 2 ft) apart. Very robust plants will appear, which will die down at the end of the year. The following spring the sea kale is earthed up (as described for asparagus). The young shoots will grow inside the cover soil and stay white. As soon as they show signs of growing up into the light they must be harvested. Boil before eating.

It is also possible to dig out sea kale in the autumn and force it by giving it extra warmth – not above 15°C (59°F). If the surroundings are completely dark no cover soil is needed.

Sea kale left in the garden produces new shoots and then flowers. The next year, the covering process can be repeated. Besides using seed, sea kale can be propagated by division or root cuttings. To take cuttings, use the side roots, cut them into sections 10–15 cm (4–6 in) long and lay them in boxes of moist sand. A little extra warmth helps the roots to shoot quickly. Then the new plants are transferred to the beds.

Fruiting plants

General information

When we talk about fruiting plants in this book we are referring to a large number of plants whose large fruit we eat. The name may be a bit confusing, because we eat bush fruits as well, but we have given these a separate chapter. Reason: bush fruits are always perennial, while the fruiting plants in this chapter die off at the end of the season.

And there was another exception: legumes, which are also fruiting plants, of course, but with their fruits in the form of a pod.

All the fruiting plants dealt with in this chapter need plenty of warmth to grow well, without exception. So it's not surprising that they are often grown in a greenhouse or under plastic sheets. In cold wet weather a lot of fungus diseases strike and the fruits do not ripen.

All the fruiting plants discussed here are especially sensitive to night frosts.

Early sowing is perfectly possible, but then the plants must be grown fully sheltered and with plenty of warmth through to mid-May. This works well with tomatoes, for example: you can sow as early as February, and after potting-on you will have sizeable plants by mid-May. Courgettes, which grow a lot faster, do not need to be sown so early. April is early enough – after another month and a half the plants will be very tall indeed.

Most fruiting plants are very vigorous (as long as everything goes well). So vigorous, in fact, that they can fail to fruit. To prevent this, we need to give the plants a hand, by stopping and removing side shoots. This inhibits the growth and encourages the formation and development of the fruits.

You will often have to wait a long time before you can pick fruit from these plants. Grafted cucumbers and courgettes can be harvested from the end of June onwards, but the other plants will not be ready until the end of August. To prolong the picking season of tomatoes (among other plants), the plants are often covered with plastic to combat night frost and raise the temperature a little.

Fruiting plants are not storing vegetables. Sometimes the fruit can be bottled, but in general it has to be eaten fresh.

Finally, feeding: during the growing season a weekly feed with organic or inorganic fertilizer is strongly advised. The food requirements are high, and if you do not provide plenty of fertilizer the plants will stop growing early.

PREVIOUS PAGE: A trug filled with the harvest from fruiting plants, including tomatoes, cucumbers, courgettes and gherkins. Growing these foods is not always that easy, as they demand plenty of warmth.

LEFT: Covering with perforated polythene keeps the temperature high.

Tomatoes

Lycopersicon lycopersicum

Tomatoes are grown the world over, in vast numbers: they are the most important of all vegetables. Today's tomatoes are very different compared with the time around 1500, when the first, still very modest 'love-apples' or 'paradise apples' reached Europe from South America via Italy. In this country its cultivation has only been really popular for some eighty years, but it has now taken on enormous dimensions.

Commercial tomato growing is quite a big industry, particularly on the south coast of England. Often they are given plenty of nitrogen to make them grow bigger, but then the fruits lose their taste.

If you grow your tomatoes properly you should steer clear of this problem, which is why home-grown tomatoes are more tasty, at least as long as you make the right choice of variety.

Tomatoes come in all shapes and sizes, and even in a choice of colours, although orangey-red is still the favourite. The large, irregularly-shaped 'beef-steak tomatoes' have become very popular over the last few years. At the other end of the scale there are cocktail or cherry tomatoes, mini-fruits which are very good for growing in pots on the balcony.

Tomatoes are generally eaten raw, but are also cooked in numerous dishes, including soups.

Varieties. In deciding on a variety, the amateur gardener will mainly be concerned with taste and with suitability for growing out of doors. Not everyone has a greenhouse, nor wants to give it over to tomatoes. This means that resistance to cold and diseases are important characteristics.

Taking beef-steak tomatoes first, good results can be achieved with 'Big Boy', 'Dombello', 'Dombito', 'Golden Boy', 'Marmande', and 'Super Marmande'.

A standard red tomato which does well is 'Ailsa Craig'. The widely grown variety 'Moneymaker' grows well, but has less of a taste. Others you can buy are: 'Alicante', 'Eurocross BB', 'Herald', 'Piranto', 'Shirley', 'Sioux', and 'Sonato'.

'The Amateur' is a good variety of the tomato plants which do not grow tall. Besides this there are: 'Alfresco', 'Minibel', 'Red Alert', 'Roma', 'Sigmabush' and 'Sleaford Abundance'. All of these varieties are self-topping.

In the field of cherry or cocktail tomatoes we can mention: 'Gardener's Delight', 'Sweet 100' and 'Tiny Tim'.

Finally, an odd-man-out: 'Yellow Perfection', which stays yellow.

Soil type. The most desirable ground is a humus-rich, permeable soil with a pH roughly between 6.5 and 7.0 Manuring must be heavy and extra fertilizer will always need to be given during growth.

Tomatoes are decorative plants which can be grown very well in large pots, especially the dwarf varieties.

It is said that tomatoes can be grown for years on end in the same spot, and that they do well on a compost made from . . . tomato plants. This is not untrue, but it will increase the risk of fungus diseases.

More and more tomatoes are being grown in pots or in growing-bags. In place of growing-bags you can use ordinary sacks of potting compost with one or two openings cut in them. All this standard potting compost, of course, contains artificial (chemical) fertilizer. If this is not what you want, you should be able to put together your own organic potting compost from garden compost, rotted cow manure, peat, bonemeal and a little lime.

When to sow. Professional growers sow tomatoes all year round, but the most common sowing time for amateurs is February or March.

How to sow. Tomatoes need a lot of warmth to germinate well, so we always sow in a heated seed tray at 20–25°C (68–77°F). Within a week the seedlings will be showing through the soil. At this point the thing is to lower the temperature quickly, or the tomatoes will keep on growing at the same rate – and that is certainly not the aim. So provide a high temperature until germination, then cool the plants off at once, especially at night.

Once the first true leaves have appeared you can prick out the seedlings: we always do this in 9 cm (3½ in) plastic pots. After a few days the night-time temperature can drop to 10°C (50°F) with 16°C (61°F) by day. If there is enough light it can be warmer. Make sure the growth doesn't come to a halt: this means it is too cold; but the plants must not be allowed to grow limp and thin – in which case it is too warm.

Usually you will have to pot on the

Growing tomatoes in the greenhouse gives you the best results and the earliest crop.

Besides side shoots, unwanted growth on the trusses must also be removed.

plants in April, this time in 12.5 cm (5 in) pots. Now you begin the gradual hardening off of the plants destined for the outdoors, a most important part of the growing process.

The seeds retain their germinative power for four to six years.

Growing tips. If you were to ask the tomatoes themselves, they'd tell you they would rather stay indoors, in the greenhouse. They like their warmth, and nearly all problems besetting growers are due to the cold and damp that summers in our lovely country are prone to. But having said all that, given a good summer and a sheltered location the plants can be grown very successfully out of doors, so why not give it a try?

Once the plants have been hardened off as far as possible in the greenhouse or, better still, once they have stood in their pots for a few days somewhere well-sheltered in the open, you can start planting out. For standard, large tomato plants the distance is 60 × 60 cm (2 × 2 ft). Smaller tomatoes can be planted closer together. A good place to plant is in front of a wall facing the south. But whatever else, the spot must get the full benefit of the sun.

Large tomatoes need a sturdy cane for support. Set this up at the same time. The handiest are 3 m (10 ft) bean poles that you have sawn in half. The tying in is done as the tomatoes grow, preferably with soft twine.

A very important point concerns the removal of the side shoots. These are the shoots that appear in the leaf axils. Tall

tomatoes must never be allowed to grow with more than one shoot. Some growers have a lot of trouble spotting these side shoots, but check your plants every week throughout the growing season. Sometimes shoots will appear through the soil, and these also have to be removed. Now and then a truss will overgrow and produce a growing shoot. If that happens, this must be removed as well.

Outdoor tomatoes can be allowed three to five trusses, but no more, or the top truss of fruit will not ripen. Five, in a good warm spot in a very warm summer, and three in a less-perfect position or in a poor summer. Usually the top is removed after the permitted number of trusses have developed. All unwanted shoots are removed after this as well, so that all the plant's energy goes into the fruit.

However, some people prefer not to top the plants, but only to remove the trusses beyond the number wanted. We suggest you try both ways.

There are also dwarf tomatoes, that is, plants which do not grow tall, and you will hear it said that they don't need staking. But you know, or you will find out, how it is with dwarf peas, beans, etc.: if you don't give them support they flop. It's the same with dwarf tomatoes, so it's best to give them a cane. A very accommodating characteristic of dwarf tomatoes is that they are 'self-topping': after the fourth truss they stop growing.

Now a few words about growing tomatoes in the greenhouse. As we said, this will give you better results, and the fruit will ripen earlier. Most amateurs choose to grow in an unheated greenhouse, but it is also possible to grow tall tomatoes sown in the autumn and grown in the winter with plenty of artificial warmth. It's an expensive game, though, and the taste of these tomatoes is decidedly inferior compared to those grown in the summer.

In the greenhouse you can grow dwarf or tall tomatoes, just the same as outside. Tall tomatoes are tied to canes or trained upward on wires. It goes without saying that the greenhouse must be protected against the strongest sunlight, but in the spring it is quite often kept closed to maintain a high temperature. In summer, of course, it must be kept well ventilated to prevent extensively high temperatures.

In the greenhouse you can grow six to

oration developing in the fruits.

Aphids and spider mites are two of the pests which infest tomatoes. Besides these, there must be a hundred other tomato troubles, which we won't tire you with. Given good growing conditions and sufficient rotation you are not likely to have many problems.

Picking. The tastiest tomatoes are the ones that ripen completely on the plant. For this you need the sun to shine on the fruits. Often some of the higher leaves are removed so that the sun can get through. The ripening of the top trusses often doesn't go as smoothly as we would like, because the weather doesn't co-operate. For tomatoes grown out of doors perforated polythene can be put over them to keep the warmth in, which helps enormously. It is also possible to pick green tomatoes and let them ripen inside on the windowsill. In only a few weeks the green will turn to a fine orangey-red.

LEFT: The cherry tomato 'Sweet 100' with a fine display of fruit.
BELOW: Irregularly shaped beef-steak tomatoes.

Successional and complementary planting. For crop rotation, tomatoes belong to group A. Before planting the tomatoes you can use the spot to grow kohl-rabi, lettuce, radishes or spinach. Disputed crop combinations are kohl-rabi and potatoes. Good complementary crops are asparagus, beets, brassicas, carrots, celery, chicory, garden cress, dwarf beans, garlic, leeks, lettuce, onions, parsley, radishes, black radishes, spinach and sweet corn, along with African marigolds – the last of these as protection against various pests. Planting with cucumbers, fennel, gherkins, peas, stinging nettles or turnips is not recommended.

eight trusses before topping. This means you can pick earlier, and longer as well. Greenhouse growing may give you problems with fruit setting, because the self-pollination process doesn't work. You can easily do something about that by giving the stems a tap now and again during the day. This will distribute the pollen.

Time to maturity. In the greenhouse: from 120 days. In the open: up to about 200 days.

Pests and diseases. Tomatoes can be attacked by various diseases, of which fungus diseases are the most serious. To start with blight: the first signs of this are dark brown spots on the leaves and stalks. In damp weather, there is a fair risk of botrytis or greymould. Greenback is the name for fruit which is a lurid green colour round the stalk. The cause is excessive nitrogen fertilizer, a stagnant atmosphere or too much sun.

Wide variations in temperature and/or air humidity can result in brown discol-

Cucumbers

Cucumis sativus

We will be dealing with cucumbers and gherkins separately in this book, although they belong to the same botanical species. In some countries, for example Germany, both vegetables are called by the same genus name: *Gurken*, and they are distinguished as *Gurken* for salad, that is, cucumbers, and *Gurken* for pickling, which we call gherkins.

The most obvious difference lies in the size and in the skin, respectively smooth and knobbly. It's a curious thing that we rarely eat pickling gherkins fresh and seldom pickle cucumbers. And it's equally odd that cucumbers are hardly ever cooked. There's certainly room for experiment in this area, but that's outside the scope of this book.

There used to be a type of bitter cucumber, but it didn't suit most people's taste. Nowadays nearly all varieties are non-bitter.

Another point concerns the pollination. This, too, can lead to bitterness and seed formation in the cucumbers. Older varieties produce both male and female flowers. To prevent pollination, the male flowers need to be removed. We will not bore you with this problem, because modern varieties nearly always produce only female flowers. They fruit without pollination.

Cucumbers are very fond of warmth, which means that in principle they are greenhouse plants, too. Nowadays, however, there are also outdoor cucumbers which produce shorter fruits within a reasonable time. Under cloches this will certainly work very well. You will have even more success with grafted outdoor cucumbers. With this technique, of which more below, young seed-grown cucumbers are grafted on to marrows, which are resistant to soil fungus. The result is a large, early crop of excellent cucumbers.

Varieties. First the greenhouse cucumbers, normal size: 'Amslic', 'Femspot', 'Landora', 'Monique', 'Pepinex 69'.

There are also mini-cucumbers for the greenhouse, such as 'Pepita'. These are also recommended for growing on a sheltered balcony.

A new type is the apple cucumber, which comes from New Zealand, and

Cucumbers can be grafted on to a marrow, after which they will grow better.

grows small fruit in the shape of a kiwi fruit. Suitable for both greenhouse and outdoor growing.

Cucumbers for outdoor growing are 'Bush Crop', 'King of the Ridge', 'Tokyo Slicer' and 'Pacer'. 'Pepita' can also be grown outdoors.

Grafted cucumbers are usually bought from a garden centre, and you often don't know what variety you are getting in this case.

Soil type. The best soil is a warm, humus-rich, permeable one, constantly supplied with plenty of nutrients. Cucumbers are rather sensitive to high concentrations of salt. Rotted horse manure is their favourite food.

When to sow. Greenhouse cucumbers can be grown all the year round, but for amateurs the sowing season really begins in February (otherwise the light is too poor). Sowing can continue until the end of July for an October crop. For outdoor growing you can sow in pots from the beginning of April.

How to sow. A lot of warmth is required for the seed to germinate: preferably 25°c (77°F). It is often recommended to let the seeds start their germination between damp sheets of tissue paper for a few days. After germination grow in the warm at 20–25°c (68–77°F). If you have started in small pots, you can pot on to larger pots after a few weeks.

If the plants stay in the greenhouse they can be planted out about four or five weeks after sowing. If the cucumbers are going outside they must first be well

Stopping a cucumber plant serves to curtail growth a little.

hardened off before they are planted out on a mild and preferably rather rainy day, and not before mid-May.

The seeds retain their germinative power for five to seven years.

Grafting. As mentioned above, cucumbers can be grafted on to a marrow, such as *Cucurbita beningasa* or *Cucurbita ficifolia*. Both the stock (of which it is difficult to get seeds) and the cucumber must be sown in warmth, as described earlier. The cucumber needs to be a little larger when grafting, so it is sown a week or so earlier than the stock.

As soon as the first true leaf of the stock begins to form and once the first true leaf of the cucumber has a diameter of 5 cm (2 in), grafting can take place. For this, both plants are lifted and cleaned up. The stock is cut, about 1 cm (½ in) deep, in a downwards direction, at the height of the true leaf. A similar cut is made in the cucumber, but this time in an upward direction. The plants now fit into each other exactly, and are fastened together with a strip of polythene. Then both plants are potted together and grown in high humidity (place a plastic bag over them).

After a few days harden off a little (remove the bag), and a few days later remove the head of the stock and any side shoots. Leave the lower leaves on the stock for the time being. After about a fortnight both plants will normally be strong enough for the roots of the cucumber to be removed. Now harden off some more, and later, after the plant has been planted out in its final position, don't forget to remove the last (round) leaves from the stock.

Growing tips. We'll begin with cucumber growing in the greenhouse. Plants that have been raised in warmth are set in well-prepared greenhouse soil from the end of March onwards (it can be done quite a bit later, even as late as the beginning of August). You can also grow plants in growing-bags (see tomatoes). Cucumbers are also grown in bales of straw soaked in manure. Leave 50 cm (20 in) between plants. A strong cane is set next to the cucumber, or a good strong piece of twine is hung from the roof of the greenhouse. The top of the cucumber is always securely tied in or wound round the twine. Remove the bottom side shoots and leave the rest to grow. As soon as the growing point reaches the roof, it is stopped. Flowers will now grow on the side shoots – all female, if all is well – and as soon as you see the beginnings of a cucumber growing, the side shoot is also stopped, so that each side shoot grows only one fruit. Any shoots that grow after this should be stopped after three to five leaves have grown.

When growing cucumbers in a coldframe or under cloches, the best way of working is this: put the cucumbers under glass or plastic at the beginning of May (after hardening off). Allow 1 m² per plant (about 40 × 40 in). Leave to grow until there are four leaves on the plant.

Then stop. Four new shoots should now grow from the four leaf axils, and these should be spread well apart to occupy the available space. When they have all grown out, stop these side shoots as well.

Only the very strongest varieties can be grown without any cover at all, or you could try it with grafted cucumbers. The location must be very sheltered and sunny. Trim as described above for coldframe growing.

Finally, growing in pots (preferably buckets with drainage holes). Mini-cucumbers are the right varieties for this. Give them a cane support, as described for the greenhouse, and keep the side shoots short.

Time to maturity. You will get the quickest results from grafted cucumbers: about 90 days after sowing you can pick the first fruit. Cucumbers in a heated greenhouse will grow faster than those in the open. The maximum growing time is around 180 days.

Pests and diseases. Cucumbers frequently suffer from diseases. Grafting to marrows as described helps prevent trouble. Virus diseases can also plague your crop. These turn the leaves various colours. Downy mildew mainly occurs in cold, damp weather, as does botrytis. In the greenhouse the main pests are whitefly and red spider mites.

Picking. Pick the cucumbers that look big enough to eat. Cut through the stalk carefully with a knife. Greenhouse

Grafted cucumbers will give you a rich and early crop.

cucumbers can grow to 30 cm (1 ft) long; outdoor cucumbers are best picked when they are half this length. Mini-cucumbers and apple cucumbers are picked even smaller.

Successional and complementary planting. For crop rotation, cucumbers belong to group A. Suitable early crops are kohl-rabi, radishes and black radishes. Good complementary plants are asparagus, beans, beets, brassicas, celery, coriander, fennel, dill, lettuce, onions, peas, sunflowers and sweet corn. Potatoes, radishes and tomatoes make bad partners. For a late crop you can grow spinach or corn salad.

The apple cucumber is still very little known; it comes from New Zealand but is quite at home here.

Gherkins

Cucumis sativus

You can see from the Latin name that there is a great deal in common between gherkins and the cucumbers we have just been dealing with. However, gherkins (or ridge cucumbers) are much less popular with amateur gardeners because they are nearly always eaten as a pickle. Pickling takes time and trouble, so people prefer to buy them ready-made and put up with the nasty taste of the inferior vinegar that is generally used. For those who would rather pickle their own, the following describes the growing method.

Gherkins usually grow out of doors. They must be picked young, otherwise they contain too many seeds. In contrast to cucumbers, gherkins need pollinating before they will produce fruit.

The newest varieties, like modern cucumbers, only grow female flowers, which do not need pollinating.

Varieties. You will find the following in seed catalogues: 'Bestal', 'Conda', 'Hokus', 'Parisian Pickling', and 'Venlo Pickling'.

Soil type. See cucumbers.

When to sow. The easiest way to grow the plants is under glass, as with cucumbers. The beginning of April is early enough. If you would rather sow outdoors, don't do it before mid-May.

How to sow. Germination temperature should be around 25°c (77°F). Sow directly into 9 cm (3½ in) pots or prick out later. Grow at 20°c (68°F). The seeds retain their germinative power for five to seven years.

Growing tips. The plants should be given about 1 m² (a little over a square yard) each. If you prefer, you can grow in rows – 50 cm (20 in) between each plant in the row, 2 m (7 ft) between rows. Usually the stems are allowed to lie flat on the ground, but it is also possible to grow gherkins up strong netting. Pruning is not usually necessary.

Another method is direct potting into buckets with drainage holes. In this case, supply a cane with cross-pieces on it. Stop the plant after the sixth leaf. The side shoots are trained along the cross-bars.

Time to maturity. 90 to 120 days.

Pests and diseases. As with cucumbers, virus diseases and downy mildew can cause a lot of problems. Modern varieties are more resistant. In bad weather botrytis can appear very quickly. As well as these, aphids and red spider mite can also make trouble for you.

Picking. Gherkins should be picked small. This means that the plants need constant checking during July, because this is when the fruits can rapidly become too big. Preservation is usually a matter of pickling in vinegar.

Successional and complementary planting. See cucumbers (page 145).

Gherkin 'Hokus', from small to too large. They quickly become too big.

Melons

Cucumis melo

Thanks to the nature of our climate, melons can only really be successfully grown under glass or plastic. What is more, water melons, so popular in France, are so difficult to grow that we shall only be dealing with what are known as sugar melons.

Varieties. 'Charantais', 'Early Sweet', 'No Name', 'Ogen', and 'Sweetheart'.

Soil type. Very fertile, warm soil with good drainage.

When to sow. From mid-March for growing under heated glass. For cold growing best sown at the end of April.

How to sow. Preferably directly into pots, germination temperature 20–22°c (68–72°F). The seeds retain their germinative power for four to six years.

Growing tips. Grow in warmth and with plenty of light. Stop plants after the fourth leaf. Usually grown on the ground, because the fruits become quite heavy. But it is also possible to grow melons in the greenhouse on a strong cord. Planting out is done at the end of May or the beginning of June. A maximum of four shoots grow from the leaf axils of the four leaves, and these are later stopped after the fifth or sixth leaf. Now fresh shoots will appear in the leaf axils of the side shoots, and these are stopped after the second or third leaf. That is all the training there is, and now it's a matter of waiting for the flowers. Often the first flowers are removed so that more melons can be grown on the plant. The maximum is four to six.

In contrast to modern cucumbers, the fruits need to be well pollinated. If there are no bees in your neighbourhood, you can do it yourself with a soft brush.

In sunny weather good ventilation must be provided, so that the temperature under the glass or the plastic does not become too high.

Time to maturity. About 120 days.

Pests and diseases. Soil fungi can destroy your plants, especially if you grow them in the same place every year. Grafting on to a rootstock which is resistant to soil-borne diseases is a solution, but not one much used by amateurs.

Risk of various fungal diseases, as with cucumbers. Light grey, sunken patches on the fruits result from direct sunlight.

Picking. Melons must ripen on the plant. Because the fruits rot very readily if they come in contact with soil it is a good idea to lay them on a board. Once the stalk begins to crinkle, the fruit is ripe. It also begins to smell good at this point.

Successional and complementary planting. Melons are in group A for crop rotation. Suitable plants for an early crop are kohl-rabi, radishes and early lettuce. Sweet corn seems to make a good complementary crop.

Melon 'Ogen' is a well-known variety, which can if necessary be grown outdoors, especially if a cloche is used.

Melons in the greenhouse, supported on cords.

147

Courgettes and marrows

Cucurbita pepo and *C. maxima*

Two distinct species, but as the method of growing is the same we are dealing with them together.

Cucurbita pepo includes courgettes, custard marrows and decorative gourds. The plants usually grow on a short stalk and do not throw out long tendrils.

Cucurbita maxima – the marrow or squash and the pumpkin – does produce tendrils, and can grow enormous fruits, such as the giant pumpkin or mammoth gourd of a full 75 kilos (165 lbs) apiece.

Courgettes usually form long, cucumber-like fruits coloured yellow or green. They are eaten after boiling or frying. The custard marrow is different in shape, and looks like a yellow flying saucer.

Marrows are used to make sweet pickles, and also jams and chutneys.

Varieties. Among the courgettes we can mention 'Green Bush' and 'Zucchini' with green fruits, and the yellow varieties 'Burpee Golden Zucchini' and 'Gold Rush'.

Well-known custard marrows are 'Custard White' and 'Custard Yellow'.

The small marrows include 'Golden Delicious' with 10 cm (8 in) long orange-yellow fruits, and 'Vegetable Spaghetti', a marrow with stringy flesh which does look like the pasta it's named after. Others are 'White Bush', with white fruits, 'Long Green Trailing', and 'Long White Trailing'.

The giant pumpkins such as 'Atlantic Giant' and 'Mammoth', have less tasty flesh. These are more for showing. The new 'Jackpot' has much smaller fruits and is better for the kitchen.

Soil type. Fertile to very fertile, loose, warm soil with good drainage. Giant types will grow well on the compost heap.

When to sow. Mid-April is early enough, as the young plants grow very quickly.

ABOVE: Young courgette plants in the greenhouse.

LEFT: Yellow courgettes are even more delicious than green ones. This is the right size for picking.

BELOW: Marrows must be stopped when the main shoot is 60 cm (2 ft) long.

Various types of
courgette. Some
varieties have their
origin in Italy.

BELOW: 'Vegetable
Spaghetti', easily
grown in our
climate.

BELOW RIGHT: We
consider custard
marrows to be very
tasty. It is a good
idea to reduce the
superabundance of
flower buds by at
least 50 per cent.

How to sow. Preferably straight into good-sized pots, temperature 20–25°C (68–77°F). Harden off slowly.

Growing tips. Plant out in mild weather after mid-May, preferably towards the end of the month, whether under plastic sheeting or not. Courgettes are sturdy plants, not so much affected by bad or rainy weather as cucumbers or tomatoes. Each courgette plant needs around 1 m² (square yard) of ground. Don't plant too many, because they will produce plenty of fruits.

Marrows are usually stopped when the shoots are 60 cm (2 ft) long. Side shoots then grow from the leaf axils, and

The sturdy green courgette 'Zucchini'.

Pests and diseases. Fruit-rot in wet weather. The plants are very sturdy in themselves, but may be affected on occasion by virus disease or downy mildew. Whitefly can also be a nuisance outdoors.

Picking. Courgettes and custard marrows are better picked young – there will be plenty of them, after all. We cut the courgettes as soon as they are 10 cm (4 in) long. These 'baby courgettes' often have the flower still attached. This can be eaten as well. Marrows are not picked until they are fully ripe, when the leaves have fallen victim to the first night frosts. They can be saved for a little while after this.

Successional and complementary planting. Group A for crop rotation. Before planting courgettes and marrows you can grow a little kohl-rabi. Good complementary planting with peas, beans, onions and sweet corn. Avoid potatoes. Courgettes can be picked for a long time, but when you have had enough of them you can dig up the plants and – after a freshener of manure – grow some spinach or corn salad, or possibly a few bush beans.

develop male and female flowers. They will produce fruits more readily if, when the weather is dry, you pick off the male flowers, fold back the petals and push them into the female flowers. You can also dust all the flowers with a soft brush. Courgettes also profit from this if insects are scarce in your garden. After setting up a hive of bees we had twice the crop of courgettes on our plants!

With custard marrows we have noticed that they are far too inclined to branch out, which makes the growth too thick. We removed a number of growing points, after which the fruits came on very quickly.

With courgettes, especially, which are always picked when small, it is important to manure regularly during the summer. The plants form a short stem, but this usually flops. To prevent this, we stick short, thick bamboo canes in the ground and tie up the plants from time to time.

Time to maturity. Courgettes can be picked from mid-June, so the minimum growing time is 60 days. Marrows do not ripen until autumn, after a good 150 days.

Marrow 'Zebra Cross', a new bush variety.

Peppers

Capsicum annum

Red and green peppers are the same species as the long, thin, hot-tasting Chilli peppers. They are grown in very much the same way. Both types of vegetable need plenty of warmth and light. In warm summers you can be confident of a good crop out of doors, but in rainy weather they will grow far better in an unheated greenhouse.

Varieties. Capsicum plants used in market gardening may grow as high as 250 cm (100 in). Well-known varieties are: 'Yellow Lantern' and 'Goldstar', both of which start off green then turn yellow. Bush varieties with red fruits, more suitable for the amateur: 'Canape', 'Early Prolific', 'Ace', 'Gypsy', and 'Triton'.

A true mini-variety is 'Twiggy' which forms very compact plants with small fruits. They can be grown in pots.

The main chilli pepper varieties are 'Red Chilli' (red) and 'Hot Gold Spike' with yellow fruits. These have thin, pointed peppers.

Soil type. Both types require a warm, fertile soil with good drainage. Extra fertilizer is necessary during the growing period.

When to sow. Mid-March is early enough.

How to sow. In seed trays in warmth, with the temperature around 25°C (77°F). A little cooler after germination. Prick out the seedlings in individual plastic pots and continue to grow in a warm place. To plant in the greenhouse: around the end of April, tall plants at 60 × 60 cm (2 × 2 ft), bush varieties 30 × 30 cm (1 × 1 ft). Plants for outdoors should be hardened off slowly, first pricked out into large pots if necessary, and planted in the garden no earlier than the end of May.

The seeds retain their germinative power for three to four years.

Growing tips. Lots of sun and warmth are needed for a good result. In warm summers you can be confident of a good crop out of doors, but if it is cold and wet you will naturally be more successful using cloches.

Peppers pollinate themselves. They produce abundant flowers, but not all the flowers become fruits, which is just

Capsicum 'Goldstar', which turns yellow after its green stage.

Chilli peppers will only turn red in a very good summer.

as well, since that would make for too dense a crop. There is no real need to stop the taller varieties or remove the side shoots. The bush varieties are 'self-topping', which means that they produce no more shoots once they have reached a certain height.

The taller varieties must always be tied to canes or strings, and the bush varieties are also likely to profit from some support.

Time to maturity. At least 90 days in a well-heated greenhouse, to much longer outdoors in cold weather.

Pests and diseases. In general, few problems, but sometimes aphids or red spider mite in the greenhouse. In wet weather botrytis can appear on the plant or the fruit.

Picking. Both types can be picked either green or red. Remember that the mini-varieties will also produce mini-fruit, and don't pick too late.

Peppers picked while they are green can ripen later and still become red. The fruits can be kept for some time in the fridge.

Successional and complementary planting. For crop rotation these vegetables belong to group B. For an early crop you can grow kohl-rabi, radishes or spinach. We know of no plants suited or unsuited as complementary crops, and in any case we don't recommend interplanting as peppers need all the light and sun they can get.

Aubergines

Solanum melongena

These long, violet fruits, which originated in India, have become part of the British vegetable basket for good. Aubergines used to be white and more egg-shaped, hence the name 'egg-plant'. Seeds of these varieties can still be bought.

Growing requires even more warmth than for peppers. Growing in the open is pretty chancy, but you can grow them well in an unheated greenhouse. Aubergines are eaten boiled or baked.

Varieties. Well-known varieties are 'Black Prince', 'Claresse', 'Dusky', 'Long Purple', 'Moneymaker' and 'Slim Jim', all compact plants; and the white, oval 'Easter Egg'.

Soil type. Loose, nutritious, humus-rich soil with good drainage.

When to sow. From the end of February. Early sowing is the best guarantee of good plants.

How to sow. In seed trays, heated to a temperature of 20–25°C (68–77°F). Prick out as soon as the first true leaves appear, preferably in individual plastic pots. Continue growing in warmth until mid-April, then plant out in the greenhouse. Compact varieties can also be grown in large pots or buckets. Spacing 60 × 60 cm (2 × 2 ft) for tall varieties, 30 × 30 cm (1 × 1 ft) for very compact types.

The seeds retain their germinative power for four or five years.

Growing tips. Young plants with only one growing point must be stopped to encourage extra shoots. In the greenhouse, no more than four shoots should be trained upwards on sticks or twine. All the side shoots that appear on these

Aubergines must not be allowed to produce too many shoots, so side shoots should be removed.

shoots should be carefully removed.

In the open (under glass or plastic), it is better to grow no more than two shoots on each plant, and when growing in pots or growing-bags it is best not to attempt to grow more than one shoot per plant.

The attractive purple flowers will appear very quickly. If they are too densely crowded together take out some of the flowers or the fruits will not develop fully. Six to eight aubergines per plant is quite enough. The fruits will develop beneath the flower without the need for pollination. Remove the dried-out flower, because this often gives rise to rotting.

When tying up, bend the stalks downwards a little, so that light and air can get to the centre of the plants. The bottom leaves are often removed for the same reason.

Several extra helpings of fertilizer are necessary during the growing season.

Time to maturity. About 180 days, longer out of doors.

Pests and diseases. Aphids are crazy about aubergine leaves, and turn them knobbly. Spider mite and whitefly are common pests, especially in the greenhouse. Botrytis occurs if air humidity is too high.

Picking. Aubergines are ready for picking when the skin turns slightly dull in colour. Fruits picked too early may still contain poisonous solanines. If picked too late they often go spongy from the inside.

Successional and complementary planting. Include in crop rotation group B. Suitably early crops include kohl-rabi, radishes, spinach and early lettuce. We know no complementary crops to try or to avoid. Late crops are unlikely, thanks to the long growing time.

Aubergine 'Black Prince' is a sturdy variety and one of the earliest to mature.

Sweet corn (maize)

Zea mays var. *saccharata*

Strictly speaking, an intruder among these fruiting plants, this type of maize should not be confused with the maize that is so widely grown for fodder in this country. Sweet corn, or corn-on-the-cob, is a grain crop, very popular here in Britain. It is planted in small quantities and eaten boiled.

Varieties. Choose early-ripening varieties like 'Aztec', 'Earlibelle', 'First of All', 'Kelvedon Glory', 'Kelvedon Sweetheart', 'North Star' and 'Sundance'. The newer, extra-sweet hybrid varieties, such as 'Early Xtra Sweet', are also well worth growing. They also ripen very early.

Soil type. Maize is widely cropped in the intensive cattle-breeding areas of our country to work off excess manure; from which you can see that its nutritional requirements are very high. Nitrogen and phosphate, in particular, are components you can't supply too much of. Extra phosphate needs to be worked into the soil before planting, and extra nitrogen can be added at intervals during growth. The acidity level must lie between 5.5. and 7.0.

When to sow. First half of April.

How to sow. Place two seeds in a 9 cm (3½ in) pot filled with potting compost and leave the stronger of the two seedlings. The best germinating temperature is 10–15°c (50–60°F). Start hardening off the plants at the end of April.

Growing tips. Sweet corn needs to grow in a warm, sheltered spot. Wait until the night frosts are over, then plant out in rows 70 cm (28 in) apart. Spacing within the row is 20 cm (8 in). Remember to hoe and water regularly. Break off the side shoots: these are not wanted.

Provide extra nitrogen fertilizer in July and August (dried blood or artificial fertilizer, according to preference).

Maize forms a male inflorescence at the top, from which pollen is wafted by wind down to the female flower (the cob). If maize is being grown for fodder in your neighbourhood, there is a risk that its pollen may land on your extra-sweet plants, with floury cobs as a result.

Time to maturity. 180 days.

Pests and diseases. In the main, sweet corn is not troubled by diseases.

Sweet corn with the protective husk removed. The black brush at the top indicates the right time for picking.

Side shoots at the base of the plant must be removed.

Picking. When the silky threads on the cob start to wither (they turn black), it is close to picking time. Part the protecting leaves (the husk), and press into one of the grains with your fingernail. If a milky sap comes out, the cob is ready to pick.

Cooks will tell you that you should bring the cob to the kitchen at a trot.

There is something in this, because the taste is much poorer after only a day. This makes corn cobs a difficult commodity to market, and the quality of home-grown corn all the better.

Successional and complementary planting. Given the high food requirements, you will not be surprised to learn that for crop rotation sweet corn is a member of group A. An advance crop of kohl-rabi, radishes or spinach is a good possibility, so long as you dig in fresh fertilizer before you plant the corn. Good complementary vegetables are bush beans, courgettes, cucumbers, dill, early potatoes, gherkins, lettuce, melons, peas and tomatoes. Beets and celery are combinations to avoid. A late crop is not a real possibility.

Artichokes

Cynara scolymus

The artichoke is a perennial plant from which we eat the large flower buds before they open. The flower bud is cooked in its entirety, and the lower, fleshy parts of the scales, along with the base of the flower, are destined for the table.

It is only in very sheltered and warm locations that sufficiently large flower buds can be grown in Britain. The plants are not fully winter-hardy.

Varieties. 'Gros Camus d'Angers', 'Gros Camus de Bretagne', and 'Green Globe'.

Soil type. Warm, fertile, moisture-retaining soil.

When to sow. From March.

How to sow. Under glass, germinating temperature 20°c (68°F). Prick out seedlings in pots, harden off and plant out no sooner than the end of May at a spacing of 1 × 1 m (40 × 40 in).

The seeds retain their germinative power for four or five years.

Because artichokes are not especially uniform in flower production it is a good idea to pick out the best plants yourself. These can then be further propagated by dividing.

Artichokes form an attractive plant which looks a little like the cardoon and is also closely related to it. In our climate the flower buds will not grow as large as they do in southern climes.

This flower bud is at the right stage for harvesting.

Growing tips. You have no hopes of a crop from new plants for the first year. Water well and keep fertilized so that they put on good growth. Protect against the frost in winter with evergreen twigs.

It is often recommended that artichokes should be moved every two to four years. This is probably not necessary if the plants are well manured every year.

Time to maturity. The crop should be ready for picking every year around the end of August or into September.

Pests and diseases. Sometimes a few aphids.

Picking. The flower buds must be picked before they open. You can collect four to eight buds per plant. They can be stored for some time in the cold.

Successional and complementary planting. Not applicable, as artichokes are perennials.

Soft fruit

General information

Bush fruits is a term which quite literally describes the sort of fruit we have included in this book: the fruit that grows on perennial bushes and shrubs, plants that do not grow very tall. The fruits themselves are not very large either. They are also popularly known as soft fruits. 'Tree fruits', such as the 'stone fruits' (apples, pears and cherries) are beyond the scope of this book.

It is much easier to find space in a small kitchen garden for a few bush fruits than for a sizeable apple tree – although it must be said that a well-trained tree does not have to be large to produce a good crop of apples. But that aside . . .

Bush fruits in most cases require a very sunny spot as is really the case with nearly all vegetables. However, blackberries and bilberries can get by with a little less sun.

If you are short of room, you can select types that will grow against a wall or a pergola, such as blackberries or kiwi fruit. Red currants and gooseberries can also be very successfully trained against a wall, as the photograph shows. And strawberries can also be trained tall against a wall or a trellis.

Bush fruits do not demand a lot of attention. The main things are a bit of pruning, manuring and weeding; apart from that the only other thing is picking the fruit. The greatest problem, in fact, is that bush fruits are such a delicious treat for the birds that they can't stay away. So we have to do something to keep our feathered friends off, or there'll be very little left for us to pick.

Aerial defence can operate through things designed to frighten, such as scarecrows, dazzling foil and humming wires, but it is more effective to use netting. Unfortunately, the birds often get caught up in it, and sometimes you have to do quite a bit of damage to the net when cutting them free. The most satisfying solution is a special fruit cage, complete with a door.

Because most fruit bushes stay in the same place for years on end, there's not much to say about successional planting. Complementary crops are rarely possible either. Fertilizing with lime is usually very effective, but high doses of nitrogen, on the other hand, can lead to problems.

Besides birds, bush fruits can also suffer from a number of diseases. In wet weather you will above all see the signs of fungal diseases, especially with strawberries. If you don't want to spray the plants, the best thing is to provide a dry underlay for the fruit (straw, plastic). There are a number of pests, but in the main these are no great problem.

Bush fruits are a treat for most children, and they will be delighted to join in, as here, where they are helping to pick strawberries.

Strawberries

Fragaria × magna

The present-day varieties of strawberry, with their large fruits, have been created by crossing with various botanical species. The mail-order catalogues are full of pictures which make your mouth water. But we should not forget the small strawberries, such as the alpine strawberry. These have a particularly delicate taste, and are popular with the best restaurants.

Strawberries are perennials with great growing power. They produce runners which give birth to new plants. The fruits are mostly eaten fresh.

Varieties. New strawberry varieties regularly appear, excelling in size, length of picking season, size of crop, etc. Taste isn't always paid proper attention to, and although the typical marketing varieties, like 'Gorella' and 'Redgauntlet', are fine to look at, their

In its first year the seed-raised strawberry 'Sweetheart' produces countless smallish tasty fruits.

Strawberries can be planted to grow through black plastic, and some varieties produce two crops per year.

taste is something short of wonderful. Tastier varieties are 'Aromel', 'Pantagruella', 'Vigour', 'Cambridge Favourite', 'Totem' and 'Domanil'.

Most strawberries produce a crop once a year but there are also varieties which produce two crops, such as 'Aromel'. The first crop is harvested in early to mid-summer, and the second in late summer or early autumn.

Climbing strawberries which have to be trained upwards on netting or stakes have not become very popular in Britain and are not now too easy to obtain.

Among the small-fruiting strawberries are the alpine strawberry, *Fragaria*

vesca, and the seed-raised strawberry 'Sweetheart'.

Soil type. Strawberries grow best in a humus-rich, fertile soil which never dries out too much. The best pH is between 6.0 and 6.5. Although they are perennial, it is generally preferred not to leave strawberry plants in the same spot for more than two or at most three years. They are very susceptible to soil fungi, which can quickly lead to poor cropping.

When to sow or plant. Strawberries can indeed be grown from seed, in which case it will always be a small-fruiting variety. March is a good time to sow, but it can also be done in September.

Planting, which is more common, is usually done in July or August, preferably not later than 10 August, but is also possible in April. In the latter case there will be no crop until the second year.

How to sow or plant. Seed is best sown in seed trays. Provide a measure of warmth. Prick out in pots and plant outside after mid-May, at a spacing of 40 × 40 cm (16 × 16 in).

Young plants should be given the same spacing. If you prefer to plant in rows, keep them 60–80 cm (24–32 in) apart and plant 20–30 cm (8–12 in) apart in the row.

The crown of the plant must be level with the surface of the soil. Keep moist in a dry period.

Growing tips. Strawberries are often mulched to keep the fruit clean and dry. An even easier way to do this is by using black mulching polythene in which you cut little holes when you plant. Make the bed slightly raised so that water can run off. Straw is often used for the mulching, but this is not applied until the fruits begin to grow.

When the fruits ripen the plants must be protected from birds by netting, or you will not have many strawberries left.

With double-cropping strawberries, such as 'Aromel', the first flower trusses are often removed to encourage the plant to produce more leaves. When the fruit is picked it is not just the strawberries that are taken from the truss, but the whole truss, including the small or unripe fruits. This stimulates the forma-

Strawberry blossom, the promise of a rich crop, so long as the strawberry seed beetle stays away . . .

LEFT TO RIGHT:
Planting strawberries in plastic sheeting. First wet the soil, then fasten black plastic sheeting over it.

Small holes are cut in the sheet with a knife the right distance apart. An excellent tool for making the holes is a bulb planter; after this the strawberry plant is placed in the hole.

tion of new flower trusses and thus new, larger fruits.

For an extra-early harvest you can stand tunnel cloches over the strawberries. In warm weather and at blossoming time these must be well ventilated. When the fruit is nearly ready to pick you can replace the plastic with netting to keep the birds off.

If you are the possessor of a heated greenhouse you can grow strawberries in it for an even earlier crop. 'Gorella' is very suitable for this. Give it 5–10°c (41–50°F) in mid-January, and 10–18°c (50–65°F) in March. It is a good idea to distribute pollen with a soft brush when the plants flower: this will help you to get more fruit.

Strawberries are often heavily manured, but too much nitrogen produces a watery taste and increases the risk of fungus diseases. It's better to cut down on the nitrogen and feed the plants with a little extra lime and phosphate – half in the spring and the rest after the fruit has been picked.

In summer most strawberries will produce runners, which produce roots and then a new plant. These young plants can be used for propagation. It is worth cutting off all the leaves from the tired plants a week or two after picking the fruit, and removing the runners. A few of the young plants are put in a new bed, where they stay for two or three years. This way, part of your strawberry patch is always being rejuvenated, and old beds are cleared after two or three

You can buy special plastic 'collars' designed to keep the fruits clean and dry, which reduces the risk of infection.

years. If this isn't done the risk of infections is greatly increased.

Strawberries which produce no runners can be divided in the course of the summer or early autumn.

Time to maturity. Varies, according to whether you are growing early, late or double-cropping strawberries and whether you are using a greenhouse.

Pests and diseases. The most dangerous enemy is botrytis or grey mould, which causes the fruits to rot. Professional growers keep it off by spraying with fungicides. Strawberry seed beetles, strawberry mites, aphids and slugs are the most common pests besides this.

FAR LEFT: After the fruit has been picked the leaves must be completely cut from the strawberry plants.
LEFT: Young plants that have grown from runners can now be taken and planted in a separate bed, where they are left for two years. You can see these being planted out in the next photograph, here without using black plastic.

Crop rotation is the best protection against virus diseases, along with the occasional buying in of new, virus-free plants.

Picking. Strawberries must be left to ripen fully on the plant. The plants should be picked though a few times per week, then the fruits should be eaten or preserved as soon as possible, because they cannot be kept at all, even in the fridge.

Successional and complementary planting. If the strawberries are not planted until autumn, practically anything can be grown beforehand, even early potatoes.

Good complementary crops are borage, dwarf beans, carrots, garlic, leeks, lettuce, onions, parsley, radishes and black radishes and spinach. In practice you don't see this very often, but it is a good thing to do. Do not combine with gherkins or brassicas. Late crops do not come into it, because strawberries stay in the bed. After clearing a bed, however, you could grow some corn salad, spinach or maybe kohl-rabi. In this case, add some nitrogen first.

Red currants

Ribes rubrum

When the magnificent red clusters ripen in the summer it is our greatest delight to eat them straight from the bush. In the kitchen they are also made into jam.

There are also white currants (actually, they are pale yellow), which we will include in this section.

Varieties. A well-known variety is 'Jonkheer van Tets', early and excellent for taste. Also early is 'Laxton's No. 1'. Mid-season varieties include 'Red Lake'.

Late varieties: 'Rondom'.

Among white currant varieties we can mention 'White Grape' and 'White Versailles'. They are not widely planted.

Only buy red currants from a reputable grower, as there are also virus-infected varieties on the market.

Soil type. Red currants are not particular finicky when it comes to soil. The ground must be a bit on the acid side (pH between 6 and 7). It should contain plenty of potash. We always spread a lot of wood ash from the bonfire around the plants, as this contains quite a lot of potassium.

When to plant. From the end of October to the end of March, except when the ground is frozen.

How to plant. Make a good planting hole, improve it with organic material (horse manure, peat, etc.) and plant the bushes 1.5 m (5 ft) apart. Water in well after planting.

Growing tips. During the first year it's a matter of making sure of a well-shaped bush. You can choose from several shapes: bush, standard or espalier (fan shape).

For the bush we want to end up with about eight main branches growing diagonally outwards and upwards. They should grow out of the stem about 10–20 cm (4–8 in) above the ground. If there are not enough, simply nip out the top of the bush, and more will grow. Make sure these main branches are well distributed over the plant.

You can also grow a spindle shape: a strong main stem with maybe 12 side shoots evenly spaced up its length.

A standard is produced by regularly removing side shoots from the trunk until it is about 1 m (40 in) tall. Then you

Red currants can be trained very successfully against a wall or fence in the shape of a fan.

allow some six side shoots to grow out on all sides.

An espalier, which can be grown free-standing but is usually trained against a wall or a fence, is produced by leaving only one shoot on the bush you have bought, and pruning it back until it is 60 cm (2 ft) above the ground. In the spring, only allow the three top buds to grow out. One should go straight up, one out to the left and one to the right. In the following autumn snip off the main shoot about 25 cm (10 in) above the lowest tier. Again, let only three shoots grow. You can continue in the same way: every year one more tier is added. After four tiers the work is usually considered to be complete.

Once your fruit bushes have a good shape it's a question of getting as many berries as you can. Most varieties fruit best on two- or three-year-old wood. This wood is formed by side shoots growing from the main branches. In summer, after fruiting, the side shoots must be stopped after the fifth leaf. After two or three years cut the side shoots right back to the main branches. New side shoots will now grow, which are again pruned back as described above. With varieties which fruit better on

one-year-old wood, such as 'Rondom', you can cut away all the side shoots after picking the fruit.

The birds are not just interested in the berries: they will also go for the young

A well-known red currant is 'Jonkheer van Tets', an early and tasty variety.

shoots, which seem to be a delicacy in early spring. This means that netting is needed then as well. During blossom, the nets are often taken away, because it is believed that the insects needed to ensure pollination are sometimes kept out by them.

Time to maturity. Not applicable to these shrubs, which can supply fruit for as much as 10 years if well looked after.
Pests and diseases. A good many red-currant diseases are known, but in general you should not be bothered with them. Aphids can be kept at bay with the usual treatments. Leaf spot is a fungus infection that begins with small red spots on the leaves.
Picking. The first berries will be ripe around the beginning of June, the last in August. Pick the clusters carefully, and eat or preserve them as quickly as possible, because they do not keep.
Successional and complementary planting. Does not apply.

Red currants can be grown almost anywhere: they are shown here by the front steps.

Black currants

Ribes nigrum

Black currants are more popular than red, although they are a bit too sour to eat fresh. Black-currant jam, on the other hand, is indescribably delicious. The modern varieties have long fruit clusters, which makes them easy to pick.

Varieties. Early and mid-season ripeners include: 'Boskoop Giant', 'Wellington XXX', and 'Ben Lomond', all three productive varieties.

Late ripeners: 'Baldwin', a very old variety, and the new one, 'Jet'.

Soil type. Black currants like a very moist soil enriched with a generous amount of humus and a pH around 6.5.

When to plant. Young bushes can be planted from the end of October to early in the spring.

How to plant. Prepare a good planting hole and improve the soil with horse manure and peat. Spacing 1.5 × 1.5 m (60 × 60 in) for normal varieties, 2 × 2 m (80 × 80 in) for the strong growers. After planting, cut down the plants to about 10 cm (4 in) above the ground.

Growing tips. After the hard pruning you should not be expecting any berries for the first year. Black currants produce most fruit on shoots that have grown in the previous year. The flowering is early and can be destroyed by night frosts, so protection should be provided against these, whether with plastic sheeting or old curtains, or by sprinkling with water throughout the night.

Little pruning needs to be done for the first two years. Make sure that the bushes take on a good, open shape, and only remove the branches that are growing too close together or trying to grow across the others. Leave new basal shoots alone: that is the fruiting wood for the next season.

Branches more than three seasons old are best removed altogether, as they will not be producing much more fruit. Cut them off as close to the ground as you can.

To encourage the growth of new basal shoots it is worth feeding during the growing season with a compound organic or chemical fertilizer. Mulching beneath the bushes helps to keep the topsoil moist.

Black currants, just like red currants, need protecting from birds with the help of netting.

Time to maturity. Not applicable.

Pests and diseases. Black-currant gall mite gets into the buds in the winter, which makes them swell up. Leaf spot, as with red currants, also aphids and spider mite.

Picking. Black currants are ripe as soon as they become a good dark colour and have not yet fallen off. They can be kept for a short time.

Successional and complementary planting. Not applicable.

Black currants are mostly used in the making of jam, etc. Good pruning is essential if you want a large crop.

Gooseberries

Ribes uva-crispa var. *sativum*

These low thorny bushes produce round, veined fruits with a hard skin and sweet centre. The skin is not usually eaten with the raw fruit, but used in cooking (jams, jellies).

There are hairy and bald gooseberries varying in colour between green, yellow, cream and red.

Varieties. 'Careless' is a very old variety with a fairly good taste. 'Whitesmith' has a very good taste; its fruits are pale green. 'Winham's Industry' produces a lot of good berries of a purple colour. All these varieties go back to the last century!

Mildew-resistant varieties are 'Invicta', 'Lancashire Lad', and 'Jubilee'.

There are also crosses between gooseberry and blackberry, such as 'Josta', with dark red fruits in clusters. The bushes do not bear thorns. The Worcesterberry is another such cross.

Soil type. As for red currants. pH 6.5–7.0, plenty of lime.

When to plant. From the end of October to early March.

How to plant. Make good planting holes, work in organic material such as horse manure, plant the bushes at least 1 m (40 in) apart.

Growing tips. Gooseberries fruit on short shoots growing from older branches, just as with red currants; so the pruning is generally the same. You can choose from a bush shape, a standard, a fan, and an espalier. For the shrub shape you should first grow a short trunk – 10–15 cm (4–6 in) – from which a maximum of eight main branches can then grow diagonally upwards. The branches are limp and have a tendency to sag outwards; so the main branches are usually pruned at an inward-facing bud so that the new shoots point more inwards.

Especially when you consider this tendency to droop, it is not a bad idea to grow a standard. To do this, one shoot is trained upwards until it is 1 m (40 in) tall. A strong stake is provided next to it for support. Then about half-a-dozen main branches are grown from the crown.

For growing an espalier see under red currants. This is an excellent shape for growing against a sunny wall or fence. A

Gooseberry 'Whinham's Industry', a variety that dates from before the turn of the century.

The fan shape often encourages a better yield from the gooseberry plant.

fan is also grown against a wall: some 10 main branches are spread across the surface in the shape of a fan.

Every winter the main branches are pruned back to about half their length, to keep them strong.

In the first week of July the side shoots growing from the main branches must be pruned back to between three and five leaves. This applies to all the shapes.

Finally, the side branches are again cut back in the autumn. If you are after small numbers of large fruits prune hard, back to two buds. If you want a lot of small berries, prune less severely.

Time to maturity. Not applicable.

Pests and diseases. A particularly bad disease is American gooseberry mildew. Affected shoots can often be removed during summer pruning. Keep the centre of the bush open and make sure it always has plenty of water, because dry soil encourages infection. Besides this, aphids and sawfly caterpillars can be troublesome.

Picking. Only pick the ripe, soft fruits and leave the rest on the plant for harvesting later. Protect your arm against the vicious spines.

Successional and complementary planting. Not applicable.

Raspberries

Rubus idaeus

You really need to grow raspberries yourself because they are easily squashed during transport, so they are not very often sold by greengrocers. It is not a difficult plant, so long as you know how to go about pruning it, which is actually quite a simple task, and not too much of a chore. Raspberries are eaten fresh and cooked, and can be made into jam, jelly, etc.

Varieties. All modern varieties are thornless. There are early and late raspberries, and even yellow varieties.

Early varieties are: 'Glen Clova' and 'Malling Promise'. 'Malling Jewel', 'Malling Orion', 'Delight' and 'Malling Admiral' are mid-season.

'Leo' is a late variety. Autumn-fruiting varieties are 'September', 'Zeva' and 'Heritage'. 'Golden Everest' is a yellow raspberry.

Soil type. Raspberries do not make great demands of the soil. The best pH is between 6 and 7. It is always good to have organic material worked into the ground and only stagnant water can have bad effects on growth.

When to plant. From the end of October to March.

How to plant. Raspberries can be

Raspberries growing against a south-facing wall: the guarantee of a good crop.

grown in a variety of ways: each plant separately, supported by a stake; plants in rows supported with two or three horizontal wires. For this, sturdy stakes are driven into the ground at the end of each row in such a way that they lean outwards. The stakes should stick out of the ground by about 1.5 m (5 ft). The rows should if possible run north-south. The young raspberry plants should be 30 cm (1 ft) apart within the row.

Between the outermost stakes we then stretch galvanised or plastic-coated wires with the help of straining bolts. If the row is longer than 4 m (13 ft), you will need extra posts in between, and the wires should be stapled to these in such a way that they can still be tensioned (don't staple fully tight).

After planting, the plants must be pruned back to 30 cm (1 ft) above the ground.

Growing tips. In the first year raspberries produce shoots or 'canes' which will bear fruit in the second year. These canes then die off. New shoots regularly emerge from the ground, and these must be carefully tied in, because these are the ones that will produce fruits the next year.

This means that for the first year you will not see much fruit. Take the shoots that appear and tie them firmly to the wires in a well-spread fan shape. Only concern yourself with the shoots that appear directly under the wire and show no mercy to those that grow too far away: cut them off with the hoe. There will be plenty without them: you only need to ensure 10–15 shoots per metre (between three and five per foot).

In the second year the shoots you have tied in will bear fruit. At the same time new shoots will appear from the soil, and these must be threaded between the fruiting ones, because these will give you your fruit for the following year. Hold on to the same number as before, concentrating on the ones directly under the wires and well spread out; and cut off the rest.

At the end of September or the beginning of October the old shoots are cut off at ground level and the new ones spread out along the wires. To keep the

Raspberries can look enticing, but they vary greatly in taste.

plant open (less risk of fungal diseases) it is a good idea to keep no more than eight shoots per metre (two to three per foot) to the very end. Pick out the best ones for this. If they are longer than 1.5 m (5 ft), tie the final length horizontally along the wire.

At the end of February the new shoots are cut back, a little above the top wire.

Time to maturity. The growing pattern is biennial, so you could think in terms of a year and a half from planting to the first crop.

Pests and diseases. Unfortunately, raspberries are prone to a number of diseases. Aphids can easily be dealt with. The raspberry beetle, which causes the familiar grubs in the fruits, can also be killed.

It is more difficult with fungal and virus diseases. Try to buy virus-free planting stock and make sure you have an open plant to limit fungal attack. Spur blight and cane spot, as a result of which the shoots completely die off, can be combatted by spraying with copper fungicide.

Picking. Raspberries only take on a good taste when they are fully ripe. Eat or preserve them at once, because they will not keep for long.

Successional and complementary planting. Not applicable.

Blackberrries

Rubus procerus and *Rubus laciniatus*

Wild brambles grow everywhere in this country and many readers will remember picking the delicious fruits when they were children, precariously balanced between a soaking in the ditch and a tumble among the prickly thorns.

Numerous hybrids have been developed, which grow rather larger in the garden than the ordinary blackberry. Even better news is that there are now thornless varieties, although it is alleged that these are not so good for taste. Finally, there are a number of crosses between raspberries and blackberries, with exotic names like Boysenberry, Loganberry and Tayberry. Their poor winter-hardiness is usually the reason why these crosses are not planted much in very cold areas.

Varieties. Good varieties of blackberries are 'Bedford Giant' and 'Himalaya Giant', both very strong growers, and both with thorns. Thornless and slightly less-prolific varieties are 'Oregon Thornless' and 'Merton Thornless'.

Better known among the crosses are the thornless Boysenberry and Loganberry L654. For completeness we will also mention the Japanese wineberry (*Rubus phoenicolasius*), a nice plant to look at, but not very productive; and Tayberry 'Medana', a virus-free strain.

Soil type. Brambles grow so strongly that you are better off growing them on poor soil, so that you can keep them under control. Further, the less nitrogen, the better the taste. It's precisely this that makes wild blackberries so delicious: they do not get any fertilizer.

When to plant. From the end of October to the beginning of March.

How to plant. The best way to grow blackberries is by the method described for raspberries. Like raspberries, they fruit on two-year-old wood which dies off afterwards, so pruning is exactly the same.

The support system can be made a bit sturdier and taller: up to 2 m (7 ft). The strongest growers must be kept a good 4 m (13 or 14 ft) from each other, so there's hardly room to grow them in a small garden, and even for medium-sized kitchen gardens one plant is quite enough.

Where in the end we held on to eight stems per metre for raspberries, half of this is enough for blackberries.

Threading the new shoots between the blossoming branches is not a task for the faint-hearted if you have a plant with thorns. We usually duck out of it, with the result that the next year we have a scruffy bush which has to be trained back up on the wires with much cursing and sorely scratched forearms.

Strangely, blackberries are not plagued by birds very much, so they can be grown without nets.

Time to maturity. A two-year process, as with raspberries, so the first fruits will appear almost two years after planting.

Pests and diseases. Not as many as the raspberry, although they can all occur. If the fruits stay red instead of turning dark, the blackberry sap mite has been at work.

Picking. Brambles are only ripe when they have turned dark red or red-black – this stage differs according to the variety. Eat or preserve at once, because they will not keep very long, though a little longer than the raspberry.

Pruning thorn-bearing blackberry bushes is not a pleasant task, and many are turning to thornless varieties, even though they are not quite so tasty.

Successional and complementary planting. Not applicable.

Thornless blackberries are shown here in various stages of ripening. Moral: pick regularly.

Bilberries, blueberries and cowberries

Vaccinium myrtillus, V. corymbosum and *V. vitis-idaea*

Bilberries still occur in the wild in several places in our country, e.g. on the North Yorkshire Moors. They do especially well in years with a damp spring and a not too dry summer, and are soon picked by eager crowds. But besides this you can also grow them in your garden.

The blueberry is much larger: the bushes reach a height of 1–2 m (40–80 in). There is a number of familiar varieties.

The cowberry (also known under the name of mountain cranberry and red bilberry) is a low bush 25 cm (10 in) high, which is evergreen, the leaves resembling those of box, and it produces round, dark red, rather sour-tasting berries.

Bilberries, blueberries and cowberries can be eaten fresh, but are more often used in the preparation of jams, jellies, juices, etc.

Varieties. No cultivated forms of the common bilberry are known. In the Alps you will find the type *leucocarpum*, which produces very tasty white berries.

By far the best-known of the berries discussed on this page: the bilberry.

Quite a few crosses have been developed from the blueberry, with a few good varieties as a result, such as 'Bluecrop' and 'Earliblue'.

It is usually the silver kind of cowberry that is used.

Soil type. The common bilberry crops up on the thin humus layer of pine forests. Here, the soil is very acid and fairly moisture-retaining. In the garden you must also make sure of an acid soil, pH 4.0–5.0. Not much food is needed; rich manuring may improve the yield but will spoil the taste. At all events never use lime-containing fertilizers like bonemeal or chicken manure.

This all applies even more strongly to the blueberry, which demands an even lower pH: between 3.5 and 5.0. This plant would be at home in the heather garden, among the rhododendrons, etc. Soil improvement with large quantities of garden peat, shredded pine bark or peat is needed, or you will have to grow the plants in large barrels full of the required soil mixture. Rotted cow manure is permissible, or you might be better using a compound artificial fertilizer with a mildly acidifying effect.

The soil must always be moist, so water well in dry periods (with water low in lime!). Stagnant water is bad for growth, however, so the drainage must be good.

The cowberry requires a pH between 4.0 and 5.0 – that is, quite acid soil.

When to sow and when to plant. Although the common bilberry easily propagates itself from seed (transported by birds), you can buy better plants and plant them in the spring or autumn. This also goes for blueberries and cowberries.

How to plant. Bilberry bushes, about 30 cm (1 ft) high, grow by covering the ground. They produce long stems, which, incidentally, offer a simple means of propagation, too. Plant in rows or in beds, spacing plants 40 × 40 cm (16 × 16 in). Very soon the whole surface will be covered with bilberries.

The blueberry demands an acid soil, which usually has to be specially prepared.

For blueberries a good planting hole must be dug, its size at least 50 × 50 × 50 cm (20 × 20 × 20 in). This is filled with the acid and humus-rich materials already mentioned. Space the bushes 1.5 × 1.5 m (5 × 5 ft) apart.

After a few years the ground-covering cowberries will form a dense, dark green carpet. The roots do not grow deep. Plant 25 × 25 cm (10 × 10 in) apart.

Growing tips. Bilberries have no objection to a fair bit of shade, blueberries require sunshine or at worst very slight shade, and cowberries, again, can be allowed quite a bit of shade. Only use acid fertilizer, very little for bilberries, 50 g of compound artificial fertilizer per square metre for the blueberries (1½ oz per square yard), and a reasonable amount for cowberries.

Bilberries do not need pruning, but with blueberries you should aim at growing six to eight main branches, well spread over the bush. From time to time remove the oldest branches and grow new, younger main branches. Beyond this do not prune appreciably. Don't prune cowberries at all: they can look after themselves quite well.

Birds and even ground foragers will not turn up their noses at a berry or two, so nets and possibly fences will be needed to preserve your crop from unwanted attentions.

Cowberries, also called mountain cranberries or red bilberries, form low-growing shrubs that do not need pruning.

Time to maturity. Not applicable.
Pests and diseases. Generally free from diseases. In very damp weather the blueberry sometimes suffers blossom rot (botrytis). Sometimes you will be faced with dieback, also caused by fungus. The caterpillars of the winter moth can be disposed of by the usual means.
Picking. Picking the small, soil-hugging bilberries is no easy job. Ripe berries are bluish-black. The harvest begins in June, and there is often a second harvest in August.

Blueberries are also blue-black in colour, with a white bloom over them. Once they become soft it is time to pick them. This will usually be in August. They can be kept for a short time in a cool place. The cowberry ripens last, from September to the end of October.
Successional and complementary planting. Not applicable, or not known. Blueberries interplanted with bilberries might not be such a bad idea.

Cranberries

Vaccinium macrocarpum

The cranberry usually grown is the American cranberry, but there is also a smaller species, *V. oxycoccus*, which occurs naturally in Europe.

The American cranberry is a marsh plant, which is widely grown at present for the market, because the fruit is a delicacy enjoyed with game and other dishes. They are seldom eaten raw.
Varieties. Selections of a number of varieties have been developed in the U.S.A. such as 'Early Black', 'Howes', 'McFarlin' and 'Searles'. Modern crosses are 'Ben Lear', 'Bergman', 'Franklin' and 'Stevens'. So far, though, it seems these are not available in the U.K., although the species are certainly available.
Soil type. The cranberry demands a particularly moist, acid soil. The pH must be between 4.0 and 4.5. As most garden soils will be too inclined to dry out, it is worth making an artificial marsh for your cranberries. The easiest way of doing this is to dig a sheet of plastic into the ground in such a way that it produces a 30 cm (1 ft) deep pool. You can, of course, sink a shallow ready-made pool or, at a pinch, if you're only growing one bush, a bucket. Fill your marsh with completely acid soil, such as peat. Mix in some artificial fertilizer, 20 g per m² ($\frac{1}{2}$ oz per square yard), as the peat does not contain any nutrients. As there is nowhere for rainwater to drain to, the marsh will come about by itself. In very dry periods, however, you will have to top it up with water.
When to plant. April-May.
How to plant. Directly in the marsh, 30×30 cm (1×1 ft) apart.
Growing tips. The soil must be kept very moist, but the water should not stand above the soil. Full sun is desirable for good production of fruit. Pruning is not necessary; at most, you could shorten excessively long shoots a little. Be sparing with fertilizer, especially for the first few years. Only if growth slows down perceptibly should you apply fertilizer.

Cranberries are very winter-hardy, but the branches can easily dry out over the winter, so in freezing weather cover with fir branches or straw. A good spot would be sheltered against the east wind.
Time to maturity. Not applicable.
Pests and diseases. No diseases are known in Europe.
Picking. Ripe cranberries are an orange-red in colour. The plants need to be picked over several times because the fruits do not all ripen at the same time. Once over-ripe they are difficult to keep, but if a little under-ripe they can be kept in a cool place for quite a while.
Successional and complementary planting. Not applicable.

Cranberries, picked when not quite ripe, will keep well.

Kiwi fruit

Actinidia chinensis

The kiwi is the national bird of New Zealand, and the country has adopted this fruit, too. Originally it came from China. The fruits, which are eaten raw and in jam, will ripen out of doors in our climate; and since this discovery was made, growing kiwi fruit is catching on. It is not always successful, because the fruit's winter-hardiness is limited and the ripening process often takes too long.

Varieties. Usually simply 'Kiwi fruit' is supplied.

Soil type. Nutritious, humus-rich soil with not too much lime, pH around 5.0–6.0.

When to plant. Best done in spring, March-April.

How to plant. Because kiwi fruit is usually planted against a wall or a pergola, where the soil is often very poor, we recommend that you make large planting holes. Fill these with plenty of horse manure, and especially peat.

Growing tips. Kiwi plants are dioecious, which means that male and female flowers grow on separate plants. This means that along with the female plants you obviously have to have at least one male plant, otherwise you will not have any fruit. In this instance, one 'man' is the match of up to ten 'women'. The plants will twine themselves round any support provided, but they will need some help against a plain wall. Because the winter-hardiness is far from optimal, a very sheltered spot (south-east-facing wall) deserves recommendation. Protection from sub-zero winds is especially important. In spring, night frosts can cause a lot of damage to plants which have already thrown shoots, so they should be covered or kept wet throughout the night with a sprinkler. The long stems are trained, well spread out, along the wall or the pergola. If they are as long as you want, stop them. The side shoots are stopped after the fifth leaf.

When growing against a wall the best thing to do with the female plant is to make an espalier it. Keep only the main stem, which will grow straight up. This is stopped at 1 m (40 in). From the three top buds you grow shoots, of which two are trained horizontally and one vertically. Quickly stop the vertical shoot again; and the following year you can grow a second tier from it.

Side shoots will grow from the horizontal branches, and these must be stopped after the fifth leaf. Expect no fruits until the third year, when more new side shoots will have appeared from the side branches to blossom and later to fruit. Stop again seven leaves after the last fruit. After all the fruit has been picked, superfluous wood can be removed. Prune away everything beyond the last fruit.

If you have a huge number of fruits they will be very small. In that case you will need to thin them out.

After a few years you can rejuvenate your kiwi plant by completely removing some of the older fruiting branches. Choose a well-positioned young shoot to replace it.

In dry weather the plants must be well watered. Extra feeding during the growing season is not a luxury for the plant.

Time to maturity. Not applicable.

Pests and diseases. If the soil contains too much lime the kiwi fruit is unable to absorb enough iron. This leads to yellow areas between the veins of the leaves. The problem can be cured by a more acid soil or spraying with iron chelate.

Picking. As we mentioned, kiwi fruit ripens with difficulty and very late on. It will not be until the end of October that you can pick the fruit, and then it will still be rock-hard. Ripening through at room temperature can take a good four weeks or more. To protect the fruits against drying out they will need to be wrapped in plastic while they are ripening. At lower temperatures this ripening may even take a few months, so that with a little bit of luck you should be able to keep the fruit in the fridge, at 4–5°c (39–41°F), for a very long time.

Successional and complementary planting. Not applicable.

If your prune your kiwi fruit well, you can expect a very good crop of fruit, but they ripen very late indeed in our climate.

Herbs

General information

You certainly didn't buy this book to find out about herbs, but as we see it herbs and vegetables are inseparably linked. So we are going to take a few pages to deal with the most important herbs for daily use.

Herbs go with vegetables because they are often paired as complementary plants with the aim of improving taste or deterring insects. Dill, for instance, is not only planted between rows of carrots, but also in the company of potatoes, gherkins, beans, peas, brassicas and cabbage lettuce. Parsley is planted alongside black radishes, gherkins, onions, strawberries and tomatoes. And there are dozens of complementary combinations of this sort, of which the usefulness, admittedly, is not always proven, but which are certainly used a great deal.

Secondly, of course, herbs are used to give vegetables extra flavour. This use has increased a lot in recent years, with the better restaurants giving a lead. Is this a result of the fact that most vegetables don't have much taste any more? It's not at all difficult for a dish to end up tasting of nothing but thyme and marjoram: a bad pizza may have nothing in it worth mentioning, but as long as there is enough 'oregano' in it the customer enjoys it, because it's the marjoram taste that makes a pizza.

It seems to us that the true art of cooking with herbs must be to allow vegetables, fish and meat to retain their true flavour and to enhance them with the taste of specific herbs until a truly harmonious whole has been achieved. But this is not a cook book, so we will leave that subject aside. Nor are we going to tell you whether thyme goes with meat and dill with fish, as they always tell you on condiment sets. You will have to sort that out for yourself. Unusual combinations can be quite an experience as well. All we shall tell you is whether a herb loses its taste or keeps it when it is dried or cooked. All the herbs described in this book are first and foremost kitchen herbs.

From time immemorial, many herbs have had curative or other specific effects ascribed to them. Many books have been written on this subject, and we assume that you will buy one of them if you want to know more about it. Because this is another topic that falls outside the scope of this book, we will not be dealing with herbs that have only a medicinal effect and no culinary use. Under the heading of 'History', the most we shall include is an amusing anecdote from the (often long) life of the herb.

You can let your herbs grow anywhere: as we have said, this works well in complementary arrangements with the vegetables. A small herb garden brightens the view a good deal, and must in that case be laid out as close as possible to the kitchen: in winter, especially, it is important to be able to nip out for a sprig or two. Herb gardens are usually laid out in old-fashioned, geometric shapes, which makes them look a bit like mediaeval gardens, but if you are short of space you can also grow them in large pots, buckets or other containers. In general they require a fairly fertile soil and sunshine. Some herbs can also be grown in half-shade.

PREVIOUS PAGE: Herb garden at Sissinghurst Castle, Kent.
BELOW: The herb garden at the Royal Horticultural Society's Garden, Wisley, Surrey.

chives

Chives

Allium schoenoprasum

This widely-grown herb is a member of the onion family: it is a perennial plant with bulb-like roots. It is the hollow, tubular leaves, however, that are eaten. Later in the summer it also grows a purple, globe-shaped cluster of flowers, which makes chives by no means out of place in the flower garden.

Chives grow wild throughout Europe.

On page 93 you will find a plant described under the name of Welsh onion, also known as 'coarse chives' (*Allium fistulosum*). There is also a Chinese chives, *Allium odoratum*, a plant with long, flat leaves.

History. Chives have been known since at least the Middle Ages, but there is little of interest to tell about them. Even old herbals only indicate that chives can be compared with leeks. "Eaten raw, leeks produce coarse bloode, winde and heavye dreames", but we have never observed any of this after using raw chives!

In parts of Holland, chives are used in a traditional herb stew.

Growing. Chives like to stand in the sun and hate soil that becomes too dry. They can be sown from mid-March, direct in the open, in rows 20 cm (8 in) apart. Seedlings can be thinned out a little, but this is not absolutely necessary. The leaves die off in the winter, but new leaves will appear in early spring.

Picking. Chives can be picked the whole year round. Young leaves are the best, so regular cutting will make for a tastier product.

Chives are sometimes cooked after drying, but the drying process kills off most of the taste. Cooking also makes chives tasteless, so only add to hot dishes immediately before serving.

dill

Dill

Anethum graveolens var. *hortorum*

Annual plant, up to 1 m (40 in) tall, with round, stripey stalks and very finely divided leaves. The soft-yellow flowers appear from June to September. After this the oval seeds appear. Dill is not only a herb plant, but also well suited to the flower garden, not least thanks to the attractive colour of the flowers. Besides this, dill is used quite a lot as a complementary plant because it has gained the reputation of keeping pests away (especially aphids).

History. Dill is known from as far back as Ancient Egypt, while in mediaeval Europe it was first and foremost a lucky charm that kept witches and magic at bay. Young brides put salt and dill in their shoes.

Growing. Dill can be sown from the beginning of April onwards, preferably in rows, which should be 25 cm (10 in) apart. The seedlings can be thinned until they are 30 cm (12 in) apart. Do not prick out seedlings: this usually goes wrong. Once the plants flower there are not many leaves left, so it is a good idea to sow again in June for autumn picking. In the winter dill dies off, but the plants often seed themselves.

If you have fennel growing nearby there is a risk of cross-pollination. The offspring is neither dill nor fennel and tastes of nothing much at all.

The narrow leaves can be picked at all stages, but they are most aromatic when young. Dried dill leaves can be bought in small jars, but do not have much taste. Boiling also spoils the aroma. Unripe flower clusters are often picked and used when pickling gherkins and the like. They can also be dried, when they keep some of their taste. Finally, the aromatic seeds can also be kept.

chervil

Chervil

Anthriscus cerefolium ssp. *cerefolium*

Annual, with hollow stalks and pinnate leaves. White flowers appear later. Height up to 60 cm (2 ft). Related plants are cow chervil (or sweet chervil, sweet bracken or sweet-fern), *Myrrhis odorata*, which has striped stalks; and hemlock, *Conium maculatum*, which usually has red-brown spotted stalks. It is as well to know these plants apart, because, while the first two are edible, spotted hemlock is extremely poisonous: Socrates' poison goblet was filled with it. Chervil has a pleasant smell, of chervil, naturally enough, whereas hemlock smells nasty. It occurs very widely.

History. Used in mediaeval times to purify the blood, remove gallstones, etc. The difference between the various plants that looked like chervil was very well known; there is also *Chaerophyllum temulum*, a hemlock which is mildly poisonous and usually has red-spotted stalks.

The 'domestic chervil' pictured on the

previous page is now a widely used kitchen herb, which can be bought almost everywhere.

Growing. Chervil can be sown out of doors from April in rows 20 cm (8 in) apart. The soil should not be allowed to dry out too much, or the seeds will germinate very poorly. Thin out seedlings to 15 cm (6 in). Chervil grows well in full sun, but also in light shade. It is a good idea to sow several times in the course of the season, because young leaves are the tastiest.

Picking. Chervil can be picked as soon as the leaves stand 10 cm (4 in) above the soil. Don't cut too hard, as the plants will then grow out again. The leaves must be used fresh; they can be bought dried, but then the taste will largely have disappeared. Do not add to the cooking: the most you should do is warm it up for half a minute (e.g. for chervil soup). Chervil seeds can be kept: they are also used for seasoning.

cated to Pluto. The Romans, on the other hand, considered celery a plant of good fortune, but in the Middle Ages it once again became part of the witch's craft. Nowadays we can find various forms of celery lying quite innocently among the greengrocer's wares. Besides being a kitchen herb, it also dispels moisture, as can be easily confirmed.

Growing. Celery germinates slowly, so, as with parsley, the seeds are often mixed with moist sand and kept at 20°c (68°F) for a while, then sown outdoors in rows 20 cm (8 in) apart. Thin out seedlings a little. A second sowing can be made in the summer, for winter use. Moist soil and a spot out of the strongest sun is best. Heavy soil is no problem.

Picking. Fresh leaves can be cut as soon as the plants are large enough. Drying drives out the flavour, as does cooking. Despite this, celery leaf is listed in many recipes. The seeds are also used on occasion as a seasoning.

horseradish was not used very much as a medical remedy; later attempts were made to cure scurvy with it. Nowadays horseradish is mainly sold in jars, conserved wet because the taste is lost if it is dried.

Growing. Preferably fertile, loose, moisture-retaining soil. It can be sown in the open in the spring, and the plants should eventually be 40–50 cm (16–20 in) apart. The more usual practice is to plant out pieces of root in the autumn, or, of course, to buy ready-grown plants, which are cheap enough. Horseradish loses its leaves in the winter, but shoots again in the spring.

Picking. As you will have gathered by now, it is the roots we are after. They may as well be left in the ground, because the taste disappears if they dry out. They can be added to a dish for brief cooking, but the taste becomes weaker the longer they are cooked.

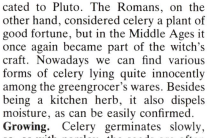

southernwood

Celery

celery

Apium graveolens var. *secalinum*

After parsley, celery is without doubt the best-known herb in our national cuisine. The celery used for this purpose is an annual with shining green compound leaves and, later, green-white flowers in umbrella-shaped clusters.

For celeriac see page 81, and for self-blanching celery see page 135.

History. The plant originally came from Western Asia, from where it was brought to the West. The Greeks laid this herb on gravestones: it was dedi-

Horseradish

horseradish

Armoracia rusticana

A perennial plant with large, dark green leaves on 30 cm (1 ft) long stalks which grow directly from the roots. That is, there is no stem, apart from a flower stem with small white flowers in ears at the end of it.

The thick, white root can grow to 60 cm (2 ft).

History. Horseradish grows naturally in the eastern part of the Soviet Union, in moist spots, such as along the banks of streams and rivers. In the Middle Ages

Southernwood

Artemisia abrotanum

Southernwood (the wormwood of southern Europe, or Lad's Love), belongs to the same genus as the mugwort and others. See under the latter for more details. Southernwood has very fine, almost thread-like leaves, grey-green in colour. It smells of lemons, and takes its name in some countries from this. The small, inconspicuous flower heads are located in the leaf axils and are a pale yellow colour. Overall, it may grow to 1 m (3 ft) tall.

History. For the origin of its Latin

name, see the mugwort. Southernwood was cultivated in Europe back in antiquity; where its ultimate origins lie is unknown. At all events, it has always been good for keeping demons, witches and spiders away. So it's a 'good' herb, and has also been credited with healing powers.

Growing. Like all members of the genus *Artemisia*, southernwood likes a sunny location in dry, limy soil. In spring the plant can be propagated from seed, and existing plants can be divided in spring or autumn. Because this herb turns woody from below, it is advisable to cut back the plants very hard every spring, so that they stay low and produce new, fresh shoots.

tarragon

Tarragon

Artemisia dracunculus

The genus *Artemisia* is well represented among the herbs. See also under mugwort. Tarragon is a perennial, which can grow to 1 m (3 ft) in height. It grows naturally in dry areas, e.g. in Russia and the USA. On the branching stems are sword-shaped leaves, which can be 10 cm (4 in) long and up to 1 cm (½ in) wide. They are hairless and a gleaming green. When the plant comes into flower, which occurs from August onwards, you can see tiny, globe-shaped, white to pale red heads in very loose clusters.

History. The name *dracunculus* means 'little dragon' in Latin, and probably derives from the snake-like roots. Pliny tells us that tarragon gives good protection against dragons and snakes, and this

might also be a reason for the name. Tarragon has been grown in this part of the world since the 13th century, and more as a kitchen herb than a medicinal one.

Growing. There is quite a lot of tarragon on the market which looks like the one we are talking about, but is not at all aromatic. So have a good sniff before you buy a plant! You can also sow seeds, which you should do in the spring, but there is then an even greater risk that you will have got the wrong tarragon. The best plants are descendants of the French tarragon, which must be propagated vegetatively, that is, by dividing or taking cuttings. Unfortunately, French tarragon is not so winter hardy. No seed is produced by the plants in this country. Russian tarragon can be propagated from seed, but has little taste, so is not really worth your while.

Picking. We use the leaves, which must be fresh. You can freeze them successfully; and tarragon also retains its taste well in vinegar, for example, so the herb is often used in the making of sour pickles. Drying the leaves does not get you far, and you should avoid adding them to the cooking, as this will also chase the taste away.

mugwort

Mugwort

Artemisia vulgaris

Also called wormwood. A perennial with grooved stalks and pinnate, dark green leaflets, which are only hairy on the underside. Height up to 1.5 m (5 ft). The flowers are grouped in egg-shaped

heads on a leaf-covered stem. They are yellowish or reddish-brown in colour and appear from July to September.

History. Artemis or Diana, the daughter of Jupiter, was the goddess of the hunt. In the Middle Ages mugwort was a popular magic herb, giving protection against storms and thieves. But wormwood was also used by witches in preparing potions (absinthe). It is still regarded as a plant that will see off vermin, such as lice.

Growing. Mugwort grows naturally in fertile, moist spots in full sun, but will also prosper in drier soil. Propagate by sowing in the heat in March-April, or in the open in May. Later, the plants can be set out at 40 × 40 cm (16 × 16 in). Or divide older plants in October or March.

Picking. Leaves and tips must be picked before the flower buds open. They can be used fresh, but are also dried. Mugwort will keep its taste after cooking.

borage

Borage

Borago officinalis

This is an annual plant covered everywhere by rough hairs. Height to 50 cm (20 in). The sword-shaped leaves are narrower on the stem and grey-green in colour. The hanging flowers are a magnificent violet-blue, the reason why the herb is used so widely in flower gardens. Bees can't stay away.

History. The name could be derived from bora, which means 'hair'. Borage is very old as a cultivated plant, and also grows wild on poor soil on the shores of the Mediterranean. Formerly often used as a medicinal herb, especially against infections, but it was also said to give pleasant dreams if kept in a vase beside the bed.

Growing. Can be sown in the open from March. A few plants will usually be enough, and should be spaced 50 × 50 cm (20 × 20 in) in fairly poor soil, as they can easily fall over otherwise. Full sun is very good for them. After the blossom, seeds are usually formed in abundance, so that you will find new borage plants all over the place next year. They are easy to recognize by their seed-leaves.

Picking. The leaves, preferably young, can be used raw, or lightly stewed. The attractive flowers are also edible raw and give a cheery effect to salads. The leaves can be dried, but most of the taste is then lost. The same goes for a long spell in the cooking pot.

coriander

Coriander

Coriandrum sativum

An annual from western Asia and North Africa, this plant has grooved stalks and pinnate, unpleasant-smelling leaves. The small white flowers are grouped in compact heads and appear in July, after which the bulb-shaped seeds ripen.

History. The name is derived from the Greek koros, which means bed-bug. As far as the smell goes, the insect and the plant, especially the unripe seed, have a lot in common. Coriander seed has been found in ancient Egyptian tombs: it was considered to have a healing effect,

especially against complaints of the stomach and the intestines. Coriander seeds were also mixed into wine.

Growing. Sow coriander in rows 30 cm (1 ft) apart at the beginning of May. Thin out seedlings to 15 cm (6 in). Be sure to give it a sunny spot; the soil type is less important. Flowers will appear in abundance and attract swarms of bees.

Picking. Coriander seeds ripen irregularly, so the plant must be picked over a few times. Only after being kept for a while do they take on their characteristic, sweet flavour. The taste survives cooking.

fennel

Fennel

Foeniculum vulgare ssp. *vulgare* var. *dulce*

Herb fennel must not be confused with the Florence fennel you will find described on page 83 as a vegetable. The ordinary variety hardly produces tubers, but instead long, round, fine-ribbed stalks on which very finely distributed leaves grow, and later, large yellow umbrellas of flowers. Fennel is sometimes a biennial and sometimes a perennial.

This herb is very like dill, and can spontaneously cross with it, but the result has no flavour. There is also a type with russet leaves.

History. Fennel originally came from the Mediterranean area. It was in use as a curative even before the birth of Christ, especially against snake bites and eye diseases. It is also an excellent defence against witches. These days,

fennel is, first and foremost, a kitchen herb.

Growing. Sow from the beginning of March, in rows 30 cm (1 ft) apart. The seedlings should be thinned to at least 80 cm (32 in) apart – that is, if you intend to grow more than one. As you cannot be certain whether the fennel will reappear after the winter, it is worth sowing afresh every year. The soil should contain some lime and the location must be sunny.

Picking. It is particularly important to use the leaves fresh, but the seeds also have uses in the kitchen. They must be kept in the deep-freeze, as the taste is mostly lost when they are dried. The seed can, of course, be stored dry. Fennel leaves should not be cooked.

hyssop

Hyssop

Hyssopus officinalis

This is a perennial which can grow 30–60 cm (1–2 ft) high. The angular, branching stalks go woody at the base and have a dull brown, peeling bark. The leaves may be everygreen in warmer regions. Flowers are usually blue. There are also forms with purple or white flowers.

History. Hyssopos is a Greek plant name. This herb is mentioned as early as the Bible: 'Purge me with hyssop, and I shall be clean' is a familiar line from the Psalms. In the Middle Ages it was naturally among the healing herbs, specifically for colds. At the present day it is an important kitchen herb.

Growing. Hyssop demands a warm,

sheltered and sunny location to be able to grow well. In harsh winters the plants need to be covered a little, because they are not fully winter-hardy. The soil can be on the dry side, but must above all drain well and contain lime.

Propagation by sowing in April, preferably under glass and in gentle warmth. Later plant out at 50 × 50 cm (20 × 20 in). In summer, hyssop can also be propagated from tip cuttings rooted in heat; and propagation by division is possible in autumn and spring.

Picking. Leaves can be picked fresh throughout the summer, and it is possible to dry them. Sometimes they are then ground to powder. If cooked in the pot, the flavour goes.

sweet bay

Sweet bay

Laurus nobilis

The bay plant, also known as sweet bay or bay laurel, is the odd-man-out in the herb garden: it is a tub plant, and one we meet with very often outside apartment blocks, large stores, hotels and the like. Clearly, this is a tub plant with prestige. Sometimes yellow-white flowers will appear in the summer, followed by blue-black berries. There are various types, with differing leaf shapes.

History. The Romans bore the bay laurel high on their standards because their laurel wreaths were made from the leaves. When it's worth the expense, these (pretty expensive) leaves are still used in making laurel wreaths for Formula One winners and other high fliers. Substitutes often seen are the (cheaper) leaves of the poisonous cherry laurel.

Nowadays bay leaves, which can be dried with great success, are to be found in nearly every kitchen.

Growing. Small plants can be bought in most flower shops and garden centres. They can be pruned into the usual shapes beloved of topiarists, but it takes a lot of patience. In the winter they can be propagated by cuttings. Tops of young shoots, 7.5 cm (3 in) long are rooted under glass or plastic in cutting compost at 20°C (68°F). After a month roots will have grown.

Your bay tree will appreciate a sheltered, sunny spot in the open during the summer. In mid-October the plant must be moved to a light, but above all cool place for the winter. It is very important that the temperature does not become too high, especially in the spring, because this will result in new shoots forming too soon. At the end of April the bush can be taken outside again. Re-pot every couple of years, and feed well during growth.

Picking. Leaves can be used either fresh or dried. The best way to dry the leaves is in an oven at 35°C (95°F). Bay leaves are never used raw, but cooked in the pot, after which they are taken out of the dish before eating.

lovage

Lovage

Levisticum officinale

A sturdy perennial from Asia Minor, which can grow up to 2 m (7 ft), with strong stalks and pinnate, shiny green leaves. The yellow flowers appear in wide umbrella-like heads.

History. Lovage was known to the

Greeks and the Romans, who used the herb as a general cure-all. In the Middle Ages an oil was made from the roots, which was also good for all manner of complaints. It is also said to be an excellent cure for freckles. Lovage is in less constant use these days in medicine, but all the more common in the kitchen.

Growing. It is possible to grow the plant from seed by sowing in April, but dividing existing plants is easier. Put the plants at least 1 m (3 ft) apart – if one plant is not enough for you, that is. It will die back in the winter, but in April you will see your lovage putting out new shoots, because it is very winter-hardy.

Picking. Fresh leaves should be picked but drying leaves and seeds is also among the possibilities, and the taste barely suffers. Even the roots can be used.

Lovage can be cooked in the pot without losing its taste.

lemon balm

Lemon balm

Melissa officinalis

Also known as sweet balm, bee balm, or simply balm. A perennial from the shores of the Mediterranean, growing to 80 cm (32 in) tall. The upright stalks are square in section and the deeply toothed leaves are a pointed oval shape. In the leaf axils you will often see tiny leaf buds or white or pale purple flowers. The blossom arrives in June to August, when the whole plant smells of lemons.

History. The name Melissa means honey bee in Greek, and the plant is indeed very attractive to bees. Lemon balm was introduced to Spain by the Arabs before 1000 AD, and the monks considered it to be of great medicinal value. It was also a major plant in witchcraft, but with a positive effect: protective, rejuvenating and sedative.

Growing. Balm likes full sun and will grow in any soil that is not too dry. The plants are perennials, but some shelter is advisable during a hard winter.

Propagation is by sowing seeds in April or by dividing older plants in spring or autumn.

Picking. Leaves can be picked as soon as they have set on the plant. They are best used fresh, since they lose their taste when dried. Cooking also makes the herb tasteless.

peppermint

Mint

Mentha species

There are quite a few species, crosses and decorative forms of the genus *Mentha* around. Here is a short list:

M. aquatica var. *aquatica* is wild water mint, a plant that grows strongly in shallow water.

M. × *gentilis*, ginger mint: there is also a variegated form, 'Variegata'.

M. × *piperita*, a cross between water mint and spearmint. Usually known as peppermint.

M. rotundifolia, white round-leaved mint or Egyptian mint. Known in England as apple mint. There is also an attractive variegated form of this, while the form 'Bowles' has soft green leaves.

M. spicata is spearmint. There is also a variety called *crispa*.

All are perennials and most are amply winter-hardy.

History. Mentha is derived from the Greek nymph Minthe, who was friendly with Pluto, the ruler of the underworld. The friendship attracted the jealousy of Persephone, Pluto's wife. In her anger she turned Minthe into a plant. If jealousy still had consequences like these, there would be a lot more plants.

In the Middle Ages it was peppermint that was best known, a cross which originally came from China and reached our shores via Egypt. It was mainly used for infusing tea, as indeed it still is. More familiar products of this plant today are peppermint oil and menthol.

As a herb it is above all white mint and spearmint that are used, but it can be fun to experiment with all the different ones, because the taste is that little bit different every time.

Growing. It is a good idea to start with young plants that have a smell you like, because if you sow you could end up with unwanted bastards. It is very easy to divide existing plants in spring or autumn. Do this after a few years, too, when the mint has worked out the ground or started 'wandering' over the garden. The soil should not be too dry and the spot where you grow these herbs can lie a little in the shade.

Picking. Use fresh leaves if you can, but drying works well with most types. The leaves can even be kept in the freezer. The taste survives cooking.

basil

Basil

Ocimum basilicum

Basil is an annual, tropical plant, growing to a bushy height of 20–40 cm (8–16 in). The opposite leaves grow on stalks and are a pointed oval shape. The white or pale purple flowers are grouped in clusters but are fairly inconspicuous.

There is also a small-leaved type, *Ocimum minimum* (bush basil), no taller than 15 cm (6 in).

History. It is pleasant to re-tell the following (none too credible) story about the Three Kings who travelled to Bethlehem to attend the birth of Jesus. Balthazzar, one of the three, spotted a bush with a flower more beautiful than a rose. This bush, it is said, is the one now called *basilicum* (the King's). Have a good look at the flower . . . we prefer the rose.

Basil is an important herb: tea can be made from it, it is an ingredient of Chartreuse and any number of foods, and let's not forget Grandma's basil biscuits.

Growing. It is best to have a fertile soil and a position in full sun. In wet, cold summers the plants are unwilling to do much, but if they have sun and shelter, they turn into attractive round bushes with cheerful, shiny leaves. They also make very fine pot plants for a sunny window sill.

They can be sown in heat from the end of March. Prick out seedlings, possibly first into 9 cm (3½ in) pots: do not plant out until mid-May, after the last night frosts. Space plants 30 × 30 cm (1 × 1 ft). It will also grow well in large plastic or other pots. For indoor growing, 12 cm (5 in) pots are large enough.

You can also pot outdoor-grown plants at the end of September: they will be happy for quite a while in a cool room.

Picking. Basil is grown for its leaves. They can be used fresh, which is by far the best way. Picking can be done at any stage of growth. The herb can also be dried and even kept in the deep freeze. Basil can be cooked in the pot and will retain its aroma.

marjoram

Marjoram

Origanum vulgare

Wild marjoram, also known as oregano, is a perennial plant originating in Central Asia, and grows up to 40 cm (16 in) high. The stalks are often purplish-red in colour, and the small oval or heart-shaped leaves are entire and hairy. The reddish-purple flowers, which appear in July, are enclosed in bracts.

There is also a species, *O. majorana* (sweet or knotted marjoram), with more egg-shaped leaves, also hairy, but this is far less winter-hardy and so it is grown as an annual or biennial.

History. The name was given by the Greeks. *Oros* = mountain and *ganos* = splendour or joy, referring to the delightful appearance the flowering plants gave to a hillside. In the Middle Ages, like many present-day kitchen herbs, marjoram was a medicinal herb, used for coughs, stomach complaints and toothache, among other things. Demons, ants and snakes can be seen off with marjoram, too. Chewing on marjoram is also claimed to keep you in good humour. In our day, marjoram, or its alter ego, oregano, is known as the 'pizza herb', but it has lots more uses in the kitchen than that.

Growing. Both types can be sown in April, in rows 20 cm (8 in) apart. Prick out seedlings and plant out at 20 × 25 cm (8 × 10 in) on as sunny a day as you can find. The soil can be on the dry, limy side. In biennial growing sowing is also done in April: these plants are over-wintered under glass and flower in the second year. Flowering shoots are more aromatic, which is why this method is used. However, we have found that annual growing also gives a perfectly acceptable result. Wild marjoram can also be propagated in the summer from cuttings, while division in the autumn or the spring offers a further means of propagation.

Picking. Fresh leaves can be picked as soon as the plants are large enough. Flowering shoots of biennial marjoram have the best aroma, and indeed this species has much more flavour than wild marjoram. Drying the leaves and flowers is perfectly possible. The taste is retained in cooking, as is the case with most Mediterranean herbs.

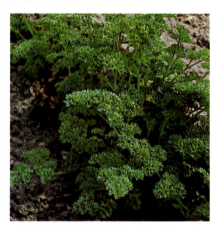
parsley

Parsley

Petroselinum crispum ssp. *crispum*

Don't keep this herb near wild parsley or spotted hemlock (see under chervil), because you probably won't survive it. Just one sniff should be enough to clear up any confusion. Parsley is a biennial or perennial plant with pinnate leaves contained in a rosette. There is a number of varieties such as: 'Consort', 'Curlina', 'Envy' and 'Moss Curled', the last of which grows very compactly.

Parsley has the highest Vitamin A content of any plant, as well as a large helping of iron.

There is also Hamburg parsley: for this, see page 82.

History. In the Middle Ages parsley was used as a purgative and febrifuge. When there were less clinics about, parsley was adopted as an abortifacient. According to superstition, parsley brought bad luck; and now, curiously enough, it's the number one kitchen herb, easily available anywhere.

Growing. Parsley seeds germinate slowly, so they're often pre-sown in sharp sand under glass and only sown outside when they have germinated. The time for this is April, not in full sun, in rows 20 cm (8 in) apart and not too densely, so that you don't have to thin out later. Often a second sowing is made in August for a winter supply. The plants are good perennials, but young leaves are tastier, which is why this is done. Parsley will grow in any not-too-dry soil and does not mind a little shade.

Picking. Parsley can be picked whenever it's needed. Use the leaves as fresh as possible: drying causes the taste to fade. This is also the case if parsley is cooked in the pot, though the writers of recipes don't always take account of it. Sometimes parsley seeds are also used. These lose their aroma with startling speed.

rosemary

Rosemary

Rosmarinus officinalis

A shrub growing up to 1.5 m (5 ft) from the Mediterranean area. Narrow leaves grow on the stems, green on top but grey and felty on the underside. These are evergreen. In summer the plant displays violet-blue or white flowers.

History. Rosemary was known in Greece as a good-luck plant and a defence against all ills. In the Middle Ages the plant was seen as an aid against many complaints: stomach, heart, nerves, you name it. In our day, rosemary leaves still supply an essential oil which gives the smell to a large number of perfumes.

Growing. In cold areas rosemary is not fully winter-hardy. It is only in a very well-sheltered location that you can keep the plant over the winter. So it's a better idea to see the plant through the winter as a tub plant in a cold greenhouse or some other frost-free room. Ordinary potting compost is fine; otherwise make sure of a light, well-drained limy soil. Propagation by seed or by rooting cuttings under glass in August.

Picking. It is usually the leaves that are used, but stems, flowers and seeds will also release an aroma. The leaves can be dried, but the flowers have to be used fresh. The taste persists after cooking.

sorrel

Sorrel

Rumex species

Garden sorrel (*Rumex acetosa* var. *hortensis*), is related to dock. In earlier times it was eaten in place of spinach by those who could not afford to shop at the greengrocer's. The leaves are spear-shaped. A tastier form is French sorrel, *Rumex scutatus*, whose leaves are wide rather than long, rounded at the end and blue-green in colour. We suspect that this last sort is difficult to come by and that what you get under the name of 'sorrel' is usually plain common sorrel, or at best a selection.

History. In Latin, rumex means spear or arrow, which refers to the spear-shaped leaves. And acetum means vine-

gar, which is how the leaves taste. (The name sorrel derives from 'sour'.) In the past, the juice of the leaf was used to quench thirst. Later, the leaves became a treatment for scurvy. Following its arrival as a popular vegetable, sorrel is now gaining importance in French haute cuisine.

Growing. Sorrel grows easily in any soil that is not too dry. It can be sown in the spring in rows 20 cm (8 in) apart, with plants 3–5 cm (1–2 in) apart after thinning. Sorrel is a perennial and can be left to grow in the same spot for years. It's perfectly normal for the plants to be attacked by the sorrel bug, which eats a lot of holes in it. It's not usually necessary to do anything about this.

Picking. There is a distinct difference in taste between young leaves and older ones. The older the leaf, the sharper and more unpleasant the taste. With this in mind, sorrel is usually cut when it is 5–7 cm (2–3 in) tall. Should this slip your mind, cut the whole plant off at ground level, and it will produce new shoots.

Sorrel leaves must be used fresh. Cooking kills off the sour taste. It can, however, be warmed up. Nothing to be gained by drying, only by freezing.

sage

Sage

Salvia officinalis

Sage is a low shrub growing to 60 cm (2 ft), completely covered with grey-green felty hairs. The leaves are oval to spear-shaped, crinkly and grey-green and will not fall in mild winters. In summer there are purple flowers in the leaf axils. There are various garden

forms, such as 'Icterina', with yellow and green leaves, and 'Purpurascens', with purple leaves.

History. Salvia derives from *salvare*, Latin for to cure. This plant has always been seen as a medicinal herb and considered active against all possible complaints. In mediaeval times it was also a magical herb, used by the famous Albertus Magnus (around 1200). Sage makes you sleepy: sage milk is drunk just before going to bed.

Nowadays sage is used in mouthwash and in some toothpastes, and also very widely in modern cooking.

Growing. Sage suffers a great deal in hard winters, so plant it in a sunny and well-sheltered spot and cover it up a little for the winter. The soil must be well drained and limy. Propagate by sowing in the spring or by cuttings.

Picking. Sage is mainly of interest for its leaves, which should be used fresh but will keep their aroma when dried. The seeds are also used as a condiment. Sage can be cooked in the pot without losing its flavour.

savory

Summer and winter savory

Satureja hortensis and *S. montana*

Summer savory is an annual, with narrow leaves and later purple flowers. Height up to 20 cm (8 in).

Winter savory is a shrubby plant with square stalks, woody at the base and narrow evergreen leaves. Height up to 40 cm (16 in). The flowers appear in late summer and are white or pale purple.

History. The annual savory is one of the oldest known herb plants. It was formerly used in medicine, but nowadays only for adding aroma to peas, beans, etc.

Growing. Summer savory is usually sown when the broad beans begin to flower. That way, the herb is precisely ready when the beans are picked. Rows 15 cm (6 in) apart, not too densely sown, so that no thinning out is needed. Needless to say, you can sow later if you wish, so as to use the herb with other legumes.

Winter savory can be propagated by sowing, dividing and taking cuttings. The plants will also seed themselves. The best location is in dry, well-drained and lime-rich soil with plenty of sun.

Picking. Summer savory should be picked young, and at all events before it flowers. The leaves can also be dried. The leaves will not lose their flavour if included in the pot.

Winter savory is more of a decorative plant than a herb. The leaves are less aromatic, but can be used all the same. Drying can also be done.

at the edges. Purple flowers in July. Any number of varieties are available.

Secondly we have true thyme, *Thymus vulgaris*, the common or garden thyme, a 20–30 cm (8–12 in) high shrub which is not very winter-hardy in our climate. The narrow leaves are hairy on the underside and curled up at the edges.

History. The name probably originates in Egypt. In Europe wild thyme used to be a defence against all ills and common thyme a curative for a wide range of sicknesses. Thyme syrup is still prepared for coughs. Both sorts are used in the kitchen, and sometimes other forms alongside them, such as lemon thyme with its lemon-scented foliage.

Growing. Thyme grows well in dry, limy soils in full sun. In winter you must protect garden thyme well, or grow it in pots. Propagation of wild thyme is by division and garden thyme by sowing seeds in April. Do not prick out, but thin out because transplanting is not successful.

Picking. In both cases the leaves are used, preferably fresh, but they will retain most of their aroma when dried.

thyme

Thyme

Thymus species

There are many species of thyme, which are also often used as decorative plants in rockeries. The main one used in the kitchen is wild thyme, *Thymus serpyllum*, also known as mother of thyme, a winter-hardy shrub. It has horizontal stems, and leaves very variable in shape, bare on the underside and slightly curled

The main organic and synthetic fertilizers

O – organic

S – synthetic

N – nitrogen

P_2O_5 – phosphoric acid

Org – organic material

K_2O – potassium

MgO – magnesium

pH+ – raises pH (lowers acidity)

pH− – lowers pH (raises acidity)

percentages given are minimum legal requirements

Fertilizer	S/O	%N	%P_2O_5	%K_2O	%lime	%MgO	%Org	pH + or −	Notes
Nitrogen fertilizers									
Nitrochalk	S	15						−	ammonium and nitrate nitrogen
Ammonium sulphate (sulphate of ammonium)	S	21						−	nitrogen from ammonia
Dried blood	O	12							releases nitrogen slowly
Nitrate of soda	O	15						+	nitrate nitrogen
Guano	O	14						+	bird droppings
Hoof and horn meal	O	13						+	acts even more slowly than dried blood
Nitrate of lime	S	15						+	ammonia and nitrate nitrogen
Calcium cyanamide	S	18						+	mainly calcium cyanamide
Urea	S	44						−	amide nitrogen
Mixed nitrogen fertilizer	S	20						−	nitrate, urea, possibly ammonium nitrate
Phosphate fertilizers									
Superphosphate of lime	S		18						raw phosphate treated with sulphuric acid
Triple superphosphate	S		45						raw phosphate treated with phosphoric acid
Basic slag	S		10						slow-acting; a waste product of the steel industry

The main organic and synthetic fertilizers

O – organic	N – nitrogen	K₂O – potassium	pH+ – raises pH (lowers acidity)
S – synthetic	P₂O₅ – phosphoric acid	MgO – magnesium	pH− – lowers pH (raises acidity)
	Org – organic material		

percentages given are minimum legal requirements

Fertilizer	S/O	%N	%P₂O₅	%K₂O	%lime	%MgO	%Org	pH + or −	Notes
Potash fertilizers									
Sulphate of potash	S			48					soluble K₂O
Lime fertilizers									
Ground burnt or lump lime	O				70			+	limestone burnt, then ground
Ground magnesium lump lime	O				70	8		+	magnesium limestone burnt, then ground
Magnesium limestone	O				50	4		+	frequently from dolomite rock, often more MgO
Hydrated lime	S				50			+	slaked calcium oxide, may also contain MgO
Magnesium fertilizers									
Magnesium sulphate (Epsom salts)						15			water soluble
Kieserite						25			water soluble
Trace element fertilizers									
Sequestrene	S								contains iron, magnesium and manganese
Seaweed fertilizer	O		0.35	0.2	45	5			rich in trace elements and minerals
Mixed fertilizers									
Growmore	S	7	7	7					an equal balance of nitrogen, phosphorus and potash

The main organic and synthetic fertilizers

O – organic   **N** – nitrogen   **K₂O** – potassium   **pH+** – raises pH (lowers acidity)

S – synthetic   **P₂O₅** – phosphoric acid   **MgO** – magnesium   **pH−** – lowers pH (raises acidity)

     Org – organic material

percentages given are minimum legal requirements

Fertilizer	S/O	%N	%P_2O_5	%K_2O	%lime	%MgO	%Org	pH + or −	Notes
Organic fertilizers									
Hoof and horn meal	O	13						+	acts very slowly
Bonemeal	O	6	18						
Mushroom compost	O	0.5	0.3	0.6	1.6	0.6			
Compost (home made)	O	0.4	0.2	0.5				+	variable in composition
Blood, fish and bone	O	7	5	7				+	
Dried blood	O	12							releases nitrogen
Sewage sludge	O	4.5	5	0.5			60		
Farmyard manure	O	0.6	0.4	0.5	0.4	0.2	12.5		variable in composition
Poultry manure	O	0.3	0.4	0.2	2.5	0.3	2.0		
Pig manure	O	0.8	0.7	0.5	0.6	0.3	12.5		
Guano	O	14						+	bird droppings
Fish emulsion	O	6	2	2					
Seaweed fertilizer	O	0.35	0.2	45	5				rich in trace elements and minerals; 45% CaO

Sowing calendar

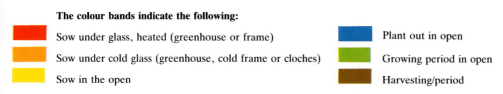

The colour bands indicate the following:

■ Sow under glass, heated (greenhouse or frame)

■ Sow under cold glass (greenhouse, cold frame or cloches)

■ Sow in the open

■ Plant out in open

■ Growing period in open

■ Harvesting/period

Earlier crop(s) may be possible under warm or cold glass and/or grown under plastic sheeting

Leaf and stalk vegetables

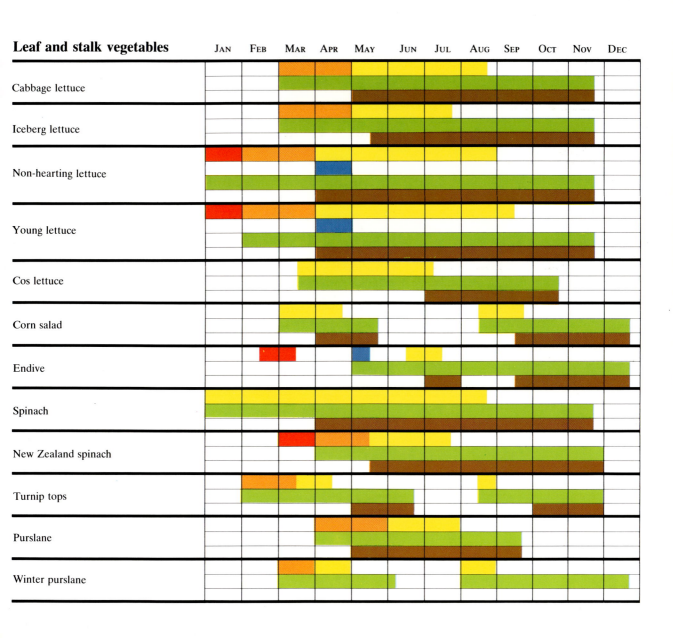

	Jan	Feb	Mar	Apr	May	Jun	Jul	Aug	Sep	Oct	Nov	Dec
Cabbage lettuce												
Iceberg lettuce												
Non-hearting lettuce												
Young lettuce												
Cos lettuce												
Corn salad												
Endive												
Spinach												
New Zealand spinach												
Turnip tops												
Purslane												
Winter purslane												

	JAN	FEB	MAR	APR	MAY	JUN	JUL	AUG	SEP	OCT	NOV	DEC

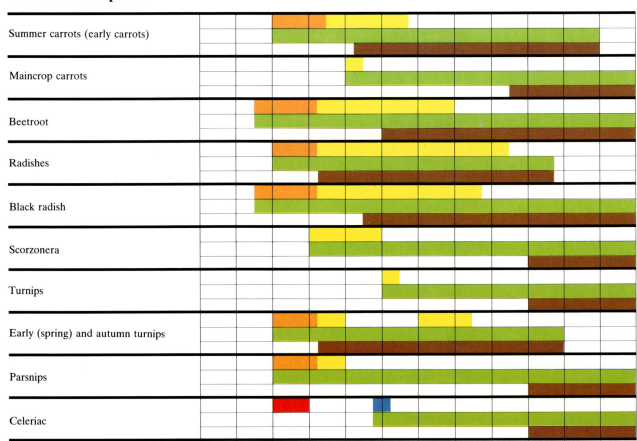

Leaf beet

Garden cress

Mustard

Watercress

American cress

Swede tops

Root and tuber plants

Summer carrots (early carrots)

Maincrop carrots

Beetroot

Radishes

Black radish

Scorzonera

Turnips

Early (spring) and autumn turnips

Parsnips

Celeriac

	JAN	FEB	MAR	APR	MAY	JUN	JUL	AUG	SEP	OCT	NOV	DEC

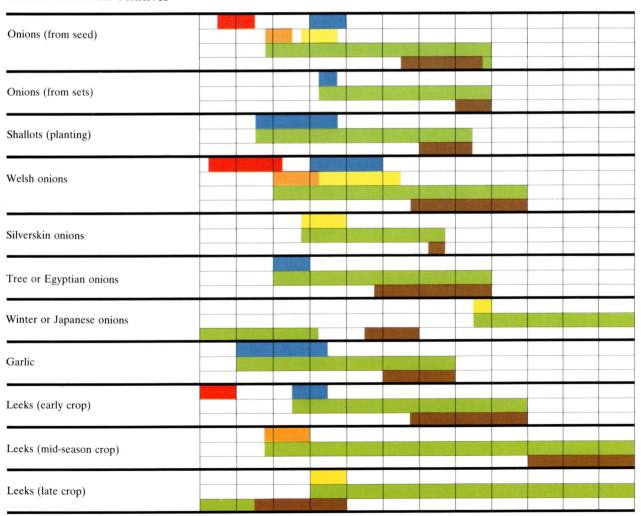

Chinese and Jerusalem artichokes

Hamburg parsley

Florence fennel

Potatoes

Onions and their relatives

Onions (from seed)

Onions (from sets)

Shallots (planting)

Welsh onions

Silverskin onions

Tree or Egyptian onions

Winter or Japanese onions

Garlic

Leeks (early crop)

Leeks (mid-season crop)

Leeks (late crop)

Brassicas

	Jan	Feb	Mar	Apr	May	Jun	Jul	Aug	Sep	Oct	Nov	Dec
Cabbage—white, pointed, savoy and red (early crop)												
Cabbage—white, pointed, savoy and red (summer crop)												
Cabbage—white, pointed, savoy and red (autumn crop)												
Cabbage—white, pointed and savoy (winter crop)												
Chinese cabbage												
Borecole or kale												
Brussels sprouts												
Cauliflower (early crop)												
Cauliflower (summer crop)												
Cauliflower (autumn crop)												
Cauliflower (winter crop)												
Broccoli, sprouting (summer)												
Broccoli, sprouting (winter)												
Kohl-rabi												

Beans and peas

	JAN	FEB	MAR	APR	MAY	JUN	JUL	AUG	SEP	OCT	NOV	DEC
Dried beans												
French beans												
Runner beans												
Broad beans												
Garden peas and sugar peas												
Asparagus pea												
Dried peas												

Blanched vegetables

	JAN	FEB	MAR	APR	MAY	JUN	JUL	AUG	SEP	OCT	NOV	DEC
Blanched chicory												
Green chicory												
Red chicory												
Blanching celery												

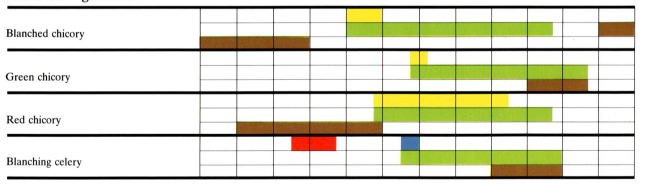

Fruiting plants

	JAN	FEB	MAR	APR	MAY	JUN	JUL	AUG	SEP	OCT	NOV	DEC
Tomatoes		red	red		blue	green	green	green	green			
								brown	brown			
Cucumbers				red	blue	green	green	green	green			
								brown	brown			
Gherkins				red	yellow		green	green	green			
							brown	brown				
Melons					red	blue/green	green	green	green			
								brown	brown			
Courgettes and marrows					red	blue/green	green	green	green	green		
						brown	brown	brown	brown	brown		
Peppers				red		blue	green	green	green	green		
								brown	brown	brown		
Aubergines			red			blue/green	green	green	green	green		
									brown			
Sweet corn (maize)				red		blue/green	green	green	green	green		
									brown	brown		

Index